Drifting Through Samsara

AMERICAN ACADEMY
of RELIGION

ACADEMY SERIES

SERIES EDITOR
Margaret D. Kamitsuka

A Publication Series of
The American Academy of Religion
and
Oxford University Press

Drifting Through Samsara

Tacit Conversion and Disengagement in Goenka's Vipassana Movement

MASOUMEH RAHMANI

OXFORD

UNIVERSITY PRESS

OXFORD
UNIVERSITY PRESS

Oxford University Press is a department of the University of Oxford. It furthers
the University's objective of excellence in research, scholarship, and education
by publishing worldwide. Oxford is a registered trade mark of Oxford University
Press in the UK and certain other countries.

Published in the United States of America by Oxford University Press
198 Madison Avenue, New York, NY 10016, United States of America.

Library of Congress Cataloging-in-Publication Data
Names: Rahmani, Masoumeh, author.
Title: Drifting through Samsara : tacit conversion and disengagement in
Goenka's Vipassana movement / Masoumeh Rahmani.
Description: 1. | New York : Oxford University Press, 2022. |
Series: Aar Academy series | Includes bibliographical references and index.
Identifiers: LCCN 2021022664 (print) | LCCN 2021022665 (ebook) |
ISBN 9780197579961 (hardcover) | ISBN 9780197579985 (epub) | ISBN 9780197579992
Subjects: LCSH: Vipaśyanā (Buddhism) | Conversion—Buddhism.
Classification: LCC BQ5630.V5 R34 2021 (print) | LCC BQ5630.V5 (ebook) |
DDC 294.3/4435—dc23
LC record available at https://lccn.loc.gov/2021022664
LC ebook record available at https://lccn.loc.gov/2021022665

DOI: 10.1093/oso/9780197579961.001.0001

1 3 5 7 9 8 6 4 2

Printed by Integrated Books International, United States of America

Acknowledgements

I would like to express my sincere gratitude to the twenty-six men and women who graciously allowed me into their worlds. I thank you for your contribution to this research and wish to remind you that I do not intend to disrespect or reduce the complexity of your outlooks by glancing at your narratives through an etic lens.

I would also like to express my sincere appreciation and gratitude to my mentors, whose wisdom has expanded my horizon in a gamut of ways. Will Sweetman, your unbounded support and patience has enabled me to carve a toehold within academia; thank you for trusting me. Ben Schonthal, you are gold; thank you for your stimulating comments. Ruth Fitzgerald, this research would not have been completed without your generous advice; thank you for uplifting my thoughts. I thank the late Cyril Schäfer, whose insights continue to colour my imagination. Miguel Farias, I am immensely grateful to you for pushing me to publish this book. I especially appreciate it given that you were my boss at the time and I could have done other work for you.

I am grateful to the University of Otago for providing me with the scholarship, resources, and the opportunity to undertake this study and to experience this corner of the world. I am thankful to Elizabeth Guthrie and Murray Rae who supported me during my time at Otago and to Henri Gooren, Margaret Kamitsuka, and my colleagues in the Faculty of Humanities and Social Sciences at Victoria University of Wellington who in various ways enabled the production of this book. I take this chance to express a wealth of gratitude to my B.A. professors, Denise Cush, Catherine Robinson, Mahinda Deegallee, Paul Reid-Bowen, and Jo Backus for shaping my career. I admire your enthusiasm for the subject matter and feel privileged to have grown under your guidance.

A special word of thanks to my family, friends, and colleagues for their continuous support: Farhad Rahmani, Lizzie Bisley, Azadeh Akhavan,

Firooz and Joanne Sefre, Anthony Stumbo, Aaron Korpal, Parul Dixit, Linda Zampol D'Ortia, Greg Faulks, and my dearest Catherine Naughtie.

I dedicate this book to my father, Mohsen Rahmani, who had selflessly endured every inch of the 9,248 miles between us so that I could embark on a life-changing journey to New Zealand; thank you for being the source of light and warmth in my life.

تقدیم به پدرم؛

او که روشنی و گرمی بازار وجود است

Contents

Figures

Figures

A Note on Terminology and Transcription

In order to ease reading, the Pali terms used in this book are not spelled with diacritical marks and do not appear in italics.

The analysis presented in this book involves a great deal of interpretation: taking account of the social, cultural, and institutional orientations of the narrators and the researcher (myself); the power dynamics between the two; and the structure and form of the language and the context of the interview. The reader should be forewarned that my analytical lens often shifts between a structural and thematic reading of the narratives. In the sections where the analysis is hinged primarily at a thematic level, I have been more conservative with the use of transcription symbols to ease reading. Nonetheless, all interview excerpts follow my conventions of transcription, most notably, my unorthodox use of punctuation and capitalization and the inclusion of false starts, grammatical errors, and other non-verbal communicative behaviour. This approach safeguards the reader from the danger of reading the excerpts simply for content (Riessman, 2002) or losing sight of an important facet of the spoken language, namely, the presupposition that individuals form coherent language and must therefore have coherent intentions (Stromberg, 1993). On the other hand, the transcriptions are more nuanced in sections where a combination of thematic and structural narrative analysis takes place. It is therefore essential for the reader to study the conventions of transcription to engage with the material at an appropriate depth. As I understand it, narrative analysis is like learning a new language; the conventions of transcriptions are its alphabet; it is like looking at a piece of sheet music and hearing the song in your head.

Conventions of Transcription

[p] Indicates pause of one second or longer

[l] Indicates laughter

[g] Indicates giggle; laughing lightly

[in] Indicates loud inhale

[ex] Indicates loud exhale

[c] Indicates cough

[vf>] Indicates voice fading from this marker onwards

[vc] Indicates voice changing from this marker onwards; or adopting an accent to signal a quote

[ntch] Indicates the single sound of 'tut' or 'tsk' formed by suction against the back of the front teeth

(?*) Bounds uncertain transcription

|| Bounds simultaneous utterances

yk Is the abbreviation of 'you know'

Underlining indicates sentences that are significant to the analysis.

Commas indicate break in speech and are not used in their grammatical sense.

Capitalised letters indicate emphasis and do not follow grammatical conventions.

The initial S. stands for Sara, the author's preferred name and indicates the author's dialogue.

Introduction

Vipassana meditation as taught by S. N. Goenka inhabits a niche in the life of many individuals who desire fulfilment through self-transformation, yet who also wish to keep religious traditions at arm's length. Goenka has achieved global popularity by divorcing his teachings of Vipassana meditation from its foundations in Theravada Buddhism and refashioning them in a scientific and world-affirming language. People from various walks of life find themselves in the unique environment of ten-day silent meditation courses where they are asked to disconnect from the external world, commit to a strict code of conduct, and meditate for ten hours per day. While some people are content to experience this novelty once and move on, others become committed meditators, advance to longer courses, and shape a life around this practice. However, regardless of their level of commitment, Vipassana practitioners in New Zealand commonly reject religious labels and conceptualise their commitment in non-religious terms. In fact, the more they are socialised into this movement, the more likely they are to conceive of it as a secular institution; the more they are converted to this movement and its Buddhist worldview, the more likely they are to deny the category of conversion.

This book explores religious disengagement in a context where the concept of conversion is ignored and taken for granted in the first place. A great deal of scholarship on conversion has been limited by taking the informants' rejection of certain categories (for instance, religion, conversion, and Buddhism) at face value. Despite the growing call to view conversion as culturally constituted phenomenon that varies across traditions, the field heavily relies on a person's self-identification as a convert to the point that for decades the etiquette for participant recruitment in conversion studies has (more or less) boiled down to one question: 'Are you a convert?' (Staples and Mauss, 1987: 138). One of the aims of this book is to disturb this etiquette in participant recruitment and the normative view of conversion as whatever 'a group or a person says it is' (Rambo, 1993: 7). I argue that this approach fails to encompass the tonalities of conversion in light of an increasing aversion to

Drifting Through Samsara. Masoumeh Rahmani, Oxford University Press. © Oxford University Press 2022.
DOI: 10.1093/oso/9780197579961.003.0001

religious labels and in contexts where people exhibit a certain anxiety about being perceived as religious.

In this book, I introduce the term *tacit conversion* to describe a peculiar form of conversion that is unacknowledged. The term describes a process whereby increased socialisation into a movement and the adoption of its language paradoxically conceals conversion to the member. Tacit conversion is the product of a complex interplay of historical, social, cultural, institutional, linguistic, ideological, and biographical structures—all of which I explore in this book. It explains circumstances where there is a disconnect between language and the lived experience, a disconnect between non-religious self-identification and representation of selves that are constructed and interpreted within a particular religious language. Tacit conversion occurs in movements with rich rhetorical repretiore for rejecting associations with religion. Goenka's Vipassana organisation is a case in point; instead of teaching Buddhist meditation, the movement claims to teach a 'scientific', 'non-sectarian', self-development 'tool' based on the 'core teachings of the Buddha' or 'pure Dhamma', which are 'universal' and do not involve religious conversion. Indeed, other studies on this movement have confirmed that almost all Vipassana practitioners reject religious (Buddhist) identities (Loss, 2010; Pagis, 2008) and often self-identify as nones, secular, and even atheists. By introducing the term *tacit conversion*, I expand the category of conversion in ways that encompass new religious movements (NRMs) with ostensibly blurred religious/secular boundaries.

In the field of religious disengagement, this book makes two contributions. First and foremost, it explores whether the contours of disengagement from the Vipassana movement are coterminous with other existing models of religious disaffiliation (Barbour, 1994; Bromley, 1998b; Coates, 2013; Ebaugh, 1988; Fazzino, 2014; Gooren, 2010; Jacobs, 1989; Shoenberger and Grayburn, 2016; Streib et. al., 2011; Wright, 1984, 2007, 2014). Second, empirical studies on religious disengagement are primarily built on the experience of individuals who exit a religious tradition after years of participation and commitment. This book explores the characteristics of disengagement narratives, particularly as they occur at early stages of conversion, before the meditator has developed a commitment to the movement. In this regard, this book aims to advance the field of meditation studies by examining what prompts practitioners to stop and effectively disengage from Vipassana meditation. Understanding how disengagement occurs from meditative movements, such as Goenka's Vipassana, has significant implications for expanding our knowledge of the kinds of needs that promote individuals to seek meditation in the first place, as well as assessing the efficacy (or inefficacy) of meditation groups in meeting those needs.

This chapter begins with an introduction to Goenka's Vipassana movement, a description of a standard ten-day Vipassana course and the field site at which ethnographic research for this book was conducted. Next, the chapter briefly introduces the participants involved in this research and provides an overview of some of their shared perspectives including their conception of categories such as religion and spirituality. Finally, the chapter reflects on the recent developments in conversion studies and situates this book within this field. Most notably, it includes my conception of conversion as a process of personal transformation reflected in the adoption of a new universe of discourse and outlines the linguistic approach I have adopted to achieve the objectives of this book.

S. N. Goenka's Vipassana Organisation

Satya Narayan Goenka (1924–2013), a former businessman of Indian descent, was the most recent leader of the international Vipassana movement, best known for its ten-day silent meditation retreats.[1] After fourteen years of practice under U Ba Khin (1899–1971), in 1969 Goenka gained the authorisation to teach Vipassana meditation in India, and thereafter, embarked on a journey to spread Vipassana across the world.[2] After the death of U Ba Khin, Goenka maintained the role of supreme authority within this organisation and did not appoint a successor prior to his own demise. Instead, in an attempt to standardise his teachings and prevent deviations, in 1982 Goenka recorded all of his teachings, trained and appointed assistant teachers to conduct courses on his behalf—albeit through the use of his pre-recorded material.

To date, Goenka's network is the largest donor-funded Vipassana organisation—with over 170 official (and over 110 non-official) centres

---

[1] A portion of the material presented in this section has been published in a co-authored (Rahmani and Pagis, 2015) profile on Goenka's movement for the World Religions & Spirituality Project.

[2] In 1979, Goenka held his first ten-day Vipassana course outside India and Burma in Gaillon, France.

worldwide—that offers meditation courses free of charge to the public. From teachers to administrators, all the individuals involved in Goenka's organisation are volunteers and receive no salary for their work. The organisation therefore functions on dhamma service,[3] and the donations it receives from 'old students' (an emic term that refers to individuals who have successfully completed a ten-day Vipassana course). All centres that operate under Goenka's tradition comply with a set of guidelines, which prohibits them from altering Goenka's teachings, instructions, recordings, and the structure of the courses. According to a Vipassana teacher in New Zealand, these tapes will be used until the English language has changed in such a way that people can no longer understand them.

Part of Goenka's global success was due to his ability to export Vipassana meditation divorced from its religious foundations in Theravada Buddhism. To understand the growth of this movement, it is essential to locate this tradition in a wider historical context. Vipassana meditation was developed within Theravada Buddhism, which is the predominant form of Buddhism in South and Southeast Asia. Contrary to the common assumptions that meditation lies at the heart of a Buddhist life, many scholars (Braun, 2013; Gombrich, 1971: 322; Sharf, 1995: 242) have argued that, historically, meditation was not central to the monastic life of Theravada monks and nuns. Instead, Theravada monks and nuns aimed for a good rebirth by accumulating merit through the development of morality (sila), observance of monastic rules (vinaya), and preserving the Buddha's teachings (Dhamma). However, by the end of the nineteenth century, many Theravada countries of Southeast Asia experienced a reform, which, amongst many changes, involved the promotion of meditation as a central component of the Buddhist tradition and the introduction of meditation to laity.

The consensus in the existing literature connects the rise of Vipassana meditation outside the gates of monasteries to European colonialism in Southeast Asian countries during the nineteenth century (Braun, 2013; Gombrich and Obeyesekere 1988; Sharf 1995). Other elements of this reform involved the rejection of the authority of clergy, values of individualism, a rational and 'instrumental' approach to Buddhist teachings, the

---

[3] 'Dhamma service' is an emic term that refers to volunteer work at the centre. All tasks including cooking, cleaning, and maintenance of the centre are done by the dhamma servers. Any individual who has completed a ten-day course can offer his/her services to the movement, provide they adhere to the organisation's moral code and commit to regular practice. Dhamma service must be done 'without expecting anything in return', and therefore it is considered the highest form of charity and instrumental towards dissolving the ego and achieving liberation.

repudiation of the supernatural or magical aspects of Buddhism and the rejection of 'empty' ritual, and a sense of 'universalism' accompanied by the insistence that Buddhism is a 'philosophy' rather than 'religion' (Sharf, 1995: 252). Finally, whereas, traditionally, meditation was taught by monks within the confines of monasteries, the abovementioned reform eventually gave rise to the development of a non-monastic approach known as 'the householder tradition' (Pagis, 2008: 94). The modern lineage of Goenka's Vipassana meditation is traced to the famous Burmese monk Ledi Sayadaw (1846–1923) who established meditation centres across Burma (Sharf, 1995: 254), and was among the first to authorise a renounced householder (someone who is not ordained), Saya Thetgyi (1873–1945), as his successor in 1915. Saya Thetgyi in turn passed the tradition to U Ba Khin, a Burmese government official who taught many householders and international students in his lifetime, including Mother Sayamagyi (Sayamagyi Daw Mya Thwin), Ruth Denison, John Coleman, Robert Hover, and S. N. Goenka (Rawlinson 1997: 593).

Thus, by claiming a 'non-sectarian' status, Goenka was following a trend commonly identified by scholars as Buddhist modernism (Bechert, 1984; McMahan, 2008) or Protestant Buddhism (Gombrich and Obeyesekere, 1988). Goenka's representation of Vipassana meditation as a 'scientific', 'non-sectarian' practice has helped establish and promoted the modern conceptions of meditation as a non-religious activity. Goenka's desire to cement this image of Vipassana meditation is echoed in his efforts to create the Vipassana Research Institute (VRI) in 1985; an organisation that is concerned with conducting research into the application of Vipassana meditation in daily life (VRI Dhamma, 2014). The VRI publications thus work in parallel with Goenka's Pariyatti press, which is focused on translating Pali scripture.

Goenka's organisation offers a diverse range of courses (from three days to sixty days), although the ten-day Vipassana courses are the required introduction to the movement and are therefore the most frequently held and best attended. Since the participants in this research (including myself) have attended at least one ten-day course, I limit my exploration to the teachings and the structure of this retreat. Accordingly, the teachings that Goenka offers at this course rest on a selective interpretation of *Satipatthana Sutta* in light of 'The Path of Purification', and the *Abhidhamma*. While the *Satipatthana Sutta* offers four objects for the practice of mindfulness—body, sensations, mind, and mental objects—Goenka's teachings (following his teacher U Ba Khin) predominantly focus on sensations.

Goenka's Vipassana technique is theoretically underpinned by the basic Buddhist doctrines of the Four Noble Truths and the Noble Eightfold Path,[4] which he sporadically explores during his courses. According to Goenka, we dwell in samsara, and our human existence is characterised by suffering, resulting from attachment and aversion to things that are impermanent. Goenka follows the Buddhist premise that all physical and mental phenomena are marked by suffering (dukkha), impermanence (anicca), and not-self (anatta).

From the Buddhist perspective, the entity we conventionally refer to as 'I', the 'self', or in Goenka's words, the 'ego', consists of five aggregates: the body (rupa), sensations (vedana), perceptions (sanna), reactions (sankhara), and consciousness (vinnana). Each aggregate is characterised by impermanence, and therefore cultivating attachment to either one or all of them ultimately leads to suffering. Within this formula, sankhara is interpreted as the 'mental habit of reactions' (Hart, 1987: 46). As a central theme in Goenka's ten-day courses, sankhara represents the idea that the mind creates patterns of disposition through encounters with the world, which in turn conditions our next behaviour (or reactions), resulting in attachments to this world, causing suffering, and leading to new birth and therefore new suffering. To achieve enlightenment and exit samsara (the cycle of rebirth), one must both refrain from generating new sankharas and eradicate all previous ones. Goenka's instructions teach the practitioners that every time they emotionally react to any internal or external stimuli, they generate new sankharas or strengthen previous ones.

In Goenka's tradition, Vipassana meditation is portrayed as an instrument that enables the process of 'de-conditioning' through a systematic observation of one's bodily sensations in a non-reactive, non-judgemental manner. Therefore, meditators are repeatedly told (by Goenka, during a ten-day course) that they are undergoing a process analogous to 'mental surgery'. This depiction resonates strongly with most modern meditators who are familiar with popular psychological terms such as 'conditioning' and often conceptualise meditation as a form of therapy, which involves de-conditioning the mind and paving the way to better control and agency (Pagis, 2008).

---

[4] The Four Noble Truths are (1) existence is suffering (dukkha), (2) the cause of suffering is craving for things that are impermanent by nature, (3) the cessation of suffering is possible, and involves the cessation of craving, and (4) the path leading to the cessation of suffering—i.e. the Noble Eightfold Path.

However, according to Goenka (1997: 12), a mere intellectual under-standing of these concepts and processes do not produce 'real wisdom', and therefore cannot lead one to liberation from suffering. To attain liberation and true happiness, one must understand the true source of this suffering at the *experiential* level. Hence, students are advised to invest their time in meditation rather than reading or engaging in intellectual endeavours. This epistemic strategy—which considers embodied experience and not intellec-tual understanding as the true source of knowledge—undergirds much of Goenka's enterprise including his efforts to abstract his movement and its teachings from the category of religion. For instance, despite teaching various Buddhist doctrines (including dukkha, anicca, anatta, sankhara, kamma, etc.), Goenka discourages his students from accepting them 'blindly' and advises them to accept only these insights as 'truths' once they have experi-enced them for themselves.

Insight into the true nature of reality, according to Goenka, can be gained through the observance of Buddha's Noble Eightfold Path, which is divided into three sections: morality (sila), concentration (samadhi), and wisdom (panna). A standard ten-day course is structured meticulously to practice these three stages and to develop insight into the true nature of reality, as it is understood within the Theravada tradition (Pagis, 2010a).

Around the world, Goenka's ten-day Vipassana courses are conducted identically, since all meditation instructions are taught via Goenka's pre-recorded tapes (in non-English-speaking countries, translated versions of in-structions follow the original passages). Thus, if and when a student returns to one of Goenka's Vipassana centres (elsewhere in the world) to attend a second ten-day course, they will be listening to the same instructions. During the course, students follow a timetable (see appendix 1) with extensive hours of meditation (approximately ten to twelve) from 4:30 to 21:00 each day. All students must adhere to a strict code of conduct, take a vow of silence, known as the Noble Silence, which restricts them from all kinds of communication with one another (whether by speech, eye contact, gesture, sign language, or written notes). Under Noble Silence, students can only speak to the as-sistant teacher and the course manager if necessary. Other restrictions such as gender segregation, possession of religious objects, practice of religious rituals, listening to music, and reading or writing are imposed in an attempt to limit external stimuli during the course (Pagis, 2010b). Despite this, each day commences with thirty minutes of pre-recorded audiotapes in which Goenka chants Pali passages from Tipitaka to enhance the environment with 'good vibrations' and ends with an hour of his evening 'discourse' (an emic term) in which he explains relevant Buddhist theories in a language replete with humorous analogies.

Contrary to its label, the ten-day course consists of twelve days: it commences on day zero and ends on day eleven. On day zero, students officially register by providing their personal details, a signature that indicates they have understood the course structure, will commit to the movement's guidelines, and turn in all prohibited objects such as intoxications, mobile phones, and valuable possessions. One of the activities on day zero involves the allotment of cushions in the meditation hall, which follows the principle of merit. Hence, one's position and proximity to the teacher's seat (front rows) depends on the individual's seniority in the practice and the number of courses they have undertaken in the past—a model which closely resembles the spatial order of Southeast Asian monasteries where senior monks occupy the front rows (Pagis, 2008: 160). Finally, the course officially commences on the evening of this day when students take the Three Refuges (Buddha, dhamma, sangha), surrender to the teacher, and formally request to be taught instructions to anapana meditation.

To practice morality, the first component of the Noble Eightfold Path, all students must take a vow to keep the Five Precepts for the duration of the course. These include abstaining from killing, abstaining from stealing, abstaining from all sexual activity, abstaining from telling lies, abstaining from all intoxicants. Three additional precepts apply to old students: abstaining from eating after midday, abstaining from sensual entertainment and bodily decorations, and abstaining from sleeping on high luxurious beds.

The second component of the path, concentration, is practiced from day one to day three, during which students learn the anapana meditation, which is a breath observation technique aimed at increasing the students' concentration. The anapana meditation consists of focusing one's attention to a limited area under the nostrils—between the tip of the nose and the upper lip—and observing the sensations that arise from the uncontrolled breath as air moves in and out of the nostrils.

To practice wisdom, the final component of the Eightfold Path, from the fourth day onwards students learn the practice of Vipassana meditation. Once again, students must officially request to be taught instructions of this practice. Vipassana instructions are provided in phases and involve extending the concentration gained during the first three days to other areas of the body. Thus, students systematically move their attention from head to toe, from toe to head, and observe only the sensations (pleasant or unpleasant) that arise on this path without reacting to it. For instance, if the attention is focused on the left arm, the student should not react or divert her attention to a tingle that suddenly arises in her right ear. Initially, the scanning of the body starts part by part, observing any sensations that arise on the surface of the skin. If the student is not able to feel any sensations on an area of the body, he/she is instructed to concentrate on that particular area for a minute until some sort of sensation crops up. Eventually when the student can feel the entire surface of the skin, he/she then extends this attention to the internal organs and continuously scans the body at a deeper level; from head to toe, from toe to head.

Throughout this exercise, as well as during each meditation session, Goenka constantly reminds the students that everything is impermanent and 'bound to pass away'—'anicca, anicca, anicca'; that they should refrain from developing attachment or aversion to the sensations in their bodies and instead, observe them in a calm, balanced, and 'equanimous' manner; that the more subtle the sensations are, the sharper the mind has become; that if one observes each sensation by remaining in the present moment, without reacting to the sensation, one is effectively eradicating past sankharas; that 'gradually you will progress towards a stage in which all sankhara leading to new birth, and therefore to new suffering, have been eradicated: the stage of total liberation, full enlightenment'; and that the secret is to work 'patiently, persistently, and continuously' (Goenka, 1997: 27).

Finally, the Noble Silence ends on the tenth day of the course. After nine days of introspection, students are now allowed to share their experiences with one another, take back their possessions, give donations, and buy CDs and books from a range of VRI publications. During this day, the students are introduced to yet another method of meditation: metta-bhavana, or meditation of loving kindness. Unlike the practice of Vipassana meditation, the instructions of metta meditation are rather simple. After an hour-long session of Vipassana, students are taught to relax their bodies, focus on the subtle flow of pleasant sensations (if possible) and extend their 'vibrations of good will' to themselves, others, and the world, wishing 'may all beings be happy' (Goenka, 1997: 63). According to Pagis (2008: 99), the purpose of mixing metta and Vipassana is to 'produce detachment that does not include aloofness'.

The Field Site

Participant observation for this piece was conducted at Dhamma Medini, the only official organisation that offers Vipassana courses under Goenka's tradition in New Zealand. Dhamma Medini is in a rural area of Kaukapakapa, approximately one-hour's drive from Auckland. On average, this centre hosts up to sixty students per course and has the capacity to provide accommodation for sixty-eight meditators in single rooms—a total of 1,280 students attended the standard ten-day Vipassana course in 2014. Dhamma Medini follows the general spatial arrangements common to all meditation centres that teach within Goenka's tradition (Pagis, 2008). During the course, almost all of the centre's areas accessible to students are segregated by gender—the accommodations, dining area, facilities, and the outside premises including separate walking paths (see figure I.1). The female section is located within a valley, surrounded by native trees, silver ferns, a stream that cuts through the land, and is the habitat of native birds, wild bunnies, and a magnificent pair of paradise ducks (see figure I.2).

The meditation hall is the only exception where both female and male students are brought under one roof, although, even within this space, the

Figure I.1 Aerial view of Dhamma Medini

The land was purchased in 1987 with the legal status of charitable trust and educational institute. The main building (now used as a kitchen and for administration) was constructed in 1994–1995. The pagoda site with fifty-four cells was under construction at the time of my second visit in 2015. Both images were downloaded from the centre's website (Medini Dhamma, 2014).

Figure I.2 Female dorms, a view from the entrance to the meditation hall

seating arrangements and entry points are separated, and students are advised to not look at each other. Accordingly, all students face the teacher, while dhamma servers are located at the closest spot to the teachers, facing sideways, and are able to view the teacher and the students at once. The teacher(s) occupy a slightly elevated seat from where he/she can view all students and sit an arm's length away from the audio/video control panel (see figure I.3). The hall is equipped with speakers and two large plasma televisions that rest under a fitted curtain. At the beginning of each meditation session, and after all students are positioned in their spots, the teacher walks into the hall and starts the session by pressing the play button and casting Goenka's voice into the space.

Behind this serene scene, there is the world of dhamma servers (volunteers), where talking, reading, writing, and limited contact with the outside world is permitted. During a ten-day course, the volunteers are in charge of cooking, cleaning, and maintenance. They do their tasks with minimal interaction with students and usually avoid the course premises. The dhamma servers spend most of their time in the kitchen and only meditate in the hall for three hours per day. The 'course managers' (one female and one male) are the only dhamma servers who interact with students; they mediate between students, teachers, and dhamma servers, and spend most of their time

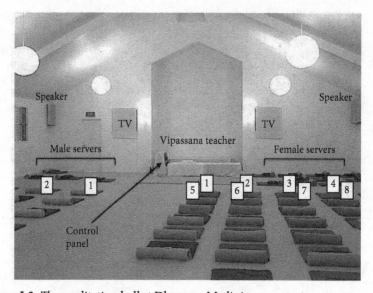

Figure I.3 The meditation hall at Dhamma Medini

The pathway in the middle separates female students (*right*) from male students (*left*). The original photo was downloaded from the centre's website (Medini Dhamma, 2014).

in the meditation hall, act out the teacher's command, manage unexpected situations, and make sure that students attend the meditation sessions, particularly the three compulsory sessions held morning, noon, and evening.

The atmosphere of the centre is completely different during the work periods. Volunteers can talk to one another to coordinate the necessary tasks for preparing the centre for the next ten-day course, and thus segregation is relatively less strict during this period. However, the general code of conduct, such as observance of sila and three hours of compulsory group meditation, still applies to all. Moreover, if a dhamma server temporarily leaves the premises during the day (for shopping or personal reasons), upon their return, he/she is advised to spend an hour ('cleansing period') meditating in the hall before they resume work.

I have visited Dhamma Medini twice during my research. On my first visit in 2014, I spent a total of sixteen days at this site, attending a ten-day course followed by dharma service, and in 2015, I paid a day visit to the centre to interview its main teacher and collect information about the history of the centre. Conducting fieldwork in these conditions was both interesting and overwhelming. Okely (2012: 78) notes that the fear of total participation is conterminous with the fear of losing analytical and observational skills and the obvious combat strategy against this sort of distress is (analytical) note taking in the field. Yet, during the first phase of fieldwork, I was strictly prohibited from reading and writing and indeed any kind of activity that involved *thinking*. As my gatekeeper had it, there was no better way to understand Vipassana other than personal experience—which in this context meant nothing but a complete surrender to Goenka's teachings and switching off the intellectual faculty.

It all began when the management of Dhamma Medini rejected my initial proposal for conducting participant observation and interviewing new students before and after a standard ten-day Vipassana course. After lengthy correspondence, it became clear that my only means of accessing the field site required my full participation at a ten-day course as a Vipassana student and not as a researcher. Consequently, my plans for data collection were postponed to a work period that immediately followed that course and my application was carried forward under certain conditions: refrain from observing others, avoid distracting participants by talking to them about this research (on day zero, throughout the course, and on metta day), and solely focus on my meditation by 'setting aside [the] project for the duration of the course'. Thus, on the day of my arrival, like any other student, I had to deposit certain possessions with the management such as keys, wallet, mobile phone, recording device, MP3 player, books, notebooks, and, of course, pens. Moreover, since I had already attended two Vipassana courses in the past (2006 and 2010), I was automatically considered an old student and was allocated a single-digit cushion number (seven), which positioned me alongside serious meditators in the front rows of the meditation hall—where I felt both out of context and under pressure to maintain a certain etiquette (see figure I.3).

For some readers, this may seem a golden opportunity; she was killing two birds with one stone, you may think. 'You can meditate and do research!' I was told by numerous friends who were neither familiar with ethnography nor had any experience with long meditation retreats. Alas this was far from reality—for the simple fact that self-transformation was not an item on my agenda. Needless to say, I wholeheartedly refused to surrender (both the cognitive and verbal performance) when Goenka's pre-recorded voice kindly urged us to do so. In fact, I was determined to remain as critical as was humanly possible in that situation.

Thus, when other students were attempting to silence their thoughts, I was preoccupied with analysing Goenka's teachings, making mental notes of the key words, and scrutinising the linguistic patterns that occurred in his discourses. When others were introspecting, I was extrospecting with my eyes shut, observing the domino effect of a single cough in the meditation hall. When other students were watching Goenka's evening discourses on the plasma screen televisions, I was watching their body language and counting the increasing number of 'sadhu, sadhu, sadhu-s'[5] at the end of each session.

Without a pen at hand, this masochistic approach slowly propelled me to the brink of a psychic collapse. My mental and emotional state was that of a caged bird. Except no one had forced me to stay at Dhamma Medini, and I was there of my own accord. Rather, it felt as if I had become imprisoned within myself. If not for the fear of embarrassment among colleagues and the idea of having to return and start the process from scratch again, I would have fled the centre ten times per day. But I stayed, despite the mental torment. Goenka's persuasive teachings of the Four Noble Truths on day five did not exactly soothe my pain either. 'Every living being suffers. Life starts with crying; birth is a great suffering. And anyone who has been born is bound to encounter the sufferings of sickness and old age. But no matter how miserable one's life may be, nobody wants to die, because death is a great suffering' (Goenka, 1997: 23–24). If anything, hearing the term 'suffering' countless times each day was becoming its own self-fulfilling prophecy.

Until I gave up and gave in. I surrendered, without making a conscious decision or having a memory of when and how this had happened. Lewis Rambo (1993: 134) is right to portray the process of surrender as 'warfare'. I felt that I had miserably failed as an ethnographer the moment I realised that I had been observing my sensations in order to ease my pain. Each day, I felt that I was stepping further away from my position as an observer, and instead, started to accept that my suffering was the result of craving objectivity. Perhaps that was my deep-rooted sankhara that must be eradicated, I thought. This was the embodied experience of what Susan Harding (1987) detailed in her excellent ethnographic piece decades ago. She wrote (1987: 178) that 'the membrane between disbelief and belief is much thinner than we think', and going under conviction, she adds, 'is a state of unconscious belief, experienced with more or less turmoil and anxiety, depending on how strong your disbelieving voices are'. The point is that contrary to my unfounded distress, anthropologists such as Harding consider this fragile

---

[5] Students are encouraged to repeat the Pali term *sadhu* three times at the end of each meditation session, which is 'an expression of agreement or approval' (Goenka, 1997: 92). Sadhu can be translated as excellent, auspicious, or well said.

space between belief and disbelief as the space that ethnographers must enter to do their work.

Unexpectedly though, on Tuesday, 29 July 2014, and after eleven days of fieldwork at Dhamma Medini, I was reunited with my pen. Never before that day had I understood the powerful image of a pen. My separation from, longing for, and reunion with my pen is a serendipitous tale that coloured aspects of my methodology and my experience as a researcher. Adhering to the centre's restrictions also impinged on my rapport with other practitioners. For instance, to respect the management's legitimate concerns for protecting students from the distractions (caused by my presence as a researcher), on day zero, I tried to consciously avoid any conversations that would reveal information about the study and/or my intentions of being there. This quickly became problematic since my nationality provoked curiosity as to what I was doing and why I was in New Zealand. In attempt to avoid these topics, I was forced to answer as briefly as possible or redirect the conversation towards the practice of Vipassana. As if this mystery was not enough, my unanticipated reunion with the pen was the straw that broke the camel's back.

With the completion of Noble Silence (on the tenth day of the course), and despite our initial agreement, I was granted permission to openly speak of my research and was provided with a small piece of paper and a pen to collect contact details of potential participants. With a pen at hand, my image of old student was suddenly transformed to an outsider, and even a potential spy. Every person I approached became highly reactive to the pen, which stood out like a sore thumb. While some participants explicitly vocalised their anxieties, others conveyed this message by withholding eye contact and effectively excluding me from conversations. In my eyes, it was evident that others perceived this sudden change as a breach of trust. For a moment I was overcome with despair. I returned to my room, sat on the side of my bed, all too aware that 'to hold a pen is to be at war'. Not only had this mundane tool influenced my position as a researcher, complicated my relationship with Vipassana practitioners, and swayed me across the insider/outsider boundaries in unforeseen ways, it had also opened my eyes to these methodological issues, and more. At that point, I had endured nine days of intensive meditation, spent between ten to twelve hours sitting in the meditation hall each day, and by no means was I prepared to concede defeat. Despite the practitioners' newly wary attitudes towards me, I tried to rebuild rapport by addressing their concerns. Soon I realised that part of the suspicion was related to matters of affiliation. A few students had imagined that I was surveying on behalf of the centre. Once that was clarified, practitioners were less hesitant and began to show interest in this project.

Introducing the Participants

The twenty-six individuals (fifteen male and eleven female) who partici-pated in this research belonged to the middle and upper-middle class.[6] Most had university education and came from various walks of life—from post-graduate students to freelance artists, from builders to accountants. All the participants were of European descent, between the ages of twenty-four and seventy-six, and each displayed different levels of commitment to this move-ment. The majority of the participants were born into Christian households,[7] and all had distinct reasons for arriving at Vipassana. Leslie was craving si-lence; Holger was prescribed meditation by his physician for his stress; Victor wanted to challenge himself; Carole wanted to become happy; and Damian was searching for a spiritual discipline that would give him a 'boot up the bum'.

In spite of this diversity, all participants represented themselves (in ex-plicit or implicit terms) as the unconventional segment of the society. At times, this characteristic was conveyed in their attitudes towards Western medicine, their critique of the consumerist culture, yet more commonly, it manifested in their stories of teenage rebellion against their parental religion. Generally speaking, the participants' narratives of disengagement from their parental religion were in line with the body of scholarly research on disaffili-ation/deconversion from Christianity (Barbour, 1994; Fazzino, 2014; Wright et al., 2011); emphasising a dissatisfaction with the behaviour of church members (as hypocritical, narrow-minded, and dogmatic), accompanied by a growing awareness and realisation that often occurred in conjunction with leaving home and/or exposure to other traditions, which led them to

---

[6] Participants in this research were asked about their preference on anonymity. Pseudonyms are used to ensure the anonymity of those who requested it. I have also respected the decision of other participants who desired to be named.

[7] Twenty-four participants came from Christian backgrounds, whereas the other two were born to atheist/socialist parents. Those with Christian backgrounds reported a varying degree of parental religiosity—often describing parents as 'moderately' or 'loosely' religious, although a small number came from more strictly religious households. Almost all of the participants had some experience of attending Sunday school at one point in their childhood.

challenge this convention. In general, most of the narratives corresponded with and confirmed Peter Berger's (1999) refined ideas about pluralism and its effect on ways of being religious (i.e. fracturing taken-for-granted beliefs and certainties).

I should stress that in spite of their dissatisfaction with Christianity, these individuals did not dwell on, discuss, or explicitly reject the ontological realities of the tradition; rather they despised its institutional, authoritarian, fanatical, and hierarchical modes of religiosity. In other words, they did not reject transcendental beliefs, instead, they expressed an incredible appetite and desire for *unconventional* understandings of reality—a characteristic that shone through their excitement for discussing abstract ideas in our formal and informal conversations. In fact, the participants in this research considered their unconventionality (particularly in spiritual, metaphysical, and cultural orientations) a courageous virtue. From the perspective of most participants, this characteristic was a requisite for a genuine search, spiritual development, and consequential to their arrival at Vipassana.

Hence, in more general terms, this unconventionality echoed the participants' values of autonomous spiritual seekership. Indeed, the vast majority of participants in this research (twenty-four out of twenty-six) constructed narratives within a seekership plot. For those who grew up in Christian households, the departure from Christianity was synonymous with the beginning of their spiritual search, while others hinged their narratives on a pursuit of spiritual fulfilment, and thus they narrated the twist and turns of their search and commonly made use of the metaphor of 'journey' and 'growth' to ascribe coherence to it. The vast majority of participants reported prior involvement with arrays of practices ranging from Transcendental Meditation to Aura healing, from Tai Chi to positive-thinking seminars. The narratives of these individuals varied in their emphasis on physical, mental, and emotional well-being and a pursuit of 'happiness'. In general, the self-representations of the participants corresponded with Colin Campbell's (2002 [1972]: 123) definition of the 'seeker' as a person who has 'adopted a problem-solving perspective while defining conventional religious institutions and beliefs as inadequate'.

In fact, similar to the sociological literature that enforces a binary framework on the fertile field of contemporary spiritualities (Heels and Woodhead, 2005; Zinnbauer et al., 1997), the participants in this research commonly conceptualised religion and spirituality in opposition to each other, and they situated Goenka's Vipassana movement under the latter

Religion	Spirituality
External Path	Internal Path
Structured, Organised	Intuitive, Organic, Authentic
Dogmatic	Experimental
Passive Recipient	Active Agent
Conventional	Idiosyncratic
Authoritarian and Controlling	Autonomous and Fluid
Absolutism	Relativism
Discourages Subjective Interpretations	Encourages Subjective Interpretations
Requires Exclusive Belonging	Open and Inclusive
Empty Rituals	Pragmatic, Transformative Tool
Anthropomorphized Deities	Impersonal Entities
Source of Conflict and War	Source of Connectedness

Figure I.4 Participants' definition of religion and spirituality.

This table was produced from my thematic analysis of interview segments in which participants defined the terms religion and spirituality.

canopy (see figure I.4 for an exhaustive list of the characteristics participants ascribed to each category). To put it bluntly, I argue that the weight that Vipassana meditators ascribed to these values (e.g. seekership, autonomy, authenticity, individualism, self-exploration, etc.) permitted them to over-look, in Goenka's movement, those characteristics that they themselves as-sociated with 'religion' (e.g. structure, required belonging, dogma, etc.). It is important to note, however, that Goenka's evening discourses are also re-plete with stories and arguments that reinforce this perceived dichotomy between religion and spirituality.

From the participants' perspective, spirituality is a broader realm that qualitatively transcends religion yet encompasses the *essence* of all religions. Its impersonal entity cannot/should not be constrained by names or labels such as 'God', 'Allah', or 'Zeus', but by evermore abstract concepts such as 'con-sciousness', 'love', 'life', 'energy', and 'vibrations'. Moreover, religion with its rules and dogmatic beliefs is seen as a source of conflict, whereas spirituality's fluidity provides participants with a sense of freedom to explore the many ways in which one can connect to the self, others, the surrounding world, and possibly beyond.

According to the participants, to be a spiritual seeker, one must first and foremost be *open* to explore alternative viewpoints—such was the charac-teristic that participants sought to project of themselves in the interviews. This curiosity for alternative worldviews and lifestyles can partially explain the participants' aversion to labels—including spirituality itself, which was rendered an 'icky word' by one participant. Needless to say, none of the participants in this research appreciated questions about their religious identity, nor were they thrilled to recap how they classified their religious affiliation on paper (i.e. on the New Zealand national census[8]). In fact, some participants strongly revolted against the idea of having to answer such questions on a national census and rendered the exercise 'irrelevant', 'bureaucratic', and 'useless'.

Interestingly, with the exception of three individuals, who felt comfortable with the fixed labels of their choice (i.e. Bright, Baptist, and an atheist), the rest of the participants were (generally speaking) eager to stress that what they state on the census is *not* how they truly feel or identify themselves, but simply what they perceived to be the closest available option on the menu or representative of their heritage (e.g. Leslie who identified with Panentheism, yet selected Jewish on the census). Consequently, while one participant refused to respond to my question, eight participants preferred idiosyncratic identities such as 'everything', mixed identities such as 'Buddhist-Pagan', and vague categories such as 'other'. The largest group consisting of ten participants represented the category of 'nones' (excluding the atheist just noted), which was a typical response of old students and Vipassana teachers. That said, while seven participants *contemplated* adopting a Buddhist identity, only four individuals self-identified as Buddhist on paper—in which case, they generally represented the disaffiliates who accepted this label *retrospectively* after their disengagement from Goenka's movement. (See appendix 2 for more detail.)

In general, their resistance to labels entailed a certain fear of being constrained, in a sense that subscribing to one label took away the participants' freedom to explore the tradition from within or experiment with other possibilities in the future. This was at times expressed by utterances such as 'I don't like putting all my eggs in one basket'. Hence, the vagueness of categories such as 'other' may have provided them with just enough space to feel unique in their understanding of the world yet, at the same time, connected to others. 'Openness' was therefore associated with spirituality. It was also an important characteristic that some participants used to distinguish Goenka's

---

[8] 'What is your religion?' is the question that appears on the New Zealand national census, for which individuals are provided with tick-box options of the following order: 'No religion, Christian, Buddhist, Hindu, Muslim, Judaism, other religion', with an additional list provided for Christian denominations and an space to specify what one means by 'other' (Statistics New Zealand, 2016).

Vipassana organisation from religion, particularly the movement's openness in accepting practitioners from all kinds of religious backgrounds.

From the participants' perspective, another important characteristic of the so-called spiritual search was authenticity—as participants put it, 'following my own intuition', 'behaving in an authentic way', 'accessing our real true authentic core'. The theme of authenticity in the context of spiritual search envelops a sense of autonomy that emphasises a break from external, demanding, fixed structures and a turn to internal, authentic, fluid guidance mechanisms. Vipassana meditation was recognised as a spiritual practice simply because it accommodated and corresponded with the individual's desire to feel authentic. For the participants in this research, religion with its strict rules and regulations was synonymous with 'constraint' and 'control' and was therefore perceived as the enemy of authenticity. Spirituality on the other hand, is intuitive, organic, idiosyncratic, and more profoundly, undemanding. Consequently, all participants categorised Vipassana under the umbrella term of spirituality because it allows for a direct experience with the self and hence alludes to a sense of autonomous exploration.

Thus, another characteristic by which Vipassana was categorised as spiritual is its focus on the *individual*, his/her subjectivism, and experiences. Evidently, all the participants in this research expressed a polarised understanding of spirituality and religion, which approximates to the perspective of scholars such as Heelas and Woodhead (2005), who draw firm descriptions and rationalisations (such as arbitrary boundaries between the former and the latter by using similar arguments such as surrender to authority and living according to an order vs. autonomous exploration).

Finally, regardless of their religious background and/or conceptualisations of spirituality and religion, the narratives of almost all (twenty-five) participants emphasised one underlying premise: that their participation at a ten-day Vipassana course had resulted in a dramatic change in their sense of self and perspectives. Utterances such as 'I walked in one person and walked out another' or 'I came out of that first course thinking . . . I've sort of unlocked the key to the universe' are examples of this trait.

In the social sciences, this process of transformation is commonly labelled as conversion, and the literatures that explore either sides of this phenomenon (engagement and disengagement) are absorbed within the large pool of conversion studies. An effort to describe the nuances of disengagement from Vipassana movement within the scope of this book requires an established set of vocabulary, framework, and parameters.

Conceptualisations

As Stromberg (2014) has accurately remarked, a sobering step in the field of conversion studies requires us to first distinguish between the two conceptually different processes that are often conflated. These include the 'experiences of personal transformation' and 'change in religious affiliation' (Stromberg, 2014: 118). While affiliating with, or disaffiliating from, a religious organisation may certainly bring about personal transformation, the association is not guaranteed (e.g. a person may formally change his/her religious affiliation to fulfil other goals, such as marriage).

In this book, I use the terms *affiliation* and *disaffiliation* to refer to the formal processes of joining and leaving an organisation. These terms are neutral to the changes/transformations prompted by the acceptance or rejection of a system of meaning. The terms disengagement, departure, and exit are also conceived to be neutral and therefore encompass a variety of pathways outlined in this study (see figure I.5 for the specific terminology on disengagement). While a discussion of the practices linked with the formal process of affiliation to this movement is provided in chapter 2, this book is primarily concerned with exploring the changes that occur at the personal level.

Moreover, I limit my review to approaches that correspond with the disciplinary standpoint within which I have conducted this research, gathered the data, and analysed them. In other words, I engage with approaches that focus on changes that are accessible to the ethnographer. These include exploring the forms of *language* that participants used in representing themselves and their experiences, as well as the non-verbal communicative behaviours they

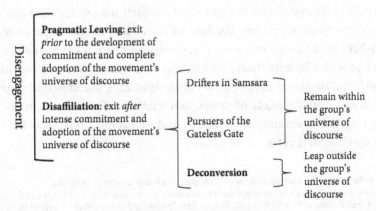

Figure I.5 Disengagement terminology and pathways.

used to perform the *role* of a Vipassana meditator in our interpersonal inter-actions (as opposed to attempting to explore the *cause* of conversion or look for factors that allegedly *motivated* conversion).

Perspectives and Approaches to Conversion

Derived from the Latin word, *convertere*, the basic meaning of conversion is 'to revolve, turn around or head in a different direction' (Gooren, 2010: 10). Hence, conversion as 'turning to' and deconversion as 'turning from' are alternative per-spectives on the same process of personal transformation (Barbour, 1994: 3). Over the last two millennia, Christianity has shaped and redefined conversion in many ways. Conversion in early Christianity was not merely a personal pro-cess; rather, it also emphasised the communal aspects of the process: people were baptised with their families, relatives, and servants (Gooren, 2010: 12). On the other hand, the early Protestant Reformation of the sixteenth century propagated a more personal form of conversion experience. Overall, (and espe-cially within the Evangelical Christian discourse) the connotation of the term is meant to be its end result, indicating 'a change of mind and a change of heart' (Gooren, 2010: 10).

Within the Western tradition, conversion is commonly conceptualised as a dramatic and solitary process, similar to Paul's experience on the road to Damascus (Glazier, 2003: 149)—known as the Pauline paradigm. The Pauline paradigm 'combines notions of an unexpected flash of revelation, a radical reversal of previous beliefs and allegiances, and an underlying as-sumption that converts are passive respondents to outside forces' (Rambo, 2003: 213). However, with the growth of scholarly interest in NRM conver-sion/recruitment after 1965, the field of conversion studies experienced a paradigm shift.[9] In the following paragraphs, and with reference to a sum-mary provided by Paloutzian, Richardson, and Rambo (1999), I provide a snapshot of the major developments in the landscape of conversion studies, including several models of conversion that vary in their emphasis on 'dispositional versus situational factors' as the most influential aspect of this process (Paloutzian et al., 1999: 1052).[10]

---

[9] Although this does not necessarily indicate that all scholars submit to these ideas.

[10] As leading scholars on conversion such as Gooren (2010), Paloutzian, Richardson, and Rambo (1999), and Rambo and Farhadian (2014) have already provided comprehensive reviews of various disciplinary approaches to conversion studies, I do not reiterate these points in detail here.

Noteworthy developments in the field of conversion studies include the *sudden* versus *gradual* mode of conversion distinguished by William James (1902) and the *active* versus *passive* conversion pioneered by Richardson (1985), which emphasises the convert's agency and seekership in pursuing a new faith against the view that assumes the change occurs under external social and psychological forces pressuring the person. Rambo (1993) provided a useful typology that distinguished the difference between *tradition transition* (conversion across traditions, e.g. Islam to Buddhism), *institutional transition* (conversion across religious denominations, e.g. Roman Catholic to Evangelical Christianity), and *intensification* (conversion as a change in levels of commitment to the religion in which one already belongs). Lofland and Skonovd's (1981) six conversion 'motifs' was an effort to describe various forms of conversion based on the blend of various factors (social pressure, temporal duration, level of affective arousal, affective content, and sequence of belief and participation). These include (Lofland and Skonovd, 1981: 375) intellectual, mystical, experiential, affectional, revivalist, and coercive conversion. Finally, surpassing theories that focus solely on the episode of religious change, Henri Gooren's (2010) 'conversion career' model offers a framework for exploring *patterns* of religious activity and inactivity across the individual's life course by offering five typologies of religious involvement: preaffiliation, affiliation, conversion, confession, and disaffiliation.

In terms of definitions, the most widely used and referenced account of conversion is provided by Rambo (1993: 5), who defines the term as 'a process of religious change that takes place in a dynamic force field of people, events, ideologies, institutions, expectations, and orientation'. This comprehensive and multifaceted definition accommodates the conceptualisation of a wide range of conversion experiences—since each conversion instance (and definition) anchors itself differently in relation to social, cultural, religious, and personal dimensions.

While the search for an all-encompassing definition of conversion has bedevilled much of the discussion of conversion, some of the scholars in this field have come to accept that there is no universal definition that could capture all aspects of religious conversion (Buckser and Glazier, 2003: xii; Rambo and Farhadian, 2014: 10). As Rambo (2003: 214) notes, 'What we are really talking about are a cluster of types of change that have been observed and discussed'.

Position Within Conversion Studies

Along the same lines, my attempt in this book is to depict and discuss one peculiar type of this so-called change. It is important to note from the outset that all individuals have voluntarily participated in this research. They have read the research's information sheet,[11] and they self-selected to be appropriate participants for this research (particularly the disengagers). Hence, what these individuals essentially have in common is that the vast majority (twenty-five) have attended (at least) one ten-day Vipassana course; gone through some process of change; gone through a process of rationalising that change; had the desire to share (with me) the many insights they gained from that change; and commonly denied labelling that change in terms of conversion. Thus, logically, at a basic level this change has taken place, otherwise they would not have self-selected themselves as suitable participants for this research in the first place (for the simple fact that they would not have much to discuss).

To be sure (and with reference to the approaches outlined in this chapter), I consider conversion to be a *gradual* process of *personal transformation*, and not a 'finished product' (Rambo, 2003: 214). I approach conversion by looking at 'experiences of transformation as the accomplishments of

---

[11] The participants' information sheet described the objective of this study in the following terms: 'The aim of this research is to understand what attracts individuals to meditative practices such as Goenka's vipassana and what stops them from continuing the practice. Participants will be asked to explain their motivations for attending and/or disaffiliating (moving away/departing) from such courses. These interviews will be analysed to explore why individuals depart from vipassana and how they experience this disaffiliation? Should you agree to take part in this project, your participation should take between 60 and 90 minutes, depending on how long you would like to talk. This project employs an open-ended questioning method. In general, I am interested to hear about your experience with vipassana meditation. The precise nature of the questions which will be asked has not been determined in advance, but will depend on the way in which the interview develops. Consequently, although the University of Otago Human Ethics Committee is aware of the general areas to be explored in the interview, the Committee has not been able to review the precise questions to be used. In the event that the line of questioning does develop in such a way that you feel hesitant or uncomfortable you are reminded of your right to decline to answer any particular question(s) and also that you may withdraw from the project at any stage without any disadvantage to yourself of any kind. Examples of the kinds of questions that will be asked include: Could you tell me a little about how you became involved with vipassana? What was the most meaningful concept you've learned from vipassana? Did you at any point in life consider yourself a Buddhist? What do you like/dislike the most about vipassana? Why did you stop practicing vipassana? Do you ever think of attending another course? What made you realise vipassana is not for you? What qualities do you seek from a spiritual tradition? Participants are welcomed to discuss anything that they believe is relevant to the topic of this research.'

agents who exploit the resources of language to bring about desired change' (Stromberg, 2014: 124). I conceptualise the convert as an *active* agent and essentially concentrate on the forms of language they use to convey this change. With this in mind, I restrict my in-depth review to studies that concentrate on the process of personal transformation, with a specific emphasis on language.

Since I am *not* concerned with making generalised claims about the *cause* or *nature* of conversion, I deliberately avoid engagement with studies that propose a psychological stage model of conversion (Lofland and Stark, 1965). Additionally, my review herein eschews reliance on sociological theories and models that exclusively promote a network approach to conversion (Greil, 1977; Stark, 1996; Stark and Bainbridge, 1985). For example, Rodney Stark (1996: 16–17) argues, 'Conversion is not about seeking or embracing an ideology; it is about bringing one's religious behaviour into alignment with that of one's friends and family members'. Despite that such a perspective implicitly and explicitly assumes a passive role for the convert, an emphasis on network did not appear in *all* of the narratives in this research (only a few). More importantly, another reason for avoiding a conception of conversion that primarily rests on network is anchored on the fact that the material I have collected does not permit me to assess the validity of these claims (as I do not know my participants outside the context of the interview, nor did I include explicit questions that address this facet in all of the interviews).

Instead, I draw inspirations from scholars who place *language* at the heart of their inquiry (Harding, 1987; Popp-Baier, 2002; Snow and Machalek, 1983; 1984; Staples and Mauss, 1987; Stromberg, 1993). First and foremost, I adopt David Snow and Richard Machalek's (1983, 1984) conception of conversion as a change in a person's 'universe of discourse'. I believe that this conception is a useful methodological standpoint and provides a framework for confining the subject of the study (conversion) into tangible material (narratives). Secondly, I support Peter Stromberg's (1993) and Clifford Staples and Armand Mauss's (1987) advocacy of the importance of language in the process of conversion. These authors essentially view language as a device that facilitates the process of change and self-transformation associated with conversion. The following pages explore the works of the aforementioned authors in more detail and clarify the ways their approach resonates with the objectives of the present research.

Conversion and Language

In 1983 Snow and Machalek published their influential article, 'Convert as a Social Type', in the *Sociological Theory* journal. This (1983: 260) work essentially criticised conversion literature that was concerned with exploring the causes and stages of conversion by presupposing the criteria for *identifying* the convert in the first place. Their argument rendered the identification of a convert based on their overt religious behaviour (such as physical aberrations, group membership and participation, and demonstration events), which is problematic in determining conversion since some institutions may apply pressure on their members to act a certain way.

Moreover, as far as their conceptions of conversion were concerned, Snow and Machalek (1983: 265) agreed with their peers that conversion involved a 'radical change', yet their concern was to clarify exactly *what is being changed* and what were the *indicators* of that change. They argued that perceiving conversion as a change in a person's belief, value, behaviour, and identity was equally problematic since these conceptions require further clarification and specification of how much change is necessary and in which direction these changes should occur for it to qualify as conversion.

Snow and Machalek tackle this problem by relying on the works of George Herbert Mead (1932, 1962 cited in Snow and Machalek) and propose that conversion should be perceived as a change in one's 'universe of discourse'. This adaptation builds upon the idea that individuals orient themselves towards the world from a set of socially constructed and taken-for-granted assumptions, which are essentially embedded in language. As a 'system of common or social meanings', a universe of discourse provides the individual with the means to interpret and structure their actions and experiences (Snow and Machalek, 1983: 265).

This conception of conversion is not unique to Snow and Machalek. Similar definitions of conversion have been applied in many anthropological studies, such as Buckser and Glazier (2003: xi), for whom conversion means, 'to change one's world, to voluntarily shift the basic presuppositions upon which both self and others are understood'. Other scholars have conceptualised conversion in the same framework, albeit under different terms. For instance, Heirich (1977) spoke of conversion as a shift in one's sense of 'ultimate grounding' or 'root reality'. By this Heirich (1977: 673) refers to that which 'provides clear basis for understanding reality, that provides meaning and orientation for understanding one's situation and acting in relation to it'. Similarly, Travisano (1970: 598–600) used the change in one's 'universe of discourse' or the 'informing aspects of one's life or biography' as a criterion to distinguish conversion ('a Jew becoming a fundamental Christian') from *alteration*. Travisano (1970: 601) defined the latter as a 'relatively easily accomplished changes of life, which do not involve a radical change in universe of discourse'. Hence, alteration is understood as 'learning well a new part of a world', or the universe of discourse the actor *already* belonged to, such as 'a Jew becoming a member of a Unitarian Society' (Travisano, 1970: 598).

The present research follows (and applies) the aforementioned understanding of conversion (Buckser and Glazier, 2003; Heirich, 1977; Snow and Machalek, 1983). Interpreted in this framework, conversion is the process of migration from one universe of discourse to another and involves the *creation* of a new self-concept; the new universe of discourse provides the individual with a system of meaning and the necessary recourse for self-construction; reorientation towards the world; and the understanding of events, experiences, and actions of self and others. By using the terms *self* and *self-concept*, I follow the largely unchanged footprints of Mead (1934, cited in Gecas, 1982: 3) who sees the former not as an organism, but as a 'reflexive phenomenon that develops in social interaction and is based on the social character of human language', and the latter as the 'product' of this reflexive activity.

That said, by confining conversion to a change in a person's universe of discourse, Snow and Machalek (1983: 260) proposed that the evidence of this transition could be sought in the changes that occur in a person's language and reasoning. Grounding their theory in Snow's (1976) research on converts to the Nichiren Shoshu Buddhist movement (and a number of secondary sources), Snow and Machalek proposed four rhetorical features by which one can identify a convert simply by paying attention to the way they speak. These include (1) biographical reconstruction, (2) adoption of a master attribution scheme, (3) suspension of analogical reasoning, and (4) embracement of the convert role—I explore these in relation to the data in chapter 1. For the purpose of this argument, it suffices to say that Snow and Machalek developed this theory out of a criticism of conversion studies that often ignored or simply assumed the characteristics of the converts.

Indeed, Snow and Machalek's theory has been the subject of criticism for two main reasons: first, for rendering the individuals' self-conception as a convert irrelevant to their analysis, and, second, as many scholars, such as Radford (2015: 5), have argued, for effectively limiting 'conversion to simply a change in words'. Staples and Mauss (1987: 138; original italics) were among the first to respond to Snow and Machalek's study, and wrote:

> Because we view conversion as an inherently subjective phenomenon, we believe that the subject, and only the subject, is qualified to tell us who he or she *really* is. Consequently, we determine whether or not someone is a convert by asking the person the question: Are you a convert?

With this methodological concern in mind, Staples and Mauss (1987: 142) proceeded to reformulate Snow and Machalek's theory within the 'functionalist' framework of language. First, however, Staples and Mauss put this theory to test. They conducted qualitative interviews with fifteen members of an Evangelical Christian community and concluded that only the first rhetorical feature—namely biographical reconstruction—is unique to (new) converts, and that the other three rhetorical features also apply to 'life-long' committed Christians (1987: 143). They further argued that biographical reconstruction should be understood as a *device* that facilitates the process of self-transformation and change associated with conversion. Moreover, whereas Snow and Machalek (1983, 1984) theoretically linked the change in a person's universe of discourse to a change in his/her 'consciousness', Staples and Mauss (1987: 142–145) primarily perceive conversion as a change in a person's self-concept, suggesting that the function of a new universe of discourse is to provide the individual with a methodology to construct the self. Hence, they conclude (1987: 144), if biographical reconstruction enables individuals to reconstruct their past and transform their present sense of self, then it is reasonable to assume that the other three rhetorical features are likely to play a role in the 'maintenance' of that self and thus indicate commitment.

In the decades following these publications, a person's self-identification as a convert remains satisfactory evidence that conversion has occurred, to the point that this approach is comfortably conceived as the etiquette for participant recruitment among many of the studies on this subject.[12] What seems to be ignored is the fact that the Western socio-religious landscape has undergone drastic transformation since the time of those publications. The point to which I am alluding is that at a grassroots level, the terms *convert* and *conversion* no longer carry the same connotation as they did during the 1980s, particularly among unconventional subcultures in Western societies (including New Zealand) that not only avoid labels but are also reluctant to be associated with traditional religious establishments—as was the case for almost all Vipassana practitioners in this research.

Thus, I strongly support Snow and Machalek's (1983; 1984) criticism of research that presupposes the characteristic of the convert and simply relies on the individuals' self-identification as convert. In the same light, I also believe that paying attention to individuals' language and reasoning is, methodologically, the most plausible approach to study conversion. The rationale for this is simple. I agree with the aforementioned authors that determining conversion solely in terms of change in a person's belief and values—as some scholars have argued (Chaves, 2004)—is methodologically problematic. This is because another person's beliefs and values are not immediately available to us for assessment but are conveyed through the medium of language in the form of narratives. These narratives must not be analysed in terms of their potential referential function (Popp-Baier, 2008; Stromberg, 2014) but should be seen and treated as 'artfully accomplished constructions' (Beckford, 1978: 250). This point is the cornerstone upon which the foundation of this book rests. Secondly, I argue that conversion may not necessarily entail a drastic alteration to one's belief system. This is particularly the case among Vipassana practitioners who often claim to have had prior affinity to Buddhist philosophy and worldviews. Thus, instead of holding a change in beliefs as criteria for conversion, I look at the language in which beliefs and values are articulated.

Theoretically, however, I also align this book with the latter position, namely Staples and Mauss's (1987: 137) *functionalist* approach to the role of language in the process of conversion. Hence, in referring to Snow and Machalek's (1983; 1984) four rhetorical 'features' of a convert's language, I approach them as rhetorical *devices* that converts utilise to both achieve and

---

[12] Indeed, a review of recent publications on religious conversion (Jindra, 2014; Radford, 2015) reveals that authors of these studies were content with recruiting participants based on self-description or and/or their membership and affiliation to religious organisations (e.g. church) or relevant associations (e.g. Muslim American Society).

convey (to others) that transformation has occurred. However, while Staples and Mauss essentially believe that self-transformation occurs through language, I do not assume that language is the *only* mechanism that assists this process; rather, I take it as an observable medium (for research). This is because the process of self-transformation within Goenka's Vipassana tradition relies on an interplay between discourse and the practice of meditation. This aspect of the movement makes this process far more complex to study than perhaps conversion to Evangelical Christianity (which Staples and Mauss have drawn their conclusions from).

Moreover, Staples and Mauss's speculation about the role of language in self-transformation remains at an abstract level, as they do not illustrate exactly how language is instrumental in this process. Thus, in scrutinising the linguistic patterns involved in this process and its performance, I draw upon, and closely engage with the work of Stromberg (1993). In doing so, my aim is *not* to attempt to provide an inclusive theory of how conversion or self-transformation occurs within language. Rather my objective is to demonstrate that in narrating their experience of self-transformation, old students engage in a distinctive linguistic process that closely resembles the structure of 'conversion narratives' in other traditions (Harding, 1987; Popp-Baier, 2001, 2002; Stromberg, 1993).

To date, there are a number of studies that have taken a somewhat similar language-based approach to conversion albeit for objectives different to that of the present study. Most notably, Harding's (1987, 2000: 37) attentiveness to verbal performances demonstrated how fundamental Baptists persuade a person to convert by appropriating certain rhetorical techniques and adopting a particular form of language that is 'intensified, focused, and virtually shot at the unwashed listener' during witnessing. Ulrike Popp-Baier's (2001) work, which was similarly inspired by Stromberg's (1993) linguistic approach, examined the narrative of a young Charismatic-Evangelical convert who understood her conversion as a remedy to her eating disorder. Popp-Baier's (2001) exploration demonstrates the efficacy of a conversion story in providing the narrator with a platform to articulate unfavourable aspects of her life story to categorise them as belonging to a temporal past and therefore move forward with the possibility of a new self constituted in a new universe of discourse. As becomes evident in the next chapter, the method of analysis used in this study inherits from these strains of thinking about conversion (Harding, 1987; Snow and Machalek, 1983, 1984; Staple and Mauss, 1987; Stromberg, 1993) and blends them in ways to inform my exploration of the collected material including disengagement narratives.

Finally, this research contributes to the relatively small body of qualitative studies about Goenka's Vipassana movement (Goldberg, 2001; Loss, 2010; Melnikova, 2014; Pagis, 2008, 2010a, 2010b; Selim, 2011), most of which have been concerned with accounting for and conceptualising the efficacy of the practice in producing various outcomes. Among the abovementioned literature, this book provides a complementary account to the sociological study of Michal Pagis (2008), which is the state of the art for theorising the process of production and maintenance of a self that is detached from external influences. In her doctoral thesis, Pagis (2008: 4) illustrates how the practice of Vipassana meditation enables individuals to cultivate a self-dependent self by replacing the 'stabilising mechanisms of selfhood'—'from verbalisation of the self to embodied self-reflexivity, from anchoring subjective experience in intersubjectivity to anchoring it in solitary practice, from emotional dependency on others to emotional autonomy'. The objective of Pagis's (2008: 61) study is to demonstrate that a mere change at the level of language is not enough for the kind of self-transformation that Vipassana meditation seeks to produce; this change must also take place at the level of embodiment and experience.

The study of non-verbal semiotics and embodied experiences are therefore the locus of Pagis's (2008) attention, and, consequently, she does not give the same significance to the role of the *movement's* language and rhetoric in this process. Even though interviews with committed Vipassana meditators constitute a large proportion of her data (as she mainly anchors her study in participant observation at two official centres in Israel and America, and autoethnography), she predominantly analyses them in terms of their referential meaning, often translating large interview passages from Hebrew to English. Moreover, while Pagis (2008: 19, 93, 157) makes note of the fact that all Vipassana instructions are taught via Goenka's pre-recorded audio and videotapes, this essential piece of information is often neglected in her analysis. In other words, Pagis (2008; 2010) partially hinges her theory on the token of silence, in a context that is not completely silent.

Research Design and Personal Orientations

This research engages in a *bricolage* (Denzin and Lincoln, 2008: 5; McLeod, 2001) to create a methodological garment tailored to the context of inquiry: [13] it is an interpretive research informed by reflexive ethnography, in-depth interviews, and a dynamic combination of thematic and structural narrative analysis.[14] This approach responds to the collage of perspectives and theories about conversion and disengagement that influenced this research (Barbour, 1994; Gooren, 2010; Harding, 1987; Snow and Mackalek, 1983; Staple and Mauss, 1987; Stromberg, 1993).

In-depth interviews constitute a substantial portion of the material collected for this research. Between June 2014 and February 2016, I conducted interviews with twenty-six individuals: six old students, four new students, and sixteen individuals who have departed from the movement, all of which were digitally recorded. Moreover, I conducted follow-up interviews with three individuals who accepted the invitation to be interviewed roughly a year after the initial interview took place. Thus, a total of twenty-nine *formal* interviews were collected. These culminated in detailed longitudinal reports on two new students (initial interviews were conducted two weeks *after* their first course and the follow-up interview took place a year later) and a

---

[13] In its contemporary French usage, the term *bricolage* means do-it-yourself, and *bricoleur* describes a handyman or a handywoman who makes use of tools available at hand to complete a task (Kincheloe, 2001: 680). These terms have found their niche in scholarship through the writings of the anthropologist Claude Lévi-Strauss (1966), who saw myths as a bricolage of signs, symbols, and intellectual resources available in a cultural repertoire. In recent years, writers such as Norman Denzin and Yvonna Lincoln (2008) have used these concepts to convey that qualitative research involves the same process of sifting through the toolbox of techniques and piecing together a methodology that responds to complex situations. According to these authors, the product of this labour is 'a reflexive collage or montage; a set of fluid, interconnected images and . . . a sequence of representations connecting parts to the whole' (Denzin and Lincoln, 2008: 12). Bricolage is elastic to uncalled circumstances (Kincheloe et al., 2011: 171) and accommodates the space for improvisation if need be. However, this does not mean that the researcher has an excuse to whimsically elect methods from the marketplace of ideas. Rather bricolage demands that the researcher maintains theoretical coherence (Kincheloe et al., 2011: 168) and resolves epistemological and ontological tensions resulting from the synthesis of juxtaposing techniques and perspectives grounded in different paradigms (Denzin and Lincoln, 2008: 12; Walcott 1992, cited in McLeod, 2001: 120). In this sense, a more appropriate portrayal of bricolage is provided by Joe Kincheloe (2001: 681) who depicts the current postmodern climate as a 'postapocalyptic' area 'where certainty and stability have long departed for parts unknown', and the bricoleur is then positioned in the 'ruins of the temple' where they 'pick up the pieces of what's left and paste them together as best they can'.

[14] This research is grounded in an interpretivist framework, which holds the ontological view that social realities are constructed and can therefore be altered by the knower (Laverty, 2008: 26). In terms of epistemology, this paradigm highlights the relationship between the knower and the known, the interviewer and the interviewee, the analyst and the reader (Bremborg, 2011: 311). According to this line of thought, the researcher is an inextricable part of the research and is interactively linked with the subject under study in the creation of meaning (Denzin and Lincoln, 2011).

disaffiliate (Damian, the key informant in chapter 4).[15] In addition to formal interviews, I had *informal* follow-up meetings and conversations with six participants, which also informed the process of this research and substantiated some of my ideas.

Since the participants in this research fall into three main categories (new student, old student, and disengagers), recruitment strategies varied depending on the level of accessibility of each group. For instance, new students could only be accessed at the centre, and therefore recruitment was in person, whereas old students were recruited with the help and promotion of my gatekeeper—the movement's administration—who kindly introduced me to a group of volunteers during the work period.

Facebook constitutes another arena from which a number of participants were recruited. There are several Vipassana public groups on Facebook with over 45,000 members in total. Memberships to these groups are free but require the approval of the page administrator (usually an active member of the community). As a member of these groups, the search graph on Facebook allowed me to identify individuals with reference to their location. Therefore, it was relatively easy to identify New Zealanders affiliated to one of these groups or have simply 'liked' Goenka's Vipassana Facebook page. Additionally, there is a specific group called Vipassana (New Zealand), which hosted approximately 360 members at the time. Through this method, sixty-one individuals were initially contacted and invited to participate in this study. The invitation briefly explained the purpose of the research, the anticipated time of commitment, and my contact details. Twenty-two individuals responded to the initial recruitment message and expressed interest in participating in the study and were thus provided with further details including a copy of the University of Otago Human Ethics consent form and participants' information sheet. From the total of twenty-six participants in this research, eleven individuals (including a number of disengagers) were recruited through this method (two of whom reside in Australia).

Snowball sampling was another method through which a number of disengagers were recruited in this research. Snowball sampling is a type of

---

[15] Note that, despite my anticipation, follow-up interviews with the other two new students was rendered unproductive because these two individuals stated they had no intentions to daily practice Vipassana meditation and did not want to follow up on this topic. On the other hand, the material derived from the follow-up interviews with the other two new students provided insight into the process of leaving the movement prior to developing a commitment. These case studies are explored in chapter 3. The follow-up interview with a disaffiliate (Damian, see chapters 4 and 5) was not initially planned, rather it was conducted to gain more insight and clarity into certain topics.

purposive sampling technique useful for accessing 'hidden populations' (Atkinson and Flint, 2004: 1044). This technique simply relies on a small pool of initial participants to nominate further eligible participants among their existing social networks (Bryman, 2001: 98). This method, although very useful for recruiting hard-to-reach participants, poses a risk of capturing a biased sample group (Morgan, 2008). To avoid this danger, the initial recruited participants were chosen from all three categories (new students, old students, and disengagers) and were asked to nominate only one potential candidate each. Thus, the recruitment of the twenty-six participants consisted of a combination of recruitment in person (ten), via Facebook (nine), and snowball sampling (seven).

Moreover, with the development of the research, the criteria for participant recruitment became narrower in order to address the tonalities of disengagement such as the case study of an individual who no longer understood the world through the prism of Vipassana meditation's teachings—a deconvert. Therefore, I made use of a theoretical sampling approach (commonly used in grounded theory research) to recruit roughly half of the participants. This is because the process of data analysis ran parallel with the data collection.

In this research, I adopted a semi-structured, open-ended interviewing technique,[16] steered to some extent by an interview guide. The aim was to maintain a level of consistency across all interviews while simultaneously allowing participants to build up their narratives at their own pace and to discuss issues they considered important. However, as a result of this flexibility, the length of the interviews varied between forty-five minutes to two hours, although the vast majority of the interviews (eighteen) exceeded sixty minutes (culminating in roughly forty hours of recordings).

Conversion (and disengagement) is not some sort of a physical object 'out there', waiting to be discovered; it is a lived experience of gradual processes (Cowan, 2014; Streib et al., 2011: 97). As a researcher, I do not have

---

[16] The interviewing process generally commenced with an introduction and a short discussion about the study. This was followed up by a brief outline of the general themes of the questions, which projected a chronological order, particularly in the first introductory section. I asked the participant to start with their background, including their religious upbringing, provide a life story, and work towards their introduction to Vipassana. The purpose was to allow the participant to create a narrative that included both factual information and stories of events and trajectories that eventually led them to encounter Vipassana for the first time. This proved to be a fruitful method as it enabled me to gather substantial background information replete with participants' interpretations on key themes such as the role of religion in their early childhood/adulthood, their attitudes towards their parental religion, and the twist and turns of their spiritual seekership, which are central facets in studies of disaffiliation and deconversion (Roof, 1993; Streib, 2014).

unmediated access to other peoples' experience; I rely on their retrospective narratives (Spickard, 2011: 342). This study thus involves a double hermeneutics; my interpretation of the participants' narratives that are already imbued with their interpretations of the phenomena. In this book, interpretations were made in relation to the aspects of the wider sociocultural and historical realities that shape and influence the participant, the phenomena, and the participants' understanding of it.

Interpretive research is inevitably value laden since the researchers' biases and assumptions are brought forth in the study (Hurworth, 2005: 210; Wilcke, 2002). This feature of hermeneutic inquiry has long been the target of oppositional criticism in the social sciences. Some have argued that hermeneutic studies are biased towards the researchers' knowledge and are not true to the participants' lived experience (Tripp-Reimer and Cohen, 1987, cited in Benner, 1994: 80). Correspondingly, Taylor (1979, cited in Abbey, 2014: 155) reminds us that human sciences are essentially 'open-ended hermeneutical endeavours' and the knowledge and findings they produce are incomparable with the knowledge desired by the natural sciences. This is directly due to the ontological property associated with human beings—as self-interpreting beings—and therefore the human sciences should not be assessed by the criteria assigned to natural sciences (Abbey, 2014: 154; Blaikie, 2004: 509). For example, what a rock may think of itself—at least at this point in history— is irrelevant to the geologist. From this perspective, the knowledge is no longer perceived as the mere reflection of some objective reality, but the construction of a social world (Kvale, 1995: 25). The anchor points have moved towards linguistics and interpretations of the meaning of the lived reality. As a result, the quest for an absolute form of knowledge and validity gives its place to multiple interpretations (or possibilities) of the lived world (Hoy, 1993).

On what basis, then, are we to assess notions of validity and credibility in hermeneutic studies? Kvale (1995:25) suggests, when the dichotomy of facts and values is forsaken, beauty and the ethics of the constructed knowledge come into the foreground. In such circumstances, validation is best understood to resemble the craftsmanship of research (Kvale, 1995: 26). Consequently, in the absence of any fixed measurements, Taylor[17] considers

---

[17] Accordingly, Taylor proposes two comparative criteria for judging interpretations: first, a better interpretation is one that encompasses and explains more of the feature of the phenomenon than its rival accounts. Second, theories can be evaluated according to their ability to give an account of rival theories, both in terms of their insight and flaws (Abbey, 2014: 155).

the justified movement from one interpretation to another to be the basis on which interpretations should be weighted (Schwandt, 2000: 202), while others (Ricoeur, 1981) emphasise reflexivity.[18] Through self-reflexivity some of the complex political and ideological agendas are brought to the foreground of the research (Richardson, 2000: 254). The aim is to partially undermine the writer's authority so that her/his interpretations become one perspective with no superior claim to truth or validity (Davies, 1999: 15–16).

Due to the interpretive nature of this research, a reflexive approach was adopted to overcome some of the limitations caused by my involvement in this group. Hence, while some researchers (Healy, 2008) may prefer to bracket their views in the hope to see anew, 'as if for the first time', my approach is to acknowledge my orientations and to reflect on the ways in which my position influenced the direction of this research (Manen, 1990; Wilcke, 2002). Moreover, Reich (2003, cited in Sutherns et al., 2014) argues that our lived experiences circumscribe the kind of research one is interested in and/or is best equipped to undertake. In saying this, I do not claim that others cannot understand the processes of conversion and disengagement in Goenka's Vipassana movement, but that it should not be surprising that the selection of this research topic was strongly intertwined with my personal experience with this movement.

I am a middle-class, Iranian woman, and although I come from a different cultural background, I shared with the participants in this book similar motivations for attending a Vipassana course and somewhat similar reasons for disengaging from it. For instance, like many participants in this research, my attraction to Vipassana was partially motivated by an interest in Buddhism, Asian philosophy, and a desire to learn meditation. Despite these similarities, there are several points of departure that lead to different horizons between my perspective and that of the participants: first, my position as a researcher, which allowed me to reflect on the nature of this organisation without affectional ties. Second, I do not perceive the practice to be evenly beneficial for everyone (including myself). Third, I do not entertain the possibility of attending another course for *personal* gain—an outlook that situated me in opposition to the vast majority of the participants consulted for this research. Finally, the process of my conversion to this movement was not tacit, and in

---

[18] Davies (1999: 4) defines reflexivity as a process of 'self-reference', which in the context of qualitative research (and ethnography) refers to the ways in which the products of research are affected by the personnel and process of doing research.

fact, upon the completion of my first Vipassana course in 2006, I comfortably appropriated a Buddhist identity.

Reflecting on my past, I consider this to be rooted in difference in individual, cultural, and political structures. I was born in a country, which despite its religious hegemony, embodies undercurrents of diversity—from Kabbalists to Eckists, from Bahá'ís to Zen Buddhists. However, these unconventional clusters are not apparent on the surface of the society (of course, except for recognised minority groups such as Armenian Christians and the Jewish community); nor are they accessible to the masses, unless one is born into these groups, or is somehow connected with these networks, for example, through friendship. In my case, access to the Vipassana movement was gained through the latter. After developing a fascination for alternative religions—thanks to Tom Cruise—I began learning about 'world religions' (Noss, 1975 [1963]), Buddhism, and eventually, I located the nearest meditation centre to my region: the Iranian branch of Goenka's Vipassana meditation (Dhamma Iran) near Tehran.

At that time, my participation at this specific centre required a signed recommendation letter from a committed member, an interview with the centre's management, attendance at an Anapana day course for teenagers, and reading the Farsi translation of *The Art of Living* (Hart, 1987). This is to say, by the time that I had sat through Goenka's first evening discourse, I was somewhat aware of the movement's origins, had a rudimentary understanding of its doctrines, and had made a certain effort to be there. In these biographical traits, I am not radically dissimilar from some of the interviewees in this research (most participants expressed prior interest in Buddhist philosophy). The important difference from my experience was that this background knowledge was coupled with the desirability of an unconventional religious identity, in this instance a Buddhist one. Of course, I did not recognise this until I saw myself through the bewildered eyes of Andy Letcher, a substitute lecturer in religious studies, who was taken aback by the presence of an Iranian-Buddhist in his class.

During a long academic break in 2009, I attended another ten-day Vipassana course at Dhamma Dipa in Herefordshire, England. During this visit, and with exposure to academic study of religions, I became interested in the discrepancies between the content of Goenka's teachings and his representations of it to the outside world and subsequently devoted my BA thesis to an analysis of this topic. Concurrently, I drifted away from the movement's ideas and eventually disclaimed the Buddhist identity in favour of atheism.

In simple terms, my disengagement was derived, to a degree, from ethical considerations and was contingent upon individual factors (e.g. the field of education, which allowed me to objectify the movement and my experience of it).

By the time I commenced my postgraduate research, every person I knew from Goenka's Vipassana movement had effectively disengaged from this practice—some had joined other movements. Given that the technique of Vipassana meditation aims for 'deconditioning' the partici- pants' understanding of the conventional self and reality, I was fascinated to understand the ramification of disengagement on the practitioners' per- spectives and worldview. For instance, I was interested in whether (and how) the individual reintegrates into mainstream culture and its dom- inant understanding of reality. However, during the early stages of data collection (and the analysis phase), it became clear that there were discon- nections between the participants' self-representations and the lived ex- periences they narrated; I became enthralled with the role of language in this process. Consequently, the anchors of my study shifted towards ex- ploring these disconnections and explaining their implications on disen- gagement trajectories.[19]

Given this biographical context, my position on the insider/outsider continuum is complex, to say the least. In a narrow sense, and based on my previous lived experiences, I am an insider: I have an understanding of the technique of Vipassana meditation and Goenka's teachings of it; I am also familiar with certain explicit and implicit codes of behaviour that define a meditator's role within the premise of the meditation centre. From an institu- tional perspective, I am considered as an old student.

However, in relation to the old students, Vipassana teacher(s), and even some of the former meditators in this research (who had several years of in- tense participation), I am an outsider to an extent. In addition to the gap be- tween the richness of our lived experiences, these individuals have certain insider knowledge that it is inaccessible to me. For instance, advanced course materials (e.g. Goenka's instructions for the twenty-day courses) are only available to advanced students who attend these courses, and therefore my understandings of these materials are not derived from personal experience.

---

[19] Thus, whereas my initial plan was to conduct interviews with disengagers as well as new students before and after a standard course, I broadened the recruitment criteria to include committed medi- tators including assistant teachers.

More importantly, regardless of my position in relation to the institutional insider/outsider boundaries, I am also an outsider to the cultural context of the research participants (New Zealand). While my cultural heritage has certainly shaped who I am as a researcher, I argue that, in the context of this research, my outsider position enabled me to question the function of certain Western cultural structures in ways that previous scholarship has neglected (simply because most scholars operate from within the same structures and consequently are at the risk of taking certain ideologies for granted). In other words, my unique outsider position to the culture of New Zealand allowed me to perform the task of the *flâneur*, classically described by Walter Benjamin (1999 [1982]).

Further complicating my position in relation to this movement and the participants in this research (i.e. old students) is my role as a researcher and the type of counter-institutional research I have undertaken in this study. That is, the comparisons I draw between the categories of religion and spirituality, conversion and self-transformation, the movement and religious organisation, and so forth are not particularly favoured, approved, or supported by the movement, or the insider's perspective. Indeed, people's attitudes towards this research ranged from interest and curiosity to suspicion, depending on where they positioned themselves on the insider/outsider boundary and how they construed my positionality.

Given that from its inception this research was focused on disengagement, within the field, I frequently faced the questions of motivation—'Why are you focusing on the negative side?' In order to negotiate my role as a researcher in such contexts, I exemplified my own previous involvement with the practice, and expressed my genuine interest in wanting to understand the effects of disengagement on participants' understanding of self and reality. In the most unexpected scenario, I became the subject of an interview myself. That is, one of my initial interviews turned on its head towards the end, as the interviewee revealed their role within the organisation and noted that their participation was partially motivated by a curiosity to learn what the research was about. While claiming that the movement is 'indifferent' to and 'ambivalent' towards outside research, this participant expressed a *personal* interest to learn whether the findings about the cause of disengagement can help the movement deliver a 'better product'. Given that this interview occurred before I gained access to the field, I suspect that my conversation with this participant influenced my access to the field.

Outline of the Book

The first chapter provides an overview of the participants' biographical narratives and scrutinises the changes associated with language at different levels of religious participation and commitment in order to distinguish disengagement pathways in subsequent chapters. In that chapter, I adopt Gooren's (2010) conversion career model as a heuristic framework to achieve the abovementioned objectives in a coherent manner. I see the linguistic transformation involved in the process of conversion analysable in two gradations of conversion and commitment. Therefore, I divide this chapter into four sections: the first section explores the participants' *preaffiliation* context by looking at their biographical narratives and the practices they engaged with prior to their introduction to Vipassana meditation. The second section reflects on practices that mark formal *affiliation* to Goenka's movement and the significance of these for the process of conversion. The third section reflects on the sociocultural and institutional factors that harbour participants' rejection of the category of conversion and the Buddhist identity. This section subsequently proceeds with detailed exploration of the participants' language, and the linguistic patterns associated with their transition to *conversion*. The final section on *commitment* depicts the characteristics of a core member identity based on the meditators' language, reasoning, and their self-representation or performance of the Vipassana meditator's role. I therefore use the linguistic markers explored in this chapter (conversion and commitment) to distinguish two *broad* disengagement pathways: (1) pragmatic leavers, who disengaged prior to the development of commitment, and (2) disaffiliates, who disengaged after years of intense commitment (see figure I.5).

The second chapter introduces the concept of *tacit conversion* as an analytical framework for conceptualising the process of personal transformation and increased commitment to Goenka's Vipassana movement. This chapter is based on a detailed examination of an old student's language and his performance of the role of a Vipassana meditator. My analysis in this chapter is inspired by Stromberg's (1993) linguistic approach to conversion narratives. By paying attention to the content of speech, as well as other modalities of communication, including the inflections, tonalities, and the delivery of the narrative, I illustrate that committed old students essentially perform a narrative that in many ways resemble what have been categorised as 'conversion narratives' in other traditions (Harding, 1987; Popp-Baier,

2001, 2002; Stromberg, 1993). Moreover, this chapter outlines several themes central to the participants' experience of self-transformation such as self-acceptance, agency, and the mind-body relationship.

The third chapter explores the linguistic characteristics of the narratives of pragmatic leavers, which represent the accounts of those individuals who disengaged *prior* to developing commitment and therefore had minimum exposure to this movement. Because empirical studies on exit are primarily built upon the experience of those individuals who leave a movement after long periods of intense devotion and commitment, this chapter prioritised a descriptive approach in order to adequately depict this phenomenon. Accordingly, I argue that pragmatic leavers are (to some extent) experience seekers, and their narrative plots were amenable to the types of meditative experiences they had (traumatic, unpleasant, or extraordinary). I present three interrelated themes that characterised the language of these disengagement narratives—(1) pragmatism, (2) dualistic discourse, and (3) ambivalence—and demonstrate how each narrative differs based on a particular dynamic between these features.

The fourth and fifth chapters explore disaffiliation narratives and disaffiliation trajectories respectively. Disaffiliation narratives describe the accounts of those individuals who disengaged after years of intense commitment to the movement. Through a detailed linguistic analysis of a case study, I argue, in the fourth chapter, that Vipassana disaffiliation narratives are characterised by an ambivalent language, which involved the participants' ongoing convictions about the transformative efficacy of the technique and a certain doubt about their own abilities to progress towards enlightenment. The fifth chapter thus goes on to outline the two common disaffiliation trajectories based on the manner these doubts were dealt with: (1) drifters in samsara, and (2) pursuers of the gateless gate. This chapter illustrates that a phenomenon known as deconversion (migration outside the movement's universe of discourse) rarely occurs in the context of tacit conversion.

The sixth chapter explores deconversion as the third and final disaffiliation trajectory. Through a detailed exploration of a single case study, this chapter explores the narrator's attempt to flee the movement's universe of discourse. In this chapter, I introduce the term *authenticity talk* to refer to a style of discourse that functions both as (1) a recourse for self-reconstruction post-exit and (2) a rhetoric that provided the narrator with a sense of autonomy, empowerment, and self-validation. I claim that the disengagement literature takes authenticity talk at face value and mistakenly conceives of it as an actual motive behind exit.

The concluding chapter summarises the findings of this study and its contributions to the existing scholarship. The chapter subsequently addresses the limitations of this work and ends with a note on the implications of this study for future research.

1

Conversion Career

My aim in this chapter is to demonstrate how the universe of discourse changes with increased participation and to identify the linguistic markers of this change. A thorough exploration of the language of participants at different levels of religious commitment will then allow me to distinguish exit pathways in subsequent chapters: pragmatic leaving (chapter 3), disaffiliation (chapter 5), and deconversion (chapter 6).

To address these points in a systematic fashion, I have adopted Gooren's (2010) conversion career model as a framework and organised this chapter in four sections: the first section draws on biographical material to depict participants' preaffiliation orientations, such as the subcultures they belonged to prior to their introduction to Goenka's movement. The second section explores activities associated with formal membership (affiliation) and highlights practices that ensure practitioners' transition to conversion. The third section explores the institutional, cultural, and linguistic structures that support participants' rejection of the category of 'conversion', and it subsequently addresses the linguistic markers of conversion. The fourth section represents the linguistic changes associated with increased levels of commitment and the characteristics of the Vipassana meditator's role. First, however, it is important to clarify my appropriation of Gooren's model.

Gooren's (2010) conversion career model offers a typology of religious involvement: preaffiliation, affiliation, conversion, confession, and disaffiliation. These types of involvement, according to Gooren, do not necessarily follow a chronological order; rather as shown in figure 1.1, they are, and should be considered as, dynamic levels of individual religious activity and inactivity (Gooren, 2010: 50).

The relevance of Gooren's model for this book is that it distinguishes between three levels of religious involvement (affiliation, conversion, and confession[1]) and that it conceives of a variety of ways in which individuals

---

[1] Gooren (2010: 3) defines conversion as 'a comprehensive personal change of religious worldview and identity, based on both self-report and on attribution by others'. These 'others', Gooren notes, can be members of the same religious group, or significant others who are outsiders. Gooren's

Drifting Through Samsara. Masoumeh Rahmani, Oxford University Press. © Oxford University Press 2022.
DOI: 10.1093/oso/9780197579961.003.0002

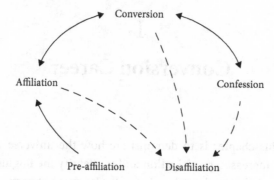

Figure 1.1 Gooren's (2010) conversion career model

can shift between these levels of religious activities, as opposed to assimilating a linear process of conversion (from preaffiliation to disaffiliation). It is this feature of Gooren's conception of the conversion career that is useful for framing various exit trajectories from Vipassana meditation, since disengagement narratives of those participants with longer and more intense commitment is *qualitatively* different from those with a relatively short-lived involvement with the practice. Note that throughout this book, I have used the term 'commitment' to refer to Gooren's category of 'confession' to avoid the Christian theological connotations of the latter term.

Preaffiliation

Preaffiliation refers to the preliminary stage where the member has made the initial contacts with the group and is assessing whether to develop affiliation on a more formal basis. Gooren's (2010: 48) preaffiliation stage aims to account for the 'worldview' and 'social context' of potential members before affiliation. It is important to note that, due to the unique structure of a ten-day Vipassana course, unaffiliated members cannot visit the centre casually and sit back and observe others while a course is in operation. While most religious organisations (e.g. the Church of Latter-day Saints) permit potential members to visit the church and observe religious services, Goenka's Vipassana movement primarily relies on word of mouth for course attendees.

(2010: 44–49) reason for adopting this narrow conceptualisation of conversion is to distinguish conversion from the 'confession' stage, which includes the 'indicators that demonstrate an ongoing...commitment after conversion'.

Hence, for the purpose of this book, and in a literal sense, the preaffiliation stage is best conceptualised as the period between the time(s) an individual has heard about Vipassana and when he/she has successfully registered for his/her first ten-day Vipassana course. Although it may be different in each individual case,[2] according to the participants consulted in this research, this period can take between six months and a decade.

Admittedly, the collected data is limited in a sense that I have only been able to conduct formal interviews with participants who have already completed a ten-day Vipassana course (although I had engaged in several *informal* conversations with new students at the centre before the course officially commenced). In general, I cannot claim to have access to unbiased material pertaining to an individual's worldview prior to his or her formal affiliation to the group, other than through retrospective accounts. There is, however, important information enclosed within these narratives which can indirectly shed light on the participants' preaffiliation mindsets. For example, information about participants' preaffiliation social networks can be sought in segments where they discuss their introduction to Vipassana through (1) a 'trusted friend', and/or (2) their prior encounter(s) with a variety of workshops, self-development courses, and holistic practices. Likewise, information regarding their preaffiliation worldviews can be abstracted from the participants' (3) attitudes about their parents' religion, and (4) descriptions of their ideal forms of religiosity, that is, spirituality (briefly depicted in the introduction). Finally, the (5) extensive list of self-help spiritual books (with Eastern philosophical undertones) and the scientific literature that participants referenced in their interviews can illustrate their ideological affinities and cultural dispositions. On the whole, these nodes reveal a complex interplay of factors—social, contingent, individual, institutional, and cultural—influencing the participants' attraction to Goenka's Vipassana movement. Hence, by taking account of the participants' narration about their interests, social circles, and the range of unconventional practices they had engaged with prior to their introduction to the movement, I was able to map broadly the subculture participants occupied at the preaffiliation stage.

As mentioned in the introduction, almost all participants in this research represented themselves as seekers and utilised a seekership plot to frame their narratives. However, this is not to suggest that because all participants

---

[2] 'Word of mouth' is Vipassana's primary means of proselytisation. This was indeed the case for all but one participant (Leslie), who sought after silent meditation retreats on the internet.

valued seekership, they were whimsically driven in any direction; rather, *most* participants seemed meticulous in their choice of practices and generally stayed within a specific subculture where the bulk of their 'journey' occurred. Broadly speaking, these subcultural realms can be distinguished between practices in which spirituality is anchored in developing the *mind* and those in which spirituality is entangled with *healing* the body and mind. The contours of these two subcultures correspond with two (of the many) categories provided by Campbell (2007: 68–111), who in support of his 'Easternization of the West' thesis, offered a thorough review of various cultural complexes, philosophies, beliefs, and practices currently popular in the West. These include (1) the human potential movement, and (2) the holistic health movement. Certainly, these are not hermetically sealed categories, and certain practices, including meditation and yoga, can be positioned under both banners depending on the participants' approach. However, although the majority of participants stayed within these general borders, two participants indicated narratives that shared both traits and hence could be positioned across these boundaries (see figure 1.2).

The following paragraphs provide a brief overview of these two subcultures, illustrate the participants' distinct approaches to Vipassana meditation, and indicate the pervasive patterns of seekership among each group—which

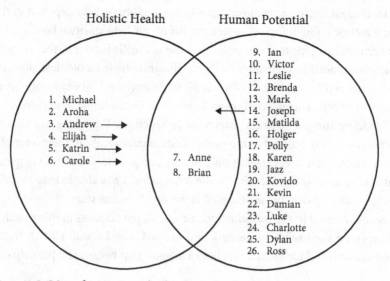

Figure 1.2 Map of participants' subcultures

Arrows indicate movement across subcultures *after* their introduction to and/or departure from Goenka's Vipassana movement.

are based on Sutcliffe's (2004: 474–479) categorisation of three distinct types of seekership 'tactics', namely 'singular', 'serial', and 'multiple'.

The Human Potential Movement

In Campbell's (2007: 91) terms, this subculture is composed of practices that enable individuals both to maximise their human potential and to get in touch with a part of themselves that 'has been supressed or imprisoned for too long'. Thus, healing the individual's mind, personality, and emotions are at the heart of this subculture's enterprise. Encompassing a wide range of practices, the human potential subculture generally bridges psychotherapy and Eastern philosophies/spiritualities.

Among the twenty-six participants interviewed for this research, eighteen individuals reported prior engagement with practices that can be categorised under the human potential movement. These included personal growth workshops, personal development, journaling, creative therapies, counselling techniques, Transcendental Meditation, mind-control training, the Presence Process, and yoga. Regarding Vipassana meditation, these individuals generally praised benefits such as hypersensitivity, attention, clarity and focus, the ability to disengage from physical and emotional pain, self-reflexivity, increased critical thinking, and a sense of calmness and peace. Holger notes:

H. before I even thought about doing Vipassana or anything you know, the span between [when] I say something that I would regret, and the time I regret it will be
three weeks away you know [. . .] but, I can say for myself that, [p] a lot of times
I, I, it is only a few seconds, you know that I realise ok, I will leave the room now
and that's what I do many times. I just walk away from things, not because I can't
handle the situation, just because I know that my personality will in the next
second will say something that I would probably regret afterwards so I actually
can hold on to that moment and leave the room before it happens. Sometimes!

Those who belonged to this subculture commonly expressed affinity towards the difficulty and rigidity of a Vipassana course (e.g. the Noble Silence, daily timetable, and the long hours of meditations) and saw it as instrumental for enabling them to regain control. This characteristic of their narratives indicated that they seek some sort of routine or structure in their lives. In addition to highlighting the more practical outcomes of the practice, a common theme in the narratives of this group was the emphasis on the element of self-discovery, becoming 'aware of what's happening in the mind', and the like.

Reflecting on my past, I would situate my preaffiliation orientations within this group. While I had not formally engaged with any other practice prior to my introduction to Vipassana, I specifically recall developing, from my exploration of Buddhist thought, a burning desire to cultivate detachment and gain control over my emotional state.

Moreover, whereas almost all participants passionately referred to a diverse collection of Hindu and Buddhist self-help spiritual guides—from authors such as Chögyam Trungpa, Deepak Chopra, Paramahansa Yogananda, and Nisargadatta Maharaj, as well as a number of their Western revivals such as Charlotte Beck, Eckhart Tolle, and Bruce Lipton—nine participants in the present group referred to various scientific publications that promote secularised versions of Buddhist meditations as a cure for all sorts of mental and physical conditions. For example, Ian notes:

I. I think the real draw for me came from, um, reading about some of the scientific literature that come back from . . . um, studies done in America with [. . .] interesting findings of just how meditation, um, restructure your brain and . . . lot of other studies just showing how it increases well-being and attention.

The interaction between secular scientific discourses and contemporary religious practitioners is nothing new. In this regard, Courtney Bender's (2010: 12–14) *The New Metaphysicals* has shown the dialectic relationship between the social sciences' understanding of religious experience in shaping the debates and meaning of religious experiences for spiritual practitioners. Therefore, it should also be of no surprise to see that some of the participants are likewise influenced by popular scientific discourse to *explore* meditational practices.

In terms of their seekership patterns, the majority of participants in this group articulated narratives that indicated a 'serial' seekership role (Sutcliffe, 2004)—which means that they experimented with numerous practices and/ or traditions before arriving at Goenka's movement. Interestingly, however, upon their introduction to Goenka's Vipassana movement, the vast majority of the participants in this group converted to a 'singular' seeking tactic

(Sutcliffe, 2004: 475)—a role type ascribed to those who commit themselves to one tradition which they then pursue with great devotion.

The Holistic Health Movement

Conversely, six participants indicated prior involvement and experimentations with practices that focused on body and 'spiritual healing', and they commonly accentuated the physical benefits of Vipassana meditation (as opposed to psychological or emotional). Their biographical narratives seamlessly fit the holistic health subculture, which involves a 'wide range of treatments and approaches to the restoration and maintenance of heath that have traditionally fallen outside of the sphere of modern orthodox medicine' (Campbell, 2007: 97–98). A desire to abandon the duality of mind/body and turning to a special focus on the human body, in addition to mind or personality, is one of the main characteristics of this group. Participants in this group were involved with practices such as acupuncture, homeopathy, massage therapy, Reiki, psychic healing, visualisation, herbal medicine, reincarnation therapies, healing by crystals, music, colour, peyote ceremonies, which were often practiced in conjunction with yoga and meditation. Take for example, the following excerpt from Michael:

M. I've been doing the inner journey for decades now. I take full responsibility for my own actions, I take full responsibility for my own health, I don't need doctors, I don't need hospitals. [. . .] I use scanning as a tool to um, determine, how healthy my body is and where, and what parts of my body needs attention or my energy, my love.

They adhered to a 'multiple' seekership patterns, which is both synchronic and multidirectional (Sutcliffe's, 2004: 477)—unlike the 'serial' seeker, whose seeking progresses sequentially. In short, the participants in this group were generally sceptical of Western medicine and pursued practices that provided a certain healing outcome, and they often mixed multiple types of techniques. Another distinctive characteristic of the participants in this group was that they tended to favour undemanding practices (those with less input and more outcome). Aroha noted, 'Vipassana is one way to enlightenment. It's a long road! But it doesn't need to be that long.'

Hence, with seekership and bricolage as inextricable features of their conversion careers, most of these individuals essentially 'adopted lifestyles that prioritise seeking over finding' (Lewis, 2013: 256). Moreover, because of this tendency to mix and match techniques, most of the individuals in this category expressed dissatisfaction with certain institutional and structural aspects of the Vipassana movement, including its strict guidelines against mixing the techniques with other practices. For example, Anne noted:

A. in my second course that I did in Auckland, um I almost couldn't participate because, at the same time I practiced Reiki, and they wouldn't allow me on the course because I was practicing Reiki!! and, and [p], and, that was, that's still, something in my mind that, um [p] I don't want, um [p] a religion or [p] um [p] something that I follow. I don't want that, to tell me that what I'm allowed and what I'm not allowed!

Finally, among the six participants whose biographical narratives indicated that they previously belonged to the holistic health subculture, after encountering and disengaging from Vipassana, four had reoriented towards the practices outlined in the human potential movement. For example, before attending a Vipassana course, Katrin engaged in colour healing practices, upon her disengagement (from Vipassana), she was pulled towards the Presence Process, which according to her account, 'explains a lot of psychological processes that makes me understand how I sometimes react and how I'm creating my own reality with emotions that are buried underneath a lot of things that I'm doing [. . .] similar to what Vipassana tries to do as well'. Thus, for many individuals who encounter Vipassana, there is a clear shift and reorientation from the holistic health practices towards spiritualities that intersect with psychotherapy. Conversely, only the narrative of one participant (Joseph[3]) indicated a reorientation in the opposite direction.

---

[3] While Joseph's initial phase of seekership took place within the human potential movement (practices with Eastern philosophical overtones) after his introduction and subsequent disengagement from Vipassana he gravitated towards the holistic healing: 'I had terrible health [. . .] I had a reading from a naturopath and a psychic healer and apart from the, one of the treatment which was also a spiritual that the naturopath gave me, all I've done was meditate, and changed my diet. So meditation has done it. Vipassana has opened the door. it was the Major mechanism that enabled me to make big steps'.

Affiliation

In Gooren's model (2010: 48), affiliation refers to the process of becoming a 'formal member', although membership has not yet become a central and leading aspect of an individual's life or identity. Due to the unique institutional features of the movement and the structure of a ten-day course, affiliation and conversion can be tightly intertwined, and, therefore, the aim of this section is to both distinguish these levels and highlight the practices that effectively enable one's transition between these levels.

As mentioned, the organisation does not permit unaffiliated members to visit the centre casually during the periods that a course is in process—one must apply to participate at a ten-day course before arriving at the centre.[4] In other words, one's formal/proper introduction to the practice and the movement is accomplished by participation at a ten-day course. Consequently, while formal affiliation and eventually conversion to most religious organisations usually occurs over an extended period, during which potential members gradually increase their participation and learn about the distinguishing features of the group, in Goenka's movement, formal affiliation, intense participation, and introduction to the practice, its teachings, doctrines, and universe of discourse (i.e. the context for personal transformation) are all condensed into twelve days. As one participant described it, one is 'thrown in the deep end'.

Affiliation strictly refers to the institutional features of membership and, therefore, corresponds with certain privileges that one gains upon completing a standard ten-day Vipassana course, as well as the practices that commence on the evening of day zero. As mentioned, when an individual has successfully completed a ten-day course, he/she automatically gains the title of old student and becomes eligible to contribute to the movement in the form of donations (dana) and offering his/her 'selfless' dhamma service (providing he/she adheres to certain guidelines).[5] Accordingly, not only will the individual be added to the centre's mailing list and receive monthly newsletters and invitations to give dhamma service (volunteer), but he/she will also be granted a password which provides access to the movement's online resources (text, audio, and video files) that are otherwise inaccessible to the

---

[4] Currently, Dhamma Medini accepts online applications via their website.
[5] The temporal distance between being a new student and an old student is simply the duration of a ten-day course.

public. Additionally, if this individual returns for subsequent courses, his/her physical position in the meditation hall will elevate towards the front rows. Hence, in a broad sense, any person that has completed a standard ten-day course is affiliated with Goenka's Vipassana organisation,[6] unless one is officially expelled from the movement by severely violating the movement's code of conduct.

At a less superficial level, we can also consider the practices that formally mark the beginning of a standard ten-day Vipassana course as formal affiliation. These include taking tiratana (refuge in the triple gems: the Buddha, dhamma, and sangha), taking pancasila (Five Precepts) or atthasila (Eight Precepts, in the case of old students), taking a vow of silence (Noble Silence), taking submission/surrender to the teacher (or guru as Goenka uses in Hindi: atmasamarpan), followed by a formal request to be taught instructions to anapana meditation. In other words, all students who have attended a ten-day Vipassana course have effectively followed a similar procedure necessary for becoming samaneras or sramaneris (novice male and female monastics in Buddhist traditions), at least for the duration of the course.

Amongst the abovementioned practices, the act of taking three refuges can be seen as formal affiliation to Goenka's Vipassana movement in the sense that, traditionally, this practice explicitly marks an individual's commitment to Buddhism (Harvey, 1990: 176). Both Goenka and a number of his followers—such as Kory Goldberg (Goldberg and Décary, 2013) and Nora Melnikova (2014)—are well aware of the tensions resulting from the conflict between propagating a non-religious, non-sectarian practice and encouraging students to take three refuges, to the point that they feel compelled to justify this inconsistency time after time.

In his evening discourses, Goenka resolves this dissonance by constantly reassuring his practitioners that no conversion is taking place and provides a gamut of reasons why this is not the case. His arguments, above all, rest on the claim that his teachings are the 'pure *dhamma*', which are the 'universal' 'law of nature'.[7] However, whereas Goenka tackles this conflict by effectively

---

[6] The organisation collects records of an individual's course attendance.

[7] In writing on this topic, Melinkova (2014: 59) adds, 'According to him [Goenka], dharma is the "rule of nature", "*qudrat kā niyam*", it is "eternal", and it applies to everyone. He says: "The law of nature is universal; the universal law of nature is dharma, truth, law". Dharma is not Hindu, Buddhist, Jain, Christian or Muslim, it has nothing to do with organised religion, it is *asāmpradāyik*, it has nothing to do with any particular tradition. Conversion can happen only from one "organised religion" to another, which is not the case here'.

utilising the most basic rhetorical device, namely repetition (Stromberg, 1993: 40),[8] Melnikova (2014: 60–65) takes a semantic route and argues that the cause of this dissonance is due to Goenka's misuse—or the inconsistencies between Goenka's understanding—of the autochthonous concepts of dhamma, sampraday, and diksa (initiation) in Hindi and his understanding of the terms religion and conversion in English.

Moreover, as noted, students are requested to surrender themselves to Goenka and his instructions for the duration of the course.[9] Goenka argues that 'this surrender [is] for the purpose of giving a fair trial to the technique. Only someone who has surrendered in this way can work putting forth full efforts. One who is full of doubts and scepticism cannot work properly' (Goenka, 1997: 55). In fact, during his earlier discourses, Goenka emphasises that 'so long as you remain immersed in doubts, you cannot take even one step on the path' (Goenka, 1997: 33). Hence, an integral component of the act of surrender to the teacher and the technique involves the abandonment of doubt and scepticism.[10]

While some scholars (Goldberg, 2001: 31–34) have rendered these practices as 'formalities', I conceive them not only as formal affiliation but also as essential steps towards conversion. Note that my aim here is not to consider these practices as a form of conversion, for as I have discussed in the introductory chapter, I do not perceive conversion as an event, rather a gradual process of adopting a new universe of discourse. Here, I want to emphasise how the performance of these practices, most notably, the act of surrender to the teacher, ensures one's transition to conversion (i.e. serves as a gateway to accepting a new universe of discourse).

---

[8] In an evening discourse on day seven, Goenka (1997: 39) notes, 'taking refuge in Dhamma has nothing to do with sectarianism; it is not a matter of being converted from one organised religion to another'. Similarly, on the discourse of day ten he (1997: 54) reminds students, 'You started your work by taking refuge in the Triple Gem, that is, in Buddha, in Dhamma, in Sangha. By doing so you were not being convened from one organised religion to another. In Vipassana the conversion is only from misery to happiness, from ignorance to wisdom, from bondage to liberation. The entire teaching is universal'. Other examples can be seen in a detailed footnote provided by Melnikova (2014: 59) which recounts the number of times this theme typically reoccurs in both the Hindi and the English versions of Goenka's evening discourses.

[9] Interestingly, Goenka's pre-recorded audio states surrender to the *present* teacher. While all the teachings are taught via Goenka's recordings, it is not clear whether surrender also includes submission to the assistant teachers.

[10] In fact, the evening discourse of day six considers doubt alongside craving, aversion, mental and physical sluggishness, and agitation as five 'enemies' or hindrances in the progress on this path: 'A great enemy is doubt, either about the teacher, or about the technique, or about one's ability to practise it. Blind acceptance is not beneficial, but neither is endless unreasoning doubt' (Goenka, 1997: 33).

The act of surrender is uniquely significant in Goenka's Vipassana movement, although it has been largely neglected in previous studies on this group (Goldberg and Décary, 2013; Melnikova, 2014; Pagis, 2008; 2010b). Instead, the concept of surrender has attracted much attention from the field of psychotherapy (Hidas, 1981; Wallace, 2009; Weber, 2003), particularly from those scholars who consider the goals of depth psychotherapy, conterminous with the spiritual quest of Buddhist meditative practices such as mindfulness. For example, by comparing the relationship between a spiritual seeker and a guru/teacher to that of a client and a therapist, Andrew M. Hidas (1981: 29) argues that the idea of surrender involves elements of 'vulnerability and risk'; in both instances, the individual exposes his or her inner life and embarks on a journey to dissolve and ultimately alter his or her sense of self and reality. Thus, the act of surrender (both in a meditative practice and therapy) involves 'giving up' and 'letting go', of the previously held conceptions (Hidas, 1981: 27), paving the way to self-transformation, 'without foreknowledge of the actual outcome' (Wallace, 2009: 145).

To understand the significance of surrender, it is fruitful to exemplify cases in which the participant refused to give up, or surrender, to the teacher and his teachings. As noted, it is often the case that new students have very little background knowledge about the course prior to their first encounter.[11] Consequently, it is not uncommon for some participants to leave a ten-day course prematurely due to experiencing dissonance between their pre-existing ideas and those propagated by the movement. Indeed, such was the case for two participants in this research. Ian, for example, had walked out of Goenka's Vipassana course on the first day as the result of experiencing an ideological conflict (although he adopted Vipassana meditation in another tradition later in life). He noted:

I. the first tapes got into a little bit of metaphysics and I just totally lost interest
S. Do you remember what it said?
I. I think something about the 'om' being the centre of, the sound of the universe or something like that and I just rolled my eyes.

---

[11] As a result, even serious meditators such as Elijah noted: 'I spent two days Walking! on Vancouver island to get to this um, random Vipassana course, that I didn't know much about, I was quite naive as to what I was getting myself into'. In the most extreme scenario, the practitioners attending a course may not even know that Vipassana meditation is a Buddhist practice. This was indeed true for many of my fellow meditators at the Goenka's Vipassana Centre in Iran—an observation also made by Pagis (2008: 21) in her study of American and Israeli Vipassana meditators.

Another example emerged in my interview with Jazz, who also declared that she 'ran away' on the first day of her third, ten-day Vipassana course. However, whereas the ideological dissonance compelled Ian to completely withdraw from Goenka's movement, Jazz's account shows that surrender is not a once-in-a-lifetime act, rather a dynamic process:

> J. I was in a bit of a torn dilemma with Vipassana [p] getting rid of the ego, and I felt like the ego needed to be there [. . .] I had been doing a lot of research into my favourite artists in which the ego played a role in their work.
>
> S. Yeah
>
> J. but I ended up resolving it and I'm definitely leaning towards the Vipassana understanding of, the ego, side of it more now [. . .] I got over it and did another course about a year later and it was really good again.

Interestingly, however, the topic of surrender as a form of affiliation did not emerge in any of the interviews with disengagers in explicit terms. This may very well be reflective of all the participants (including disengagers) highly valued ideals such as autonomous seekership (see figure I.4). Therefore, in the absence of sufficient data, I resorted to the internet where I found examples such as the following passage from an ex-Vipassana meditator (Anonymous, 2012):

> Having 'surrendered my ego centred self completely to Buddha and my present Teacher for proper guidance and protection', I certainly felt dirty. So I sent, a handwritten 'unsurrender' letter to Mr Goenka. He replied via an Assistant Teacher who weakly conveyed the pathetic comment that 'surrender was only for 10 days' [. . .] Suffice to say that I remember [. . .] the day 11 morning, in which Mr Goenka, again via his famous (non-sex, lies, and) videotape, suggests in smooching terms that 'surrender is for the whole life'.

These examples illustrate that the act of surrender (in Vipassana meditation) demands an openness to change on behalf of the practitioner, without which the completion of the course, let alone the further step towards conversion, would be impossible. It could be argued that surrender is the extrinsic demonstration of the level of compatibility between the movement's and the participants' existing universe of discourse (and self-concept). For this reason, I propose that surrender in this context should be seen as the gateway to conversion. Generally speaking, however, a student who has gone to the extreme lengths of attending a Vipassana course—stepping away from everyday life for twelve days, leaving his/her loved ones behind, preparing to follow the strict code of conduct, the Noble Silence, waking up at 4:00 a.m., and sitting cross-legged for ten to twelve hours per day—has proven his/her desire for, and amenability to, change, by virtue of being there. Therefore, it is reasonable to assume that the majority of students who have successfully finished a ten-day course were likely to take the additional leap and surrender to the teacher and (symbolically and cognitively) open up to change—unless of course they had decided to leave the course prematurely (Jazz) and/or never return to the centre again (Ian).

Conversion

This section explores conversion on an insider/outsider continuum to explain the discrepancy between the language and the self-representations of participants. On the one hand, (1) I contextualise the *participants'* understandings of conversion; (2) explain why almost every individual in this research rejected this category and/or found it irrelevant to their experience (particularly during their involvement in the movement); and (3) trace the linguistic, institutional, and cultural structures that enable/support their rejection of conversion in the context of Vipassana movement. On the other hand, I examine participants' narratives by turning to academic studies that focus on the role of language in the process of conversion (Snow and Machalek 1983, 1984; Staples and Mauss, 1987; Stromberg, 1993).

As briefly noted, I see the process of adopting a universe of discourse as analysable in two shades: conversion and commitment. Among the twenty-six participants, the narratives of twenty-two of them indicated their passage through the conversion level in their conversion career.[12] Moreover, the analysis of these narratives implied that six participants had disengaged from this stage of their conversion career, whereas others developed high

---

[12] Note that two participants (Holger and Matilda) conveyed ambiguous narratives that can be conceived at a stage between conversion and commitment. As becomes clear shortly, this classification is reflected in the conceptualisation of conversion as a change in one's universe of discourse (Snow and Machalek, 1983, 1984).

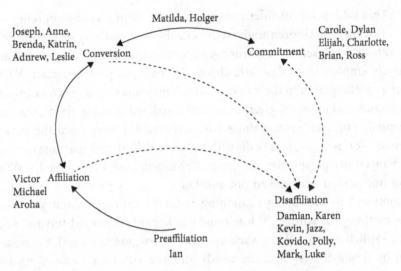

Figure 1.3 Participants' positionality across Gooren's original model

levels of commitment. Figure 1.3 illustrates the positionality of these narratives in accordance with Gooren's conversion career model (2010). The position of participants in this diagram is based on the analysis of their language at the time of their interviews. With the exception of those old students categorised under 'commitment' (Caroline, Dylan, Elijah, Charlotte, Brian, and Ross), the rest of the participants are disengagers. Their positionality on this model demonstrates the stage from which their disengagement occurred. For instance, Ian disengaged at a 'preaffiliation' level. Victor, Michael, and Aroha disengaged from the 'affiliation' level. Joseph, Anne, Brenda, Katrin, Andrew, and Leslie disengaged from the 'conversion' level. Matilda and Holger disengaged at a stage in-between conversion and commitment. Those who are categorised under 'disaffiliation', have all disengaged from the commitment level, meaning they have left the movement after years of commitment.

This diagram is a close adaptation of Gooren's (2010: 50) original model, with minor changes to accommodate the model's expansion in chapter 6 to include 'deconversion' as a separate level of religious inactivity. As becomes clear in chapter 6, the language of only one participant, Luke, warrants his recategorisation under 'deconversion'. In the meantime, however, Luke's narrative is categorised and analysed as a disaffiliate.

That said, if we consider conversion in terms of a 'change in religious worldviews', as Gooren understands it, the vast majority of the participants in this research constructed narratives that both conveyed and actively emphasised a dramatic change in their perspectives, particularly after participation in their first ten-day Vipassana course. Such examples abound, and interestingly, they are not restricted to old students, but also equally common among those who have moved away from the movement. For instance, Jazz (a disaffiliate) argued, 'it [first Vipassana course] changed my perspective on life and changed, how I felt. Like I walked in one person and walked out another [. . .] my parents once made a comment to me saying something is totally different about you, that something has shifted'. While most participants conveyed this message in explicit terms, others, such as Anne (a pragmatic leaver), expressed it by displaying (to me) the words 'this too will pass' tattooed on her wrist, which symbolised the doctrine of impermanence (anicca) for her. However, in spite of all these examples, *none* of the participants in this research used the language of conversion.

Conversely, if we consider Gooren's definition of conversion in terms of a self-declared change in identity, only a small proportion of participants claimed Buddhist identities (in most cases retrospectively, after disaffiliation). Those who did flirt with the idea of adopting Buddhist identities were ambivalent and disclaimed the label during the interview. On the other hand, the old students and Vipassana teachers who demonstrated high levels of dedication to the movement consistently insisted on presenting non-religious identities (e.g. none and atheist).

Clearly then, there is a dissonance between participation and identification as a religious person. Therefore, it is important to understand how these identities are *articulated, rationalised,* and *performed* in the context of an interview. After all, we all have multiple identities, even though we might not conceptualise ourselves that way (Barvosa, 2008). Note that by using this term (identity), I follow Stromberg's (1993: 27) notion of identity as a style—as in a 'style of self-presentation, style of motion, style of interacting, style of talking'. I thus limit the notion of identity to a behaviourally objectified definition, without assuming or attempting to imagine the concept as something that exists outside of a situational context (Stone, 2005: 143). Perceived this way, 'identity [. . .] is a congeries of styles, ways of doing things' (Stromberg, 1993: 27).

Participants' Conception of Conversion

The concept of conversion carried negative connotations for all the participants in this research. Instead, they preferred terms such as 'transformation', 'change', 'development', and 'commitment'. In order to explore conversion through the prism of Vipassana practitioners' outlook, I offer an excerpt from a conversation I had with Matilda,[13] in which we attempted to establish a definition of conversion and discussed whether it is possible to convert to Vipassana.

M. convert! the thing about the word convert, it's like <u>changing somebody's mind</u>, I guess. and changing your mind. so, you can convert, I've converted to several things in my lifetime, like veganism, for example, raw-foodism, I've done both of those. where you, you hear about a thing and you practice it and you become so committed that you decide to commit a hundred percent [. . .] I don't know about convert, whether convert is the right word when it comes to Vipassana [. . .] I feel quite uncomfortable with the word conversion for some reason . . . I think that <u>if I thought of it [Vipassana] more as a religion, and I was ok with that</u>, and I sort of 'converted' [gesture: air quotes], in my head what I think conversion is, So stop doubting, stop questioning and stop 'Shopping around' [gesture: air quotes] for other techniques or ideas. If I fully committed, there's something amazing in that step, I know that [g]. where you give up the questioning, it's Faith, it's faith really isn't it?

In many respects, Matilda's understanding of conversion was shaped by what is commonly known as the Pauline paradigm. This paradigm assumes the convert is a passive subject undergoing a radical and sudden change in beliefs due to external forces. On a scholarly level, this understanding of conversion has been jettisoned by many scholars—owing much to Richardson's (1985) influential works against the brainwashing thesis—in favour of a 'new' paradigm, which conceives the convert as an *active* agent and conversion as a gradual process (Bromley and Shupe, 1979). Nevertheless, the Pauline paradigm and, to an extent, the brainwashing hypothesis continue to influence popular perceptions of conversion.

---

[13] Matilda is a pragmatic leaver who attended two ten-day courses in the past. Although she had stopped practicing meditation, she was optimistic about returning to a course in the future.

As this excerpt suggests, converting to Vipassana for Matilda equates to a lack of agency, giving up critical engagement with an idea, exiting the spiritual marketplace. However, as we discussed this concept in depth, it became clear that commitment played a central role in Matilda's (and many other disengagers') definition of conversion. This could be partly because Matilda is not a committed meditator. In fact, the last two sentences of her statement indicate a nostalgic desire for a kind of uncritical commitment that she calls 'faith'. Hence, while rejecting conversion for themselves, some disengagers (including Matilda) had no hesitation in arguing that individuals who do invest a great deal of their lives at the centre (teachers, long-term students) can be seen as converts. Matilda continued:

M. I guess you can say, if you were too, too, [p] um, do all the um, all of the suggested um practices, the meditation everyday the um, observing the, how many principles are there I've forgotten [. . .] yeah five precepts, observing those etcetera, I guess you could say, [p] that was a kind of conversion.

Hence, Matilda also rejected conversion because from her perspective, conversion involves full (100 per cent) commitment to one's convictions. However, because she has taken a pick and mix approach to meditation, she does not see conversion fitting her experience, stating, 'commitment is a better word because I can commit to aspects without committing to the whole'. Note, however, that Matilda's definition of conversion rests on an a priori concept: 'if I thought of it more as a religion, and I was ok with that', which means Matilda (like other participants) dismisses the notion of conversion primarily because she does not see Vipassana as analogous to religion. In fact, as this example suggests, Matilda had no issues in framing her commitment to veganism as conversion. This was a common pattern across many disengagement narratives. For instance, Mark happily used the term in relation to 'running', yet offered the following argument in the context of Vipassana:

M. Convert! it's a funny word [. . .] I think conversion implies you're <u>changing</u> your <u>faith</u>. and faith by its very definition is belief in something that, you can never prove. because if you can prove it, it's no longer a Faith. Vipassana is not looking at proving anything. um it's, it's, it's simply a meditative technique.

Thus, in addition to full commitment, another reason why some participants rejected conversion in the context of Vipassana was due to the religious overtones of the term 'conversion', in particular conversion as change of faith or beliefs. As Rambo (2003: 213) accurately notes, Evangelical Christians have tended to 'own' the concept of conversion for several centuries. This is precisely why scholars, such as Dan Smyer Yü (2014: 466–467), have rendered the traditional (Christian) paradigm of conversion (which he sees as being primarily anchored in the duality of new and old, saved and unsaved) irrelevant to conversion in the Buddhist context (which he finds qualitatively distinct because it involves the 'discovery' and 'cultivation' of the 'Buddha Nature within'). Yü (2014: 466; italics added) writes, 'Theologically speaking, becoming a Buddhist is both a rational and spiritual choice', and that 'one who becomes a Buddhist, embraces *nothing new but awakens* the seed of enlightenment that was formerly dormant'.

However, such rationalisations—or more accurately narrative reconstructions—are not unique to Vipassana practitioners or converts to other Buddhist traditions (Gordon-Finlayson, 2012). Similar patterns occur in conversion narratives to Paganism (Harvey, 1999) and Islam conversion testimonies, where it is commonly conceptualised as 'reversion' (Nieuwkerk, 2014: 668). According to this perspective, instead of conversion, the practitioner of the newfound faith would argue that they 'had simply discovered what they already believed at heart' (Chryssides, 2016: 27). Hence, these narrative plots could be seen as converts rehearsing the 'appropriate' ways of talking about conversion within the specific groups he had studied (Beckford, 1978). I return to this point shortly.

Interestingly, disaffiliated individuals who had more intense involvement with the movement expressed slightly different conceptions of conversion and used the terms 'obsession', 'fanaticism', and even 'brainwashed' when describing the behaviour of old students. Take for example, the following conversation I had with Karen:

S. did you ever thought of yourself as a convert of any sort?
K. Never, I could say almost never. I was, I was converted as far as my dedication, my devotion to what the technique pointed to and where it was able to take me, absolutely whole heartedly, absolutely. but as far as a convert and making some sort of a, um, I was very aware of the people around me when I was studying it, they were very much converted I guess in that sense, they were very much converts but

there was something about fanaticism that put me off [. . .] something about the identity of being a Vipassana meditator that just didn't, didn't sit with me.

In this excerpt, Karen makes a distinction between conversion as commitment to the practice/technique (i.e. the cognitive dimension of conversion) and conversion as identity change or role taking (i.e. conversion as behavioural commitment). The former speaks of perspectives, motives, and trust in its ultimate promises—or in Riesebrodt's (2010) terminology 'conversion narrative as religious propaganda'. The latter is concerned with the *external* demonstrations of the former, albeit to some excess (by excess, I am interpreting Karen's choice of word 'fanaticism'). In a similar light, Kevin, another disaffiliate, made the following remarks: 'I don't think I was converted [long pause] yeah, not to the point of any obsession. Cause I was too slack at it [hah]'.

More importantly, most of the disaffiliates retrospectively acknowledge conversion once the language was put at their disposal. This primarily took place at the end of an interview, after participants were asked whether they would describe their involvement in terms of religious conversion. In the majority of cases (five out of eight), the disaffiliates confirmed conversion and narrated about their previous enthusiasm for proselytisation and recounted various social encounters which led them to objectify themselves through another person's 'looking-glass'. Damian noted:

D. I can remember when I was about twenty-one meeting some relatives and telling them that I had been started doing this Buddhist meditation and, and, and saying that 'I thought it was the most Truthful thing I've ever come across', at twenty-one or whatever it was and [g] [p] and these relatives who were about my age, [now] in their forties they were sort of like 'right!' you know, 'okay!' And Then I felt 'oh no I sound like a Christian ooooh God' [l] Fuck! I felt like, I sound like I've, I'm a cult convert.

Additionally, this retrospective acknowledgement of conversion was almost always accompanied by the participants' critical reflection on the institutional features of the movement. These included the movement's implicit requirements (behaviour and conduct) for allowing advancement to longer courses, witnessing the expulsion of peers, and a critical engagement with Buddhist literature that instigated a certain doubt about the movement's lineage. For example, Kevin (disaffiliate) argued:

K. when I was, I was doing [p] Vipassana, I probably [p] didn't think of it as Buddhism,
   [g] I thought of it as Vipassana and Vipassana being yk the Buddhist technique
   and therefore to call myself a Buddhist would be a bit silly [p] cause the Buddhist
   were doing it wrong!

S. yeah

K. so now I call myself a Buddhist and think that Vipassana is just one small part of
   Buddhism.

In spite of this retrospective knowledge, the majority of these individuals
shared the same views and linguistic markers with other participants: they
initially rejected conversion and/or continued to distinguish Vipassana
meditation from Buddhism and religion.

Participants' Conceptions of Buddhism

In short, all except one of the participants in this research conceptualised Buddhism in a modernist way, which emphasised and valued the
'detraditionalization, demythologization and psychologization' (McMahan,
2008: 42) of this tradition. The analysis of their narratives revealed a strong
sense of ambivalence over the links they perceived between Vipassana and
Buddhism, which influenced their rejection of the Buddhist label and/or the
creation of ambivalent non-Buddhist identities.

In most narratives, the heart of this ambivalence was anchored on a
disturbance to the participants' romanticised and 'transhistorical' (Ivy,
2005, cited in Yü, 2014: 476) view of Buddhism. From this perspective,
(1) Buddhism is not a religion, but a philosophy; (2) true Buddhism is
devoid of dogma and rituals; (3) meditation can/should be practiced
divorced from its Buddhist foundations; and (4) Buddhism is categorically different from other religions, all of which evoke an image known as
'Buddhist modernism' (Bechert, 1984; McMahan, 2008; Sharf, 1995), or
'Protestant Buddhism' (Gombrich and Obeyesekere, 1988), discussed in the
introductory chapter. This conceptualisation of Buddhism is not unique to
Vipassana practitioners, rather it captures the contemporary imagination of
Buddhism in most non-Buddhist contexts (Carrette and King, 2005; Sharf,
1995; 2015; Wallace, 2002; Yü, 2014).

To illustrate how a disturbance to the aforementioned idealised image of
Buddhism affects the participants' religious identification (or, in fact, their

rejection of Buddhist identities), I draw from my interviews with participants who were at different levels of religious involvement in Goenka's movement (both disengagers and old students). As noted, seven participants in this research claimed to have entertained the idea of adopting a Buddhist identity and/or had identified as Buddhist on New Zealand's national census yet disclaimed this label during the interview. Take for example, the following excerpt from my interview with Ian:

S. Did you consider yourself a Buddhist at any point?

I. Well, I [p], I would have to say no. I considered it, I wondered if I was [. . .] yeah I think the reason why I would never say I'm a Buddhist even though I have adopted a lot of practices in my life [. . .] I think my experience living in Thailand that, there's very much a religious side to Buddhism too. And by that I mean dogma that people just follow [. . .] That I don't think it's helpful, most of the people I know who identify as Buddhist don't actually practice Buddhism or meditation, they go to temples and give money and they pray and they have a lot of supernatural beliefs that I don't think are that helpful.

As the excerpt demonstrates, Ian (who left Goenka's Vipassana before the affiliation stage and joined another tradition) rejected the Buddhist identity because his concept of (true) Buddhism was shattered once he encountered Buddhism in its local context (Thailand). Ian identifies himself as a 'Bright' with 'naturalistic worldviews', and a '100 per cent secular approach' to meditation. In the interview, Ian represented himself as indifferent to religion and approached the topic from a scientific lens, arguing that 'religion is also a natural phenomenon' and that there are 'good explanations why people believe in religion'. Clearly, Ian views Buddhism from a rational, ahistorical, and non-cultural position. It is this position that steers Ian's non-Buddhist identity.

Many participants in this research (at different levels of their conversion career) drew similar comparisons between Vipassana and Buddhism in Asian contexts (Japan, China, and Korea). Their argument was generally value laden, trivialised the category of ritual, and indicated that the participant views himself/herself from a superior position in relation to traditional forms of Buddhism (particularly in Asian contexts). For example, Ross (current Vipassana teacher) argued: 'look at the Buddhism in Japan, I lived in Japan, it's got nothing to do with the original teaching [. . .] it's not what the Buddha was teaching'. He added:

R. monks officiate and perform ceremonies at funerals [. . .] they will chant some
prayers so that the soul of the person will get a good rebirth [. . .] and you can pay
money for that. What's that got to do with it [the teachings of the Buddha].

I return to discuss the structure of Ross's and other old students' language
shortly, arguing that these individuals identically use the same rhetorical
strategies offered by Goenka in distinguishing this movement from religion/
Buddhism.

Having contextualised the participants' rationale for rejecting conversion
in the context of the Vipassana movement and the structures that enable/
support their positions, the remainder of this section examines their narratives in light of a definition of conversion as a change in a person's universe
of discourse. In what follows, I examine the two linguistic markers of conversion: (1) biographical reconstruction and (2) adoption of a master attribution scheme. As stressed before, the abovementioned rhetorical features
originally proposed by Snow and Machalek (1983, 1984) are herein conceptualised as narrative *devices* that participants appropriate to both achieve
self-transformation and to convey that genuine transformation has taken
place. In doing so, I provide a rationale why I have selected these two linguistic features as the criteria of conversion.

Biographical Reconstruction

Biographical reconstruction is perhaps the most prominent feature of
conversion narratives and appears to be both empirically and theoretically acknowledged by the vast majority of scholars in this field (Beckford,
1978; Berger and Luckmann, 1967; Gooren, 2010; Jindra, 2014; Popp-
Baier, 2002; Rambo, 1993; Snow and Machalek, 1983; Staples and Mauss,
1987; Travisano, 1970). This concept is grounded in the symbolic interactionist framework, which posits that our self-concept is produced and
dependent on the knowledge we obtain about ourselves through interaction with others. The knowledge gained this way provides the resources
for constructing our selves in the present, past, and the future (Staples and
Mauss, 1987).

With reference to conversion, biographical reconstruction refers to the
idea that individuals who undergo a radical change reinterpret their lives
'from the vantage point of the enlightened present' (Snow and Machalek,

1983: 268). According to Snow and Machalek (1983: 267), converts tend to interpret their previous understanding of self, relationships to others, motives, and evaluations as a 'misunderstanding'. In short, the converts actively follow the formula of 'then I thought, now I know' (Berger and Luckmann, 1967: 160, cited in Snow and Mackalek, 1983: 266–267) and reassemble their biographies according to 'the new universe of discourse and its grammar'.

The specific language and rhetoric used in each conversion experience and narrative is therefore a dependent feature of the tradition or the particular universe of discourse (Staples and Mauss, 1987: 143). For instance, both Pagan Feminism and Evangelical Christianity provide individuals with rhetoric for the reconstruction of biographies, yet the senses of self created in these traditions will significantly vary due to the differences in the content of their rhetoric. Finally, as mentioned, from a functionalist approach to language, biographical reconstruction is seen as a narrative device or a mechanism used by individuals to achieve the self-transformation they desire (Staples and Mauss, 1987). This is perhaps why (new) converts 'seldom seem to tire of reminding others of how they have changed' (Snow and Machalek, 1983: 267).

In Goenka's Vipassana tradition, biographical reconstruction generally echoes the Four Noble Truths and involves the acknowledgement/acceptance of an 'unbalanced' and 'conditioned' self whose suffering in life is the result of one's 'ignorance' about the true source of suffering. For example, all past events and incidents that culminated in suffering are now interpreted as the result of one's own ignorance and/or mind conditioning. The reconstruction of the self in this paradigm is entangled with a newfound sense of responsibility for one's actions.

However, as far as the acknowledgement of the cause and nature of suffering (i.e. ignorance) is concerned, biographical reconstruction in the Vipassana movement runs parallel to general markers of conversion to Buddhism (Brekke, 2004: 181; Yü, 2014: 466). In order to distinguish biographies that were reconstructed in the light of Goenka's teachings from those that vaguely echoed Buddhist worldviews, I have attended to the *terminology/ vocabulary*, *grammar*, and, *language* of the participants and only considered accounts where there was clear overlap with the movement's universe of discourse. This point becomes clearer in the following chapter. Additionally, only segments where participants *explicitly* linked their (newfound) views to their participation in a ten-day Vipassana course were coded as biographical reconstruction to minimise the risk of biased coding.

Accordingly, only twenty-one participants construed their past in accordance with the movement's universe of discourse and with the intention to convey (to me) that their course participation resulted in a significant transformation to their self-concept.[14] However, these accounts *significantly* varied in their strength and intensity based on the participants' temporal distance from the experience. For instance, new students and recently committed old students (e.g. less than two years of involvement) appropriated this rhetorical device proportionally more than others. Note, for example, the following points raised by Leslie, whom I interviewed roughly two weeks after she successfully finished her first course:

L. three big things came up for me, one was about a relationship with my best friend and for years I hadn't understood part of it and I got real clarity around it [...] the second Big, big, big thing for me was, I think I told you that, the idea that mind and body split in me, and that's [p] it's like my heart has been protected by my mind [...] I've had a lot of trauma in my life and the idea that, that they protected my heart so beautifully is both lovely part of me thinks, 'okay it's time for that to end so I can actually feel all my feelings' and [...] Third piece that I took away which is Huge but it's been part of a lot of the conversations, is around the idea of forgiveness [...] because you do a lot of things in a kind of innocence where [...] you inherited a pattern that you didn't know that you perpetuated it up [p] and learning to forgive yourself, for that [...] I think the biggest thing, of coming out of the retreat was That notion of not setting expectations for myself that are, unrealistic, which I often do or [p] I achieve them but at great cost, kind of thing [...] and so, I almost set myself up to be more than human, then I'm disappointed when I'm just human.

While the disaffiliates constructed their narratives from a disengaged perspective, nevertheless, their biographical reconstructions functioned to implicitly accentuate the efficacy of the practice in producing self-transformation in the past. Hence, not only did disaffiliated individuals follow the formula of 'then I thought, now I know', but their rhetoric

---

[14] The twenty-one were Leslie, Katrin, Brenda, Andrew, Anne, Joseph, Holger, Matilda, Karen, Jazz, Polly, Kevin, Damian, Brian, Charlotte, Elijah, Dylan, Kovido, Mark, Aroha, and Michael.

sometimes also emphasised a *reversion* to a state prior to their introduction to Vipassana. For example, Jazz (disaffiliate) argued:

J. losing attachment and craving towards things [. . .] I think it was that kind of notion that, really, shifted me [. . .] Vipassana really made me a lot more aware of
myself, and my actions and I noticed my addictive behaviour [. . .] I definitely
think that, if I've been practicing, I would've been a lot calmer or, less frantic and,
more mindful, of my body [l] and less likely to injure myself [. . .] I like to be a lot
wiser which I think when I'm practicing Vipassana I sure do make better choices
as well.

Overall, biographical reconstruction among disaffiliates was less pronounced was centred (to varying extents) on the individuals' re-evaluation
and fabrication of their ultimate concerns and motivations for meditation.
The specifics of these narratives will be the subject of detailed analyses in
chapters 4, 5, and 6.

Conversely, the five narratives that did not feature a fundamental reconstruction in their biographies within Vipassana's universe of discourse
were made up of two individual representatives of the movement, Ross and
Carole; a deconvert Luke, whose biography was reconstructed within a rationalist secular universe of discourse (chapter 6); Ian, whose narrative did
entail biographical reconstruction, although it is not specifically influenced
by Goenka's Vipassana; and Victor, whose narrative did not emphasise a
dramatic change in his perspective and neither did he try to depict such a
change.

The absence of biographical reconstruction in the narratives of Ross and
Carole is not unexpected. Staples's and Mauss's (1987) study also showed
that this rhetoric was irrelevant to the narratives of 'life-long' Christians.
Both Ross and Carole have been involved with this movement for extensive periods of time (over twenty years), and, given their position of authority within this organisation, it was my impression that neither of them
felt the *need* to illustrate the ways in which the practice has transformed
their lives. Thus, in response to my specific questions, Carole noted, 'I'm
learning from Vipassana all the time [. . .] everyday I'm observing myself
and understanding a little bit better'. Moreover, my interview with these
two individuals was relatively forced in comparison to all other participants
who unreservedly participated in this research (some with higher levels of
enthusiasm than others). By this, I do not mean that Ross and Carole had

involuntarily talked with me for hours. Rather, I suggest that their position within the movement had some bearing on their decision and possibly obliged them to endure my presence.

On the other hand, Victor's account exemplified the case of a participant who did not (possibly) embark on the process of conversion. In addition to the lack of engagement in biographical reconstruction in his narrative, the decision to exclude Victor's account from this category rested in the manner in which Victor described the impact of the course: 'it wasn't like I walked away, oh my god I feel so much better, I know everything now, It was a very quiet and subtle change'. Moreover, Victor used a purely secular language in describing certain concepts as well as the theory behind the practice of Vipassana. Overall, Victor's narrative left the impression with me that he was not motivated to *display* a dramatic change in his self-understanding or perspective, which of course was significant given that his temporal distance from his initial course was roughly about one year. Additionally, Victor framed his motivation for attending a course in terms of an aspiration to test his limits (e.g. 'it seemed like a challenge [. . .] I wonder if I could do that') as opposed to other participants who emphasised a *desire* and even a *need* for self-transformation.

Finally, even though the vast majority of participants had reconstructed their biographies in accordance with Goenka's universe of discourse, I do not suggest, nor do I assume, that this rhetoric can stand alone as a marker of conversion. Rather, for the purpose of the present research, I argue that Snow and Machalek's (1983, 1984) second rhetorical pattern, the *adoption of a master attribution scheme*, is equally important to the conceptualisation of conversion applied in this book—as a migration to a new universe of discourse that involves the construction of a new self-concept and understanding of the world. In fact, I posit that the two go hand in hand: if I change, my world changes with me. The question is not which rhetorical device follows the other. The point is that if one's self-concept undergoes transformation through biographical reconstruction, logically, one's understanding of the world and one's position in the world should simultaneously be subjected to transformation.

This argument is grounded in the *positive* correlation between the reoccurrence of biographical reconstruction and the adoption of a master attribution scheme among the new students in this research. As noted, not all of the four new students whom I conducted interviews with immediately after their completion of a ten-day course provided detailed and extensive reconstructed accounts such as the one by Leslie quoted earlier. As I illustrate shortly, while Aroha's and Michael's narratives revealed reconstruction of their biographies in light of the insights gained from a ten-day course, they did not exclusively draw from one prevailing universe of discourse. In effect, both individuals disregarded the practice immediately after the course. On the contrary, disengagement occurred with considerable delay for both Leslie and Katrin who showed higher appropriation of both rhetorical devices. The next pages of this section explore this rhetorical strategy in the narratives of participants and in response to Gooren (2010: 47) who called for more research testing whether biographical reconstruction is 'indeed, the only true indicator of conversion' as Staples and Mauss (1987) had proposed.

Adoption of a Master Attribution Scheme

The second rhetorical feature of the convert's language and reasoning, according to Snow and Machalek (1983, 1984) is the adoption of a master attribution scheme. Grounded in social psychology, attribution is the cognitive process by which individuals form 'causal interpretations' of the behaviour and actions of themselves, others, and the events they experience in the world. However, Snow and Machalek argue that while the average person draws from a variety of interpretative schemes to attribute cause (e.g. laws of physics, divine intervention, popular psychology, etc.), converts employ a *single* causal scheme—or a rhetoric of cause and effect—which they generalise to various contexts to account for self, others, and the state of the world.

As mentioned, Staples and Mauss (1987) reject this rhetoric as a feature of converts' language and instead render it as an indicator of commitment. In short, Staples and Mauss arrived at this conclusion from the observation that while all of their fifteen Christian participants displayed evidence of the three rhetorical features (suspension of analogical reasoning, adoption of a master attribution scheme, and embracement of a master role), the language of four out of fifteen participants lacked biographical reconstruction. Staples and Mauss (1987: 141–142; original italics) wrote, 'As it turns out, these four subjects also *denied* ever having had a conversion experience . . . they considered themselves to be 'lifelong' Christians'. Thus, they reasoned since biographical reconstruction was absent from the language of these four participants, then biographical reconstruction must be the only rhetorical feature distinguishing conversion from commitment. Staples and Mauss (1987: 143–144) further proposed, while biographical reconstruction 'assists the creation of a new self', the other three rhetorics (including the adoption of a master attribution scheme) 'assist in the maintenance' of the self and are possibly the product of religious socialisation rather than the process of conversion.

My issue with this argument is that it implicitly assumes that biographical reconstruction occurs outside of a social context—as if the interviewees' accounts came out of thin air. On the contrary, it takes two to narrate. Staples and Mauss's hypothesis—or the lack of it—not only contradicts their conceptualisation of this rhetoric (biographical reconstruction) as a linguistic tool enabling the process of transformation, but such a statement also repudiates the ethos of the symbolic interactionist framework within which they operated. Moreover, the fact that the adoption of a master attribution scheme was present in the narratives of all fifteen Evangelical Christians who participated in the authors' research indicates that more careful consideration is necessary.

My immediate concern here is to reflect on the dissonance between Staples and Mauss's hypothesis and the findings of the present research. Compare, for example, two new students: Aroha and Leslie. Aroha is a spiritual healer and, in addition to her commitment to a variety of spiritual practices, she provides unique services such as 'aboriginal dream healing' and 'quantum-multidimensional-chakra-balancing'. While biographical reconstruction did appear in Aroha's narrative, she did not use a singular rhetoric of cause and effect to explain herself, others, and the state of the world:

A. you don't have to become a divine being, you fucking already are a divine being. but you forgot. we came here to forgot who we are, and now it's time to remember. it's time to remember at a fifth dimensional energy-place yk, obviously. and call it enlightened if you want to. or whatever. it's all good. and going back to Vipassana yk. I've been meaning to do it [Vipassana] since I've learnt about it in 2002 or 2001, and now I've got the opportunity and now I know Why, yk, and of course when he [Goenka] started talking about Yeshua the other day, on the cross and how equanimous he was. and Yeshua was kind of digging me in the room [gesture: poking] and I'm [like] oh yeah of course he did the teachings! he went and learnt the teachings in India, he spent a lot of time in India. and in between the time he was a boy until he was in his twenties well what happened to him. he was in India doing his training in Vipassana day after freaking day, he was in a mystery school that's where he met Mary Magdalene.

The excerpt is taken from a three-hour conversation I had with Aroha on the day that our ten-day Vipassana course had officially ended. I experienced Aroha as a light-hearted and courageously unconventional woman with exceptional narrating skills. This is reflected in the fact that Aroha not only reconstructed her own biography, but she also reconfigured the biography of the world. Even I was not excluded from this narrative reconstruction— Aroha honoured me as one of Yeshua's faithful disciples, although I am unsure as to which one. In fact, she made a point of transforming all the familiar faces at our course into historically significant characters. The point here is not whether reincarnation narratives can be seen as biographical reconstructions. Bender's (2007: 609) ethnographic research has shown that the two forms of narrative device provide similar transformative functions, enabling 'seekers to augment and creatively rethink (and replace) their relations with intimate others, providing rich experiential resources for placing the self in history and relation'.

The important point is that even if we consider Aroha's statement in which she directly speaks about herself, she does not adopt a single master attribution scheme, nor does she confine herself to a particular set of vocabulary. Rather, it seems that by summoning stories of past lives in these accounts, Aroha engages in a process of selectively translating certain elements of Vipassana's universe of discourse to a language that corresponded with her existing colourful repertoire of attribution schemes—one which amalgamated ideas as diverse as quantum physics to Greek mythology. In simple terms, there is no migration from one universe of discourse to another; rather, it is the expansion of her existing universe of discourse. This pattern was also relevant to Michael's narrative. In fact, neither of these individuals were interested in an exclusive engagement and did not take up a private placed upon their return to everyday life.

This can be contrasted with the narratives given by both Katrin and Leslie.[15] These narratives showed significant appropriation of both biographical

---

[15] Katrin noted: 'it [Vipassana] really highlighted for me what exactly [was] creating my unhappiness [. . .] it's either craving or aversion it's helping me to, [p] see where I'm creating things or where I feel aversion to things [. . .] And highlighting for me, in others, where they create their own happiness'.

reconstruction and adoption of a master attribution scheme. For instance, in her first interview, Leslie argued:

L. But I loved having made fun of all the other, you know traditions, [g] and you know some of the stories were just SO great you know [l] worshiping the doctor's prescription, you know that kind of thing. cause he [Goenka] does show just how silly, [p] but actually in the moment that's craving and aversion from things, you eventually want to give those things up.

Interestingly, while Leslie maintained certain elements of the movement's universe of discourse and incorporated them into her narrative, upon the discontinuation of her private, her follow-up interview drew heavily from another attribution scheme, namely popular psychology. In fact (for reasons that will be addressed in chapter 4), in an effort to understand her own disengagement, Leslie developed an interesting hypothesis, relying primarily on the causal psychological explanations:

L. I suspect that the personality type that ends up doing Vipassana, is already somebody that doesn't want the religious system to be a defining factor for them [. . .] for people who authority isn't a strong motivator. I have a very strong spiritual sense and I don't want a mediator between myself and the divine [. . .] it would be fascinating to see who responded to authority, who didn't, and the introvert, extrovert fascinates me around meditation, because I'm always interested whether or not introverts get nourished by it whereas extroverts get lonely by it.

Thus, within a span of one year and consequential to her disengagement, she actively sought a new system of meaning to understand and articulate not only herself and her motivations but also those of others. As these examples illustrate, there is not only a positive correlation between biographical reconstruction and the adoption of a master attribution scheme, but both of these narrative devices are also significantly relevant to the early stages of the conversion process. Admittedly this observation is quantifiably limited to four case studies. Nevertheless, it counteracts Staples and Mauss's (1987) findings that biographical reconstruction is the only indicator of converts' language.

I offer the following points to account for the dissonance between the findings of this research and that of Staples and Mauss (1987). First, as noted, Staples and Mauss based their argument on *negative* correlations. They reasoned (1987: 142; original italics) that because four individuals out of fifteen, who, coincidentally, also '*denied* ever having had a conversion experience and consistently refused to refer to themselves as being "born again"', did not feature biographical reconstruction, therefore biographical reconstruction is unique only to converts. Moreover, they (1987: 142) added, 'Two of these four subjects initially declined to participate in the study because they had heard it was about 'born again' Christians . . . and considered themselves to be 'life-long' Christians'. These statements first and foremost raise questions about the rigour of the authors' participant recruitment process, as they seem to have lacked a well-defined sample to begin with. Second, if two interviewees (out of their four counter-examples substantiating the theory) had declined participation in their research, is it possible that their initial hesitancy had a bearing on their account giving? In other words, is it possible that they were not enthusiastic to display how their faith impacted their self-understanding? Also, how were these two individuals convinced to participate? Finally—and, irrespective of the fact that I consider Staples and Mauss's functionalist reconfiguration of Snow and Machalek's theory a valuable advancement in conversion studies—it is important to consider another possible explanation influenced by sampling differences. Similar to the present research, Snow and Machalek's (1983; 1984) studies were based on accounts from converts to the Nichiren Shoshu Buddhist group, whereas Staples and Mauss looked at Evangelical Christianity. Given that the Nichiren Shoshu sect is unconventional in the mainstream American religious landscape compared to Evangelical Christianity, there is the possibility that the changes (both experienced and narrated by converts) in the former group were more radical and, thus, more *observable* than in the narratives of the latter.

This book therefore takes biographical reconstruction and the adoption of a master attribution scheme as linguistic indicators of one's embarkment on the process of conversion. However, not everyone's conversion career crosses the commitment stage, where we observe more profound (and possibly long-lasting) changes in language, behaviour, and self-representation. Accordingly, the narratives of those participants who departed from this stage of their conversion career will be analysed separately in chapter 4 (pragmatic disengagers). As mentioned, the vast majority of conversion (and exit) literature has predominantly drawn conclusions from studying those individuals who are/were at the commitment level. In other words, what will be explored in the next section under the category of commitment is the archetypal characteristic of 'convert' as it is understood in other studies.

Commitment

This section explores the narratives of participants who exhibited considerably higher levels of commitment to the movement and its universe of discourse. Judging from my participant observation and the interviews I conducted, one can identify a limited set of characteristics that constitute a member identity in Goenka's Vipassana movement—that is, 'serious Vipassana meditator', 'Dhamma meditators', or 'Dhamma children' as Goenka puts it. As mentioned in the previous section, my portrayal of the core member identity will hinge on (1) the meditators' language and reasoning and (2) their self-representation or performance of the Vipassana meditator's role. Hence, my analyses of the old students' language takes place in conjunction with Snow and Machalek's (1983, 1984) other rhetorical indicators: the suspension of analogical reasoning and the embracement of a master role—albeit the former rhetoric will be reconceptualised within the functionalist approach to language, while, in the case of the latter, I position this thesis in between structural and interactionist perspectives (Ebaugh, 1988).

Note that among the twenty-six cases, the narrative of sixteen individuals indicated passage through this level of their conversion careers.[16] Through detailed examples, in this section I demonstrate that the language and reasoning of those participants categorised under the commitment level closely resembles the language of the movement. To do this, I compare the language of three old students with different levels of commitment. My intention is to show that while all three individuals draw from a set of established rhetorical strategies—by which the movement has consistently rejected association with religion and hence rendered tacit conversion for its participants—they do so with different fluency and consistency depending on the extent of their exposure to the movement. It should be noted that except for one participant (Luke, a deconvert), all the individuals who have disengaged from this level (i.e. disaffiliated) displayed an ongoing intellectual commitment to these rhetorics. Finally, I argue that while embracing a Vipassana role involves

---

[16] Among these, six individuals who self-identify as old students (Carole, Charlotte, Ross, Dylan, Brian, and Elijah) continue to remain at the commitment level of their conversion careers, while eight individuals (Luke, Damian, Kevin, Kovido, Karen, Polly, Mark, and Jazz) had disaffiliated from this stage, whereas two participants (Holger and Matilda) represented narratives that indicated an ambiguous phase betwixt and between the two levels, although at the time of the interview, they were certainly *inactive* converts with great enthusiasm to return to the centre, and were thus considered leavers (as opposed to disaffiliates).

adherence to the movement, nonetheless, individuals take an active role in this process. First, however, it is important to account for differences in motives and seekership patterns between those categorised under conversion and commitment levels.

Shift in Ultimate Concerns

The first significant difference between the conversion and commitment stage is that committed individuals expressed a shift in their ultimate concerns and priorities: a shift from a this-worldly and pragmatic approach to meditation towards seeking salvation, that is, chasing enlightenment (full liberation, or nibbana). The following statement by Ross embodies this perspective:

R. For people who become serious meditators they feel that apart from the benefit in daily life, they have an underlying feeling that this is the path of liberation. and it's very important to make use of that in this life. otherwise we might not get that opportunity again.

The second (rather obvious) distinction is that the committed members ceased to actively seek other practices or engage in 'multiple seekership' patterns (Sutcliffe 2004). A common response to a question about whether they had engaged in any other practice after Vipassana was 'No, No . . . I haven't taken up any other religions or techniques, I just felt like I happen to land on my feet when I learnt Vipassana for the first time'. Thus, instead of 'shopping around', these individuals became devout members of the community, often lived in proximity to the centre, developed strong social networks within the community, and many *continued* to assign unique values to the practice even upon disaffiliation. Take the following comments by Karen (disaffiliate) as an example:

K. I feel that Vipassana as a technique is So Utterly sacred, it's so Utterly, I have never found anything that is So Incredibly on the ball that if you want to understand the nature of reality you will not find anything more accurate than the technique of Vipassana [. . .] Vipassana is probably the end of the road, as far as, um, I really didn't feel that I need a technique beyond that.

While the latter sentence clearly indicates the practitioners' conversion to a singular seekership strategy, the former sentences carry equally important content; it is precisely the third rhetorical feature of the convert's language that Snow and Machalek (1983) defined as the suspension of analogical reasoning.

Suspension of Analogical Reasoning

Snow and Machalek (1983: 273) developed this idea by drawing from the distinction between two forms of metaphor: *analogical metaphor*, which illustrates the similarities between two things, and *iconic metaphor*, which demonstrates the uniqueness of a thing (e.g. 'God is love' in certain Christian discourses). They (1983: 274) assert that while converts have no aversion to using iconic metaphors to describe their faith, they resist analogical metaphors because it 'violate[s] the convert's position that his or her world view is incomparable to other world views'. In other words, not only is the convert reluctant to compare his/her faith with another system of meaning, he/she also considers such a comparison irrelevant.

The suspension of analogous reasoning as articulated by Snow and Machalek (1983)—one type of metaphor overriding another—is problematic for two reasons. First, as Stromberg (2014) has rightfully pointed out, it is extremely difficult to examine for this pattern of speech. In fact, Stromberg (2014: 123–124) rejects the authors' theory as an 'incautious' generalisation grounded in evidence that actually allude to another idea (e.g. that converts assert that their new perspective is 'a unique path to truth'). Second, Snow and Machalek (1983) do not provide a theoretical link between a universe of discourse and the suspension of analogical reasoning.

To resolve this tension, I consider suspension of analogical reasoning as converts' attempts to transform the metaphoric language to a rhetorical strategy to establish a waterproof boundary around their world. Seen from this perspective, there are innumerable excerpts (cited throughout this book) in which the practitioners distinguished Vipassana from religion, some of which resulted from sociocultural influences, such as conceptions of religion, conversion, and Buddhism. While, in a narrow sense, these can be seen as indexes of suspension of analogical reasoning as originally proposed by Snow and Machalek (1983), the link between the movement's universe of discourse and the participants' language remains opaque.

Therefore, I propose that it is fruitful to conceptualise this pattern (suspension of analogical reasoning) as a rhetorical strategy only if the content of this rhetoric corresponds to the movement's universe of discourse. With reference to the present data, as well as compared to other participants, individuals who are categorised under the commitment level drew uniformly from a set of established rhetorical strategies that the movement had consistently used to disassociate itself from religion. Herein, the term 'rhetoric' is understood as 'the 'art' of persuasion, of convincing the hearer or reader of a particular line of argumentation' (Pigrum, 2008: 792).

Thus, another significant linguistic difference between conversion and commitment was the extent to which participants adopted the movement's prescribed language and reasoning to resolve this conflict. These include (1) the rhetoric of experience (Sharf, 1995), (2) rhetoric of 'here and now', (3) Vipassana as an instrumental practice or a 'tool', and (4) 'pure teachings of the Buddha'. While I will briefly explain the significance and meaning of each of these rhetorics, I do not intend to scrutinise all of them in detail. Instead, I explore the first rhetoric (experience), which was highly common among practitioners in this research, whilst providing a brief description of the other three.

(1) The Rhetoric of Experience

I am borrowing this phrase from Robert Sharf (1995: 229), whose seminal essay on the rhetoric of Buddhist meditative experience demystifies the category of 'experience' to encourage scholars to 'subject this term to rigorous critical analysis'. In short, and following Gombrich and Obeyesekere (1988), Sharf's (1995) work questions the widespread assumption that meditative experience played a central role in the monastic life of Buddhist monks. More importantly, Sharf follows Wayne Proudfoot (1985: xiii, cited in Sharf, 1995: 229) to render the contemporary emphasis on experience as a 'strategy' motivated by the agenda to free religious doctrine and practices from their dependence on metaphysical belief and religious institutions. Sharf (1995: 268; italics added) further wrote, 'The central feature of private experience that allowed it to play this role is precisely its unremitting *indeterminacy*'.

The rhetoric of experience is the most prominent pattern that appears in the language and reasoning of Vipassana practitioners, including many disaffiliates. Accordingly, these individuals rejected the notion of conversion and argued that their commitment to Vipassana was not the resultant of 'blind belief'. Rather, they reasoned that they had accepted the 'Buddha's teachings' because it corresponded with their personal experience. In other words, since they are able to experience these doctrines in an embodied way, they do not acknowledge the doctrines as beliefs rather as *experiential truths*. However, while Vipassana's emphasis on experience functioned as a successful rhetorical strategy (distinguishing the movement from religion), in practice, this very same method had failed to sustain membership and caused significant self-doubt for many practitioners who had no external resource to measure their progress towards enlightenment (see chapter 5).

To explain why I consider this rhetorical strategy as a distinguishing feature of a committed member's language, I illustrate its *function* as it appears in the language of Elijah (one-year engagement), Carole (over twenty years), and Ross (over forty years). As already highlighted, my objective is to demonstrate that the effective appropriation of this rhetorical strategy is something learnt gradually as the member becomes acculturated to the movement's universe of discourse.

The most important functions of the rhetoric of experience is to conceal the religious elements of Goenka's teachings. This is observable in the language of Carole, a serious Vipassana meditator with over twenty years of involvement in Goenka's Vipassana movement. Carole had attended countless numbers of long Vipassana courses, including a number of forty-five-day courses for which she had travelled abroad. She meditates on a regular basis and observes the Five Precepts in her daily life. Although she holds part-time employment outside of the centre, she spends most of her time volunteering at Dhamma Medini. I met Carole for the first time during my fieldwork in 2014. Given the circumstances and the extent of her engagement with the movement and its prescribed practices, I asked Carole 'whether at any point she considered herself as a Buddhist'.

C. mmm no I don't really consider myself a Buddhist, I'll, because, I'll cause I just don't ever (?) use that word, so it's the Word 'Buddhist' [p]

S. mhm

C. sort of has an implication of a um [p] religion, or [p] um, [p] a belief system or something, To me, it may not that implication to everyone and so for that reason I wouldn't call myself a Buddhist, but in a sense I Am a Buddhist I suppose, [vf>] because, I believe in [p] um or not so much believe in, but I found in my own

Experience that [p] what the Buddha Taught [p] is very helpful and useful [vf>] and um I have the utmost respect for the, the [in] Buddha's words and try to follow them. Others might say I'm a Buddhist, but I don't call [vf>] myself that.

A structural reading of Carole's narrative suggests: first, she was conscious of the weight her answers bring to this research given her status as an established member within the movement. Despite this, her responses were not black or white (I am not a Buddhist, or I am a Buddhist). Instead, she chose to vacillate between the two opposing stands using ambivalent language ('I don't really', or 'I wouldn't call myself a Buddhist'). Second, by emphasising her subjective interpretation repeatedly ('me', as opposed to you or others), Carole gained some sort of an authority to defend her stance—as in, you might think I am a Buddhist, but I don't. Her continuous emphasis on her subjective interpretation demonstrates her awareness of the conflict that exists between how the movement perceives itself from the inside (non-sectarian/non-religious) and how outsiders (a researcher) may evaluate it. Finally, after using the term 'believe'—in a slip of a tongue—Carole immediately restored to the rhetoric of experience (Goenka's phraseology, e.g. 'what the Buddha taught') to resolves this tension in the context of the interview.

I should stress that the term 'belief' is loaded with negative connotations for Vipassana meditators, not only because of its association with religion, but, more importantly, because it lacks autonomy and authenticity.[17] What I mean by authenticity here, in respect to belief, is simply the ability to doubt, question, and approach the given concept with a certain scepticism—a dogmatic vacuum which Goenka's (1997, cited in VRI Dhamma, 2014) teachings delicately convey:

> Beliefs are always sectarian. Dhamma has no belief. In Dhamma you experience, and then you believe. There is no blind belief in Dhamma. You must experience and then only believe whatever you have experienced.

As the quote suggests, personal experience is at the heart of Goenka's discourse and is consistently portrayed as the highest form of knowledge. A belief that is not verified by one's direct experience is commonly referred to as

---

[17] In using this term, I primarily draw on the definition of authenticity provided by Charles Taylor (2007: 299, 475) as expressive individualism, or the understanding in which people are encouraged to 'do their own thing', find their own fulfilment, as against 'surrendering to conformity with a model imposed on us from outside, by society, or the previous generation, or religion, or political authority'.

dogmatic or 'blind belief', which implies ignorance and naivety on behalf of the believer. The emphasis on experience, coupled with a limited Protestant notion of religion as primarily about beliefs, therefore appears as the primary rationale upon which the majority of participants, including old students, reject religious identities (e.g. Buddhist) and the notion of conversion. As Carole explains in response to a question concerning beliefs:

C. I suppose I might think there is an ultimate truth but I don't know that there is an ultimate truth um I strongly suspect that there is an ultimate truth because [p] that's where this path [p] appears to be leading

S. uhum

C. and that's where people that seem to be more advanced than me such as the Buddha for example [l] [g] um say, you know that when you achieve nirvana and you experience something beyond this realm of sensory and that's [p] probably some kind of ultimate truth but because I haven't experienced it for myself [vf>] I'm still finding that out about that [g] [...] you know there's a difference between believing in something, which in my mind is, is [p] um a sort of a tentative um [p] a tentatively held belief, because it is as yet not confirmed by my own verification, so in that sense of belief, a tentatively held a belief to yet be confirmed.

From this passage, it is clear that Carole's language and reasoning are shaped in accordance with the movement's rhetorical strategies. In fact, it could be argued that Carole constructed and formulated her responses 'appropriately' and to the movement's liking (Beckford, 1978). Moreover, Carole's approach to belief in many respects resembles John Hey's (2006) definition of 'critical believing'. Relying on Fred Dretske's (1995, cited in Hey, 2006: 58) conception of belief 'as a primary cognitive state', Hey defines 'believing' as an expression of the relationship between the self in its cultural backdrop and the world that provides the source and the context for interpreting our experiences. Believing, as Hey argues (2006: 59), is informed by an 'inner subjective dynamic interaction between knowing, feeling, and valuing'. According to Hey, human identity is created out of this complex network of interaction among the subject, culture, and world. Having explained this, Hey proceeds to distinguish two forms of believing: uncritical and critical. By 'uncritical believing', Hey refers to the type of believing that produces subjective identities that gain much of their strength by *avoiding* an engagement with the world or cultural debates (e.g. fundamentalist creationist). In contrast, 'critical believing' is introduced as a form of believing that results in the creation of an identity that is able to acknowledge and critically engage with the 'current trends in knowledge while recognising the complexity of a society of many cultures' (Hey, 2006: 60). Accordingly, 'critical believing' results in a fluid sense of identity that is less amenable to labels because the individual is open and ready to learn, change, and adapt to various cultural trends.

Carole's approach to belief and her use of the rhetoric of experience as the rationale for rejecting a Buddhist identity and beliefs correspond, to an extent, with Hey's concept of 'critical believing'. Hey attributes critical believing to an individual's openness to trends in culture and knowledge. Likewise, the critical believing involved in Vipassana's movement—that theoretically rests its anchors in embodied experience—is born out of a particular history during which Theravada Buddhism reformed itself in light of 'the culture, science, and philosophy of the West', including cultural relativism (Sharf, 1995: 268). However, while the critical believers in Hey's terms refuse to restrict themselves to any one tradition's truth claims, the Vipassana practitioner (old students such as Carole) illustrate a clear perception of what the truth is, yet they remain reluctant to acknowledge their account of the truth as dogma (Carole's passage illustrates this point in reference to the concept of ultimate reality).

Elijah draws upon the same rhetorical strategy to rationalise a difference between his previous and newfound approach to the doctrine of reincarnation. Compared to Carole, Elijah had only one year of experience within the movement at the time of this interview:

S. what about reincarnation do you think there is a past life and future life?

E. the only reason that I think I am open to that now, #in the past I think I Have# because of random fluffy things that I've heard [in] that have no real Substance but just have Been fluffy things that some spiritual person said or some clairvoyant said something like that [p] but Now I feel like, #because I'm experiencing so much stuff that Feels# um [p] Real to me

S. mhm

E. that [p] I'm much more open to what is being Said in the same arena

S. yeah

E. here. yeah so I'm far more open to what I'm being told Now, to be correct that I ever have in the past because there's been Nothing Else Solid in the past to make me have real faith in what I've been told

S. mhm

E. and I've just felt like in the past I've been [p] open and just Blindly kind of accepting
    something because it sounds better than anything else I've heard. Whereas Thisss
S. yeah
E. #<u>sounds pretty good</u># and I'm experiencing like, the, the, the top very thin, top
    layer of what I think I'm being [p] Taught here.

My first comment here involves the structure of both Elijah's and Carole's passages. From these excerpts, it is clear that the desire for authenticity and a need to substantiate doctrines with one's personal experience has created a paradox: on the one hand, they seem to be craving and wanting to accept a certain meaningful concept (e.g. 'I might think there is an ultimate truth' and 'sounds very good'); on the other hand, they seem to be actively devaluing this need both intellectually and linguistically. Conversion and commitment involve a sense of ambivalence for modern Vipassana practitioners because they function within the 'culture of authenticity' (Taylor, 2007) and favour a 'critical believing' approach to meaning making (Hey, 2006). These examples embody Diane Austine-Bross's (2003: 9) assertion that conversion in groups infused with Western modernity's values is characterised by the converts' vacillation between 'a quest for scientific authority and the creativity of a modern romantic'.

In comparison to Carole, Elijah's use of this rhetorical strategy is less developed and articulated, which demonstrates that its adoption is a gradual learning process of assimilation to the movement's universe of discourse, and it can therefore be seen as a marker of commitment. The point I am presenting is that Carole's passage exhibits both a stronger emphasis on the experiential approach to 'belief'—Hey's 'critical believing'—and that the rhetorical strategy is relatively more integrated and coherent in her speech. Whereas in Elijah's case, the use of this rhetoric is not (yet) fully developed or coherent as it theoretically contradicts his other statements (e.g. 'real faith'). This observation becomes far more evident once we compare these two case studies with an excerpt from my interview with Ross, who has been involved with this movement since 1975. In addition to coherence and fluency of style, note how Ross interweaves the rhetoric of experience with the rhetoric of 'here and now':

R. for me I felt 'this is it'. I felt a Very strong, feeling that this was going to lead to the
    purification of the mind.
S. do you ever doubt it?

R. I think there's going to be doubt, a little doubt till one has reached the first stages
of nibbana. cause, you know what I mean. one can only know the Path absolutely,
when one has had the Absolute experience of it. [hah] you know what I mean?
[. . .] so I think, it's not that I doubt the technique doesn't work. the technique
Works! um [p] I can't say, you would be dishonest in fact to say [banging on the
table] that I believe this is going to take you to nibbana; because it's a belief, it's not
yet an experience. So the whole practice should be experiential based. your level
of confidence will be depend on the level of experience

S. |but|

R. |But| Each, as you perhaps get a little deeper in each course, and as our confidence
grows, It's having a benefit in our daily lives. I don't mind it, I'm trying to live in
the present and I want to improve myself in the here and now.

With over forty years of experience, as a single, celibate centre teacher at
Dhamma Medini, and the co-ordinator area teacher for New Zealand, Ross
embodies not only the characteristics of a serious Vipassana meditator but
also the movement itself—since Goenka did not appoint a successor but
rather assigned a centre teacher for each centre.[18] I met Ross during my
second visit to Dhamma Medini in September 2015. My one-hour interview
with Ross focused on two topics. First, questions regarding the history of
the centre in New Zealand, for which Ross offered his utmost support and
provided me with a detailed summary of each developmental phase of the
centre since its inception including dates, numbers, and the cost of respective
events. The second topic involved his personal experience with Goenka and
the movement. This topic was a relatively harder conversation to carry, as
Ross seemed to have preferred discussing Goenka's biography, which, again,
he delivered identically to the narrative that is accessible on the movement's
website(s) and VRI publications.

The passage quoted developed from a question in which we discussed the
Buddhist identity, the concept of nibbana, followed by Ross's rationale in
which he argued that even though he had not experienced such a state, he
was nevertheless 'confident' that this path leads to the ultimate goal of liberation. This conversational topic continued for fifteen minutes and it was made
up of numerous themes eloquently chained to convince the listener of his

---

[18] In conjunction with his co-ordinator area obligations, and in addition to his administration
of Dhamma Medini, Ross is responsible for running the meditation courses, training assistant
teachers, and, more importantly, for the 'development and spread of Vipassana' in New Zealand (VRI
Dhamma, 2012).

line of argument. The passage shows how these ideas are utilised and linked in the interview (note, in particular, where the rhetoric of experience ends and the rhetoric of 'here and now' begins).

As the comparison between the language used by Elijah, and Carole, and Ross suggests, the adoption of the movement's language and reasoning is a gradual learning process. Furthermore, these passages illustrate that conversion and commitment to this tradition do not necessarily entail a drastic alteration in one's belief system. Yet, as I have suggested earlier, it concerns a change in the way a person approaches or *expresses* a particular belief through language. In many respects, becoming a sceptical believer, in the sense that I have discussed earlier, is itself the hallmark of commitment to Goenka's Vipassana tradition.

(2) The Rhetoric of Here and Now

Assessing the value of 'living in the present moment' is not my concern; my objective here is to explain when and how this rhetorical strategy was used and what it revealed about the participants in this research. Participants whose conversion career did not involve commitment—used this concept in contexts where they spoke about the benefit of meditation in their daily lives. In this regard, being present and aware of what goes on in the here and now was a desirable virtue and carried positive connotations such as enjoying the moment, appreciating life, and treasuring each second. Conversely, when old students used this concept, in the vast majority of cases (not exclusively), it functioned as rhetorical strategy to retreat or end a discussion about beliefs, the Buddhist identity, and the relation between Vipassana and religion. For example, when I asked to discuss their beliefs, committed members occasionally said, 'for me the goal is not some sort of theoretical understanding, or Some, some Idea. For me the goal, is to Try not to [hah], develop impurity in the present moment'.

(3) Vipassana as an Instrumental Practice or a 'Tool'

Framing Vipassana meditation as a 'tool' for personal development and transformation was another common rhetorical strategy that the committed meditators used (following Goenka) to distance the movement from religious categories. This pattern of reasoning is largely influenced by the secular and scientifically oriented vocabulary (e.g. self-exploratory technique, scientific laws) in which Goenka delivers his teachings. Moreover, in his discourses, Goenka presents Vipassana meditation in constant juxtaposition to traditional forms of religious practices (e.g. prayers, chanting, and worship), which he devalues by labelling them 'empty rituals'.

To adequately explain this, I will refer to one of Goenka's well-known analogies, the 'doctor's prescription'. This story resonates strongly with many participants (as evidenced by the fact that they commonly incorporate this analogy in their narratives) and causes laughter among the students in the meditation hall. This analogy depicts a sick man with 'great faith' in his doctor, who, instead of 'taking the medicine' prescribed, sets up a shrine in his house, bows to the doctor's statue, offers flowers, and starts reciting: 'Two pills in the morning! Two pills in the afternoon! Two pills in the evening!' The moral of the story is that 'without actually medicine, one cannot be cured of the disease' (Goenka, cited in Hart, 1987: 65–66).

Much like this analogy, this rhetorical strategy—Vipassana as 'tool'—involves two intrinsically linked ideas: autonomy and practicality. On the one hand, the movement's emphasis on individual responsibility (you must take the medicine yourself) and self-exploration alludes to a sense of spiritual autonomy which, as noted before, was the basis upon which many meditators distinguish Vipassana from traditional religions. On the other hand, because the pragmatic aspect of the practice is depicted in contrast to prayer and worship, it provokes an image of a rational and effective practice, and thus, marginalises Vipassana's religious elements in the practitioners' mind (such as chanting in Pali for 'good vibrations', the strict code of conduct, gender segregation, etc.). The committed meditators I spoke with used this rhetorical strategy to reject religious categories, resolve their ambivalences, or to abruptly end any discussion that disconfirmed their positions (i.e. their context-dependent identities).

(4) The Pure Teachings of the Buddha

The final rhetorical strategy is anchored on Goenka's claim that at once (1) authenticates his teaching and his lineage, which Goenka directly connects to the historical Buddha, and emphasises (2) the universality of the Buddha's teaching. In his teachings and in the material available on the movement's official website (Medini Dhamma, 2014), Goenka asserts that the technique of Vipassana meditation was 'rediscovered' 2,500 years ago by the Buddha, and it has been handed down through an unbroken chain of teachers who managed to preserve the technique in its 'pristine purity'. Goenka argues that any alterations to the movement's fixed set of instructions, teachings, and guidelines are threats to the purity of the technique and can lead to 'sectarianism'. These include (but are not restricted to) the guidelines pertaining to diet, segregation, physical contact, the handling of donations, proselytisation methods, and the incorporation of other practices or rituals into Vipassana (Dhamma Medini, 2017).

In his teachings, Goenka frames the Buddha's teachings as 'pure Dhamma' and the 'law of nature' that is universal and hence applies to everyone regardless of one's religious background. In fact, Goenka (1998, cited in VRI Dhamma, 2014) goes to the extent of arguing the following:

> Whoever first used the word Buddhism or Buddhist, in any language, was the biggest enemy of Buddha's teaching. Because the teaching had been universal, and now out of ignorance, he made it sectarian. Buddhism is only for Buddhists but Dhamma is for all.

An identical pattern of reasoning is evident in the language of many old students and disengagers. For example, in rejecting associations with Buddhism, Ross argued, 'An "ism" becomes when you, it's not say All the Buddha's teachings is Buddhism. it's when its moved away from the [p] the fundamental teaching of the Buddha'.

In-Between Role Taking and Role Making

A number of scholars (Bromley and Shupe, 1979; Ebaugh, 1988) have drawn from role theory to explain the importance of socialisation in the process of cognitive and behavioural transformations. Snow and Machalek (1983) also consider the embracement of a master role as the fourth indication of the convert's language and behaviour.[19] They grounded their

---

[19] Snow and Machalek later (1984) revised the title to embracement of the convert role.

idea in Hughes's (1945, cited in Snow and Machalek, 1983: 276) distinction between 'master and subordinate statuses' (such as race, sex, etc.), which posits that some of our statuses (roles) are more dominant and central to the way we perceive and present ourselves and how we behave in different contexts. Snow and Machalek (1983, 1984) suggest that instead of acting from the viewpoint of various context-specific roles, the convert primarily understands and represents himself/herself through one master role, which he/she effectively extends to *all* interactive situations. This master role thus becomes central to the convert's self-concept. Moreover, the authors asserted that as the representative of the movement, the convert acts not simply in his/her own interest but rather to spread the group's cause and mission. Hence, the convert role 'is worn like a uniform and is continuously on display' (1984: 174).

In this subsection, I depict the role of a serious Vipassana meditator based on both my participant observation at the Dhamma Medini and the interviews with committed meditators. My aim is to show how the movement and its universe of discourse influence other aspects of Vipassana meditators' lives and how these are expressed and performed in intersubjective realms. First, however, it is important to consider the two distinct theoretical positions within this framework and to clarify my standpoint.

Role theory posits that social behaviours are not random; rather they are 'patterned' (Ebaugh, 1988:16). However, there are two different understandings of how an individual adopts and assimilates a new role: the structuralist's perspective and the social interactionalist's perspective. From the structuralist's perspective (Bromley and Shupe, 1979; Snow and Machalek, 1983, 1984), individuals engage in a 'role taking' activity. This perspective assumes that the convert's 'needs and behavior are shaped by normative expectations that are a part of the social structure of groups' (Wright and Ebaugh, 1993: 124) and that role socialisation involves 'the process of internalizing the behavioral expectations associated with a given role' (Ebaugh, 1988: 18). From the social interactionalist's perspective, individuals engage in a 'role making' process, and, thus, the focus is on how the convert 'negotiates emergent meaning in order to discover and enact new roles' (Ebaugh, 1988: 18). The latter perspective therefore conceives role making as an ongoing 'process of thinking, feeling, perceiving, evaluating, and decision making' (Ebaugh, 1988: 19).

In this book, I assume a position in-between role taking and role making. I do not deny the influence of the behavioural expectations prescribed by the movement in shaping the meditator's role; nor do I deny the creative process by which the individual interpretatively engages with these structures. Instead, I consider the adoption of a Vipassana meditator's role as a dynamic process of both role taking and role making. To exemplify this, I draw on an example from a passage in which Dylan (an old student) elaborates on how he came to adopt a standardised form of proselytisation that is to the liking of the movement:

D. I came out of the course and there was a Great propensity for me to go out and just tell the world [. . .] yk, but I was um [p] I was really taken aback by these four people who had sort of communicated it to me about the course, and the Way they had communicated it to me, so I really had considered why they had done it like that [. . .] and the way I felt at the time which was, euphoric really [c]

S. mhm

D. then it can come across really, really strong and to be honest I probably, I did that with them [his family] and yk I just gave them the full barrel [. . .] [whereas now] I've pretty much done it the same way that it was done to me. So someone sort of comes into my sphere of reference and I'll mention it and I'll mention it in the same, in the Way just sort of like, I do believe it's this karmic thing, yk like if you hear it a few times, someone's gonna come to me in the next two years I think and say 'look I really think I'm gonna do that course'.

Many scholars of conversion (Beckford, 1978; Caldwell, 1985; Rambo, 1993), particularly those who have paid special attention to language and discourse, have observed that some traditions may demand a standardised form of conversion narrative from their followers. This feature, by extension, applies to forms of proselytisation. Moreover, while Gooren (2010) considers a 'strong missionary attitude' to be an indicator of commitment, I consider the adoption of the *correct* method of proselytisation as a sign of commitment. This is because individuals who successfully finish a ten-day Vipassana course rarely resist the urge to recommend the practice to their social networks. However, Goenka's movement encourages a specific form of proselytisation from its members (as Dylan's passage explained). On the last day of the course, Goenka's discourse is focused on encouraging students to 'spread Dhamma'. However, he repeatedly warns them to be wary of revealing too much detail because 'there is the danger of harming others instead of helping them' (Goenka, 1997: 64). Instead, he inspires meditators to allow prospective students to attend the course with 'fresh' minds. As a result, in recommending the practice, committed practitioners tend not to get into the specifics of the teachings.

The Vipassana Meditator's Role

Goenka's Vipassana movement has a strict set of guidelines that determine the meditator's behaviour on 'dhamma land' (the centre's premises). In addition to sila (morality), which concerns all students, there are other explicit and implicit protocols in place for dhamma servers. These cover a range of actions from interpersonal relationships (among servers, teacher assistants, and students) to personal appearance and even styles of verbal communications outside of the Noble Silence. However, the observance of sila and an *exclusive* commitment to the practice are perhaps the most important of these guidelines. It is expected that old students and dhamma servers will adhere to these standards in their everyday lives outside the movement, to the point that the violation of these guidelines can result in temporary expulsion from the community and/or limit the meditator's role within the community. For example, by restricting them from hosting group sessions outside the centre, as was the case for two participants in this research (Damian and Polly). In addition to these explicit protocols, and according to the disaffiliation narratives, there are implicit codes of behaviour imposed by the movement that concern the private aspects of a meditator's personal life, such as his/her sexual conduct (this topic will be addressed in chapter 4).

Even though students are prohibited from verbal and non-verbal communication for the most part of a ten-day Vipassana course, there are various indicators by which one can recognise who the serious meditators are on the premises. In fact, these are implicit structures which function to layout the appropriate behaviour for new students. For instance, as noted earlier, the position of students in the meditation hall is dependent on the number of the courses they have attended before. The function of this arrangement, as Pagis (2008: 160) has accurately noted, is that in the few glances that practitioners may take occasionally during meditation sessions, they observe the back of a more advanced student. While new students may not be aware of this arrangement in the beginning, they soon realise that the person in front of them sits for longer periods without movement. Consequently, for many students, non-movement becomes an indicator of 'good meditation and seniority', to the point that senior students might feel under pressure for failing this test (Pagis, 2008: 161).

In addition to non-movement, there are other indicators by which advanced students can be distinguished at the centres. Generally speaking, serious meditators tend to hold a straight posture during meditation; they project themselves to be calm and in control of their movements (particularly whilst walking); they speak 'mindfully' in a soft and gentle style. Most old students demonstrated a stronger affectionate bond with Goenka, even though they have never encountered him in person; rather this relationship was developed through his audio and video recordings. Nonetheless, most followed the Indian customary code of politeness and addressed him as 'Goenkaji'. The old students that I met during my fieldwork did not take these outward expressions lightly. In fact, during the last day of the ten-day course, one old student made a point of informing me that I had been disturbing this image by walking 'too fast' between the meditation hall and the female lavatories. A detailed analysis of the performance of the meditator's role is provided in the next chapter, 'Tacit Conversion'.

That said, perhaps one of the most important characteristics of the Vipassana meditator's role is his or her detached, non-reactive, reserved, and aloof behaviour. While the old students in this research embodied this feature in their communication, their comments about other meditators are demonstrative of just how much they value these qualities. For example, Elijah noted:

E. seeing guys that are like [in] super extroverted coming here and they're like [p] thumbs up to you and smiling [. . .] and then they are like on day four, they just like Boom, completely absorbed, crying whatever it is [. . .] and then see them at the end, they are so much calmer, so [p] like so much more relaxed and so grateful.

These characteristics can also be found in the retrospective accounts of those who had disaffiliated from the commitment level. For instance, reflecting on his past involvement, Kevin noted:

K. I remember from my second one I was flatting with some people and they thought I was too happy and one of my flatmates in particular said [. . .] 'I'm gonna burst your bubble'. I was like no you're not, No Way! I was so happy and content. she tried really hard to bum me out, which is quite funny because it must have been quite threatening to her. So yeah I was quite happy to take on the identity as the meditator and used that, isolating, aloof-type way to be. I mean at that point I was already questioning what my friends were into anyway.

S. what do you mean?

K. their lives, pretty much nihilistic some of their attitudes, well they were, taking loads of drugs, into music, kind of a hedonist thing, like there's nothing else.

As these examples demonstrate, Vipassana practitioners adopt external indicators (such as calmness) and understand them as desirable virtues. Another important theme revealed in Kevin's final sentences is related to ethics and values, which is relevant to the narrative of many participants who indicated their commitment. Accordingly, while most individuals in this research implicitly or explicitly considered the observance of sila of secondary importance (and even irrelevant) to their spiritual progress, the committed meditators emphasised the importance of morality in explicit terms. For example, Polly stated, 'I think by the time I did my fourth course, I was understanding the logic behind precepts and [. . .] not just honesty but the overall feeling of living a moral life makes me a more stable person'.

In addition to morality, some old students extend their values and the role of a Vipassana meditator to the prosaic arenas of their life, such as their business. For instance, Dylan (old student) noted:

D. I've sort of technically, or strategically gone about changing the way I work in my business model [. . .] I mean I've tended to create a business model based on a karmic principle of [p] yk I should be doing, sixty percent, seventy percent of karmic work yk, whatever it is karmic [. . .] and that's actually something that's ended up supporting me! so I do a lot of free work and a lot of community work and a lot of work [. . .] I think karma is a focused thing it's like doing dhamma service, and if you don't do it, then you don't really get the benefits.

Concluding Summary

This chapter has adopted Gooren's (2010) typology of religious involvement (preaffiliation, affiliation, conversion, and commitment) as a framework to represent the necessary context for exploring various disengagement pathways from Goenka's Vipassana movement. Accordingly, the narratives of participants who disengaged prior to the commitment level are analysed in chapter 3, while the narrative of those participants who had disengaged after years of intense commitment are analysed in chapter 4, 5, and 6.

While the first two sections of this chapter provided descriptive accounts of participants' background and practices that mark formal membership to this movement, the latter two sections examined the linguistic changes associated with increased participation. I demonstrated that the process of conversion is linguistically analysable on two levels of conversion and commitment and explored the linguistic feature of each level. I argued that both biographical reconstruction and the adoption of a master attribution scheme were relevant to conversion, while the suspension of analogical reasoning and the embracement of the master role were more accurately indicative of commitment. The next chapter, however, provides a detailed analysis of my interview with an old student to demonstrate how the role of a Vipassana meditator is performed in practice and how through this performance the individual adopts the movement's universe of discourse and achieves self-transformation.

2

Tacit Conversion

I have no recollection of the time and context in which I learnt the word 'segregation' in my mother tongue, Farsi. My second language is an entirely different story. It was Friday, 1 August 2014, fourteen days into my fieldwork at Dhamma Medini. After spending an entire morning washing, drying, and re-dressing several hundred meditation cushion covers—colour coded in blue and brown to segregate females' cushions from males'—I joined other servers in the kitchen to feast on what Julio, a traveller, had beautifully recreated from yesterday's dinner. Among us was Charlotte, a filmmaker; John, a masseur; Shoko, a cheerful backpacker; Jason, the work-period's manager, and several other part-time and long-term servers from New Zealand and elsewhere. At this point—apart from the few new students whom I interviewed the previous day—I had not been able to establish a rapport with the long-term servers, who often fled my presence. This was especially true of Jason, who had no hesitation in voicing his scepticism about my presence as a researcher. On the first day of the work-period, for example, he facetiously warned others to be careful of what they say around me because I might be 'secretly recording' their conversations—remarks which brought to mind Van Maanen's (2011: 2) accurate illustration of fieldwork as having 'instincts of an exile'. Still, I was optimistic, determined, and—borrowing a term from Goenka—'diligent' in my approach.

This static tension between the long-term servers and myself forced me to settle for a 'fly-on-the-wall' position at times (Wolcott, 2008: 53), from where I observed other servers mingle among each other. It was then that I first took notice of the word 'segregation'. I was standing in the kitchen with a bowl of food in hand when one of the centre's administrators walked in, looked at me, and uttered something about 'segregation' whilst 'eating'. Oblivious to the meaning of the term, I assumed it must concern the position in which I was consuming the food. Thus, I grabbed a stool and sat down. Long since Malinowski introduced the concept of 'context of situation', linguistic scholars have come to adopt the idea and stress the importance of context in language learning (Malmkjær and Williams, 1998). This is to say that despite

Drifting Through Samsara. Masoumeh Rahmani, Oxford University Press. © Oxford University Press 2022.
DOI: 10.1093/oso/9780197579961.003.0003

my initial misinterpretation, I eventually learnt the definition of segregation later that evening whilst interviewing Elijah. This interview (following) took place in the evening in a quiet corner of the Dhamma Medini's dining room and lasted for seventy-four minutes. During this time, our conversation was interrupted on three separate occasions by dhamma servers who were concerned that our interaction was violating the centre's segregation laws, hence my inappropriate laughter on line 9:

S. do you think vipassana is a religion?

E. um [long pause] um what, what defines religion?

S. exactly!

E. [l]

5 S. but [p] how do you understand religion yourself?

E. [p] [in] kind of a [p] 'religion' [whispering to himself] [p] Some organised, [p] something that's organised that, Has [p] [in] I was gonna say, restrictions and boundaries, |which|

S. |[l]|

10 E. in some way, there is that, there's a lot of that Here

S. uhum

E. but I can [p] understand Why, that, they keep these Spaces

S. |mhm|

E. |like this|. to keep that purity. Which, is, is, he, goenka says, there's a lot of

15 [p] [ntch] people that continued to do vipassana but have their own, Ways of doing it, which are [p] relaxed ways [p] um and Not in its pure |Form|

S. |mhm|

E. so I can understand Why there are those limitations but I don't know if I see it [p] as much of a religion [voice fades].

20 S. ok

E. I Don't know what my definition of religion is

S. [in]

E. But I don't see Vipassana as a religion.

S. |okay|

25 E. |For Me| vipassana is a tool

S. it's a tool?

E. yeah

Elijah is a young New Zealander in his thirties, who identified himself as non-religious. I met him during my participant observation in 2014 at Dhamma

Medini. At that point in time, Elijah had been intensely involved with the movement for over a year and, in fact, a few months after the interview, he committed to a year-long dhamma service at the same centre. Typical for a serious Vipassana meditator and dhamma server, Elijah appeared calm, patient, and asserted incredible control over his communication during the interview. For the most part, he spoke at an exceptionally slow pace and uttered his sentences often in a rhythmic fashion. Elijah's calmness and control over his speech was at times intimidating to an animated speaker like myself who habitually compensates for words by launching involuntary hand gestures in the air. Within the context of the meditation centre, which demands that all practitioners be calm and aware of their actions, emotions and reactions, the polarity of our behaviours impinged on the power dynamics of our conversations. That said, the segment that I just quoted was one of the few occasions in which the otherwise seamless pace of Elijah's speech was clearly disturbed.[1]

When Elijah was asked to reflect on the links between Vipassana and religion, he made use of several rhetorical strategies in an attempt to abstract the former from the later (I will explore these shortly). This behaviour is not unique to Elijah; it is rather common among *committed* Vipassana practitioners, who concurrently utilise the same reasoning to reject the category of conversion (as hinted in the previous chapter). However, I argue that their communicative behaviour suggests that a phenomenon akin to conversion is taking place.

In this chapter, I introduce the term *tacit conversion* to describe a form of conversion that is unacknowledged and/or denied. It refers to a process whereby the adoption of the movement's language paradoxically renders conversion invisible for the member. It explains circumstances where there is a disconnect between language and lived experience; a disconnect between non-religious self-identification and representation of selves that are constructed and interpreted within a particular religious language. The concept of tacit conversion provides an analytical framework for conceptualising the process of personal transformation and commitment of individuals to religious movements that deny associations with religion—such as the case at hand, Goenka's Vipassana movement. More importantly, tacit conversion

---

[1] Note the sudden intensification in Elijah's voice on lines 21–25, marked in the transcript by capital letters, through which he asserts his right to speak in response to my audible inhale on line 22 which signalled that I am waiting for a cue to ask another question. And finally, Elijah effectively puts an end to the discussion by stating that regardless of his definition of religion, he does not perceive Vipassana as one. Thereafter, the conversation became rather monosyllabic until the topic of discussion was completely changed.

allows me to conceive a theoretical link between Gooren's (2010) conversion and commitment level of religious activity, in accordance with the linguistic approach that is implemented in this book. Hence, the purpose of this chapter is to introduce the notion of tacit conversion and to use it as a conceptual framework for linguistic explorations of disaffiliation narratives (i.e. those individuals who left the movement after lengthy and intense periods of commitment).

My analysis in this chapter is inspired by Stromberg's (1993) linguistic approach to conversion narratives. I have paid close attention to the content of speech, as well as other modalities of communication, including the inflections, tonalities, and the delivery of the narrative. Through this approach, I demonstrate that committed Vipassana practitioners (such as Elijah) perform narratives that in many ways resemble what have been categorised as 'conversion narratives' in other traditions (Harding, 1987; Popp-Baier, 2001, 2002; Stromberg, 1993).

To clarify and contextualise my argument, I dedicate a substantial proportion of this chapter to a detailed analysis of Elijah's case study, whom I see as a representative of an old student, categorised under Gooren's (2010: 45) *commitment* level of religious activity. This focus on a single narrative will provide the appropriate space to scrutinise in depth both the linguistic and the performative aspect of a member's successful adoption of the movement's universe of discourse.

A close inspection of Elijah's case study demonstrates how an over-reliance on the individual to self-identify as a convert limits our understanding of conversion in the contemporary religious landscape characterised by an increasing aversion to religious categories and labels. This example unites the many points raised in the previous chapter and demonstrates their relationship to one another. The following sections of this chapter involve a brief overview of conversion narrative studies, including Stromberg's (1993) *Language and Self-Transformation*. Next, I introduce Elijah; scrutinise key passages from his interview; and highlight themes that appear to be central to his experience of self-transformation, such as self-acceptance, agency, and mind-body relationship. These are by no means an exhaustive list. Rather, I have simply chosen those themes common to most participants, including Elijah's. First, however, I will return to the interview excerpt presented at the outset of this chapter to outline a number of common rhetorical strategies that enable the movement—and, by extension participants—to rationalise a distinction between Vipassana and religion, and I illustrate how these rhetorical strategies function to conceal conversion and hence to facilitate what I refer to as tacit conversion.

In the excerpt, Elijah's immediate response (to the question regarding the links between Vipassana and religion) was to highlight the semantic issues surrounding the term 'religion'. By attempting to direct the discussion in this way, he was simultaneously indicating his awareness of the ambivalence surrounding this topic and creating a space within which he could emphasise his subjective interpretation of the term 'religion' and evaluate Vipassana accordingly (lines 21–25). This ambivalence becomes far more evident in lines 6–8, where Elijah exhibits reservations about defining religion in terms of 'restrictions and boundaries'. Elijah's hesitancy in this segment must be interpreted in the light of the incidents that had occurred during the interview. If our conversation had not been disturbed repeatedly in the name of segregation, the content and the analysis of this interview would have taken a different course.

However, since we were disturbed, Elijah was tentative in defining religion in terms of restrictions, presumably because this definition would inevitably encompass Goenka's Vipassana tradition. Yet, since Elijah had already uttered these words, and I acknowledged the irony of the situation signalled through laughter (which was not done consciously, yet implicitly communicated my position on this topic), it seems that he felt compelled to somehow distinguish Vipassana from his definition of religion. In this particular case, and in addition to emphasising his subjective viewpoint, Elijah appropriated two rhetorical strategies the movement has consistently used in distancing itself from religion: Goenka's rationale of maintaining the 'purity' of Vipassana, and the movement's emphasis on the pragmatic aspects of the practice (meditation as a 'tool', see chapter 1)—both of which are ostensibly instrumental for rationalising, if not marginalising, Vipassana's religious and institutional elements, such as the Four Noble Truths, the Five Precepts, and gender segregation laws.

The point I raise here is twofold. First, as I have illustrated, Elijah harboured ambivalence towards the links between Vipassana and religion, particularly regarding its institutional and routinised features. In the context of the interview, these ambivalences were resolved through the same rhetorical strategies that contemporary Vipassana traditions (including Goenka's movement) have commonly utilised to carve themselves a niche invulnerable to secular critique (Sharf, 1995). In other words, it is safe to conclude that Elijah's language and reasoning is, in this particular context, influenced by the movement's rhetorics (explored in the previous chapter). By this, I do not claim that the movement's discourse governs all aspects of Elijah's life and/ or language and reasoning—for I do not know Elijah beyond the scope of this interview. I am merely restricting this claim to his reactions towards the dialogue that commenced between us (or the site of the interview). Second, I argue that it is precisely through the adoption of the movement's language that participants proceed to distinguish Vipassana from religion and hence do not consider their commitment to and identification with the movement's teaching as a form of conversion.

Conversion Narratives

Conversion narrative as a subject of inquiry (in itself) has attracted much scholarly attention in recent decades. Yet no scholar (to my knowledge) has taken up the task of defining 'conversion narrative' as a genre in any comprehensive manner (Griffin, 1990: 4; Harding, 1987; Popp-Baier, 2001; Stromberg, 1993: 5). This is partly because these studies, generally speaking, gravitate towards Christian traditions, which tend to encourage 'account giving' or have conventions such as 'witnessing', or testimonies (Beckford, 1978; Harding, 1987). Therefore, in most of these studies, a story—oral or textual—that is told by a convert about a conversion event or experience is taken indisputably as a conversion narrative.

However, despite a lack of cross-cultural examination of conversion narratives, various studies have acknowledged several factors that can be arguably generalised and presented in isolation from the content of a given religious language. For example, a conversion narrative typically involves considerable biographical reconstruction (Gooren, 2010; Jindra, 2014); it is shaped in accordance with the rationales, doctrines, and ideologies of a particular religious tradition (Beckford, 1978); it is rhetoric about the transformation of the self (Harding, 1987: 167) and hence replete with the narrator's self-interpretations coloured by a particular religious language (Griffin, 1990; Stromberg, 1993); it is a 'plot' (Hindmarsh, 2005: 7) that allows for the temporal classification of the life story featuring 'a past which the narrator can leave behind and an acceptable presence which is connected to chances for the future' (Popp-Baier, 2001: 40). It is therefore a story that progresses from 'ignorance' towards 'notional knowledge' (Caldwell, 1985: 1); it is the 'site' of transformation, where conflicts and unacknowledged aims are brought to the fore, articulated, and resolved through the use of religious language (Stromberg, 1993: 56); it is above all a performance (Glazier, 2003; Stromberg, 1993), often containing poetic features (Harding, 1987); it is the tale of two lives (Griffin, 1990: 160) and the story of their metamorphosis (Barbour, 1994: 82).

These descriptions are by no means exhaustive. This being said, I acknowledge that there is a potential methodological danger in considering these descriptions of conversion narratives as a framework for studying Vipassana practitioners' narratives. Conversion narratives (both written and oral forms) are culturally constructed conventions (Caldwell, 1985; Glazier, 2003; Stromberg, 2014; Taylor, 1976). On one level, they are shaped by the tradition (or the movement) and therefore their content, language, reasoning, discourse, ideology, and symbolism would reflect the particularities of a given tradition. On a broader level, they are the products of the sociocultural trends of their historical and geographical context. This is because conversion narratives are not based monolithically on religious language and discourse. They also contain—and by extension are influenced by—secular discourses, such as political, popular psychological, gender, medical, and so on. As Beckford (1978: 260) notes, accounts of conversion are constructed based upon the resources available to the convert 'at the time of their construction'. In its broadest sense, therefore, Elijah's narrative of self-transformation has developed more or less out of the same (Western) cultural context.

The advantages of scrutinising the narratives based on their structural features is that it allows us to trace the shifting boundaries between the language of conversion and modern discourse of 'self-transformation', prevalent amongst meditation groups. However, while some contextual aspects of conversion narratives—such as the presence and role of a monotheistic God or the adoption of the sin discourse in Christian conversion narratives (Priest, 2003)—may appear irrelevant to our purpose, the act of embedding a given language within one's life story remains ubiquitous across different traditions. It is therefore the linguistic features of conversion narratives that are considered suitable for addressing the objectives of this chapter. To this end, my analyses of the passages presented in this chapter are inspired by the work of the psychological anthropologist Stromberg (1993). Therefore, it is important to briefly reflect on Stromberg's work, as it will be essential for the arguments presented henceforth.

Language and Self-Transformation

In *Language and Self-Transformation: A Study of the Christian Conversion Narrative* (1993: 9–11), Stromberg adopts an innovative analytical approach to illustrate that conversion narratives are sites in which, through the use of religious language, individuals achieve a sense of self-transformation and develop commitment. To theorise this, Stromberg identifies two distinctive forms of communicative behaviour: the 'referential' and the 'constitutive'. The referential designates the use of linguistic symbols in a manner that assumes a common consensual meaning within the society. The constitutive, refers to the visible communicative behaviours (including gestures), and their meaning depends on the situation in which they occur. For example, when I say, 'It's almost midnight', it would be a referential communicative behaviour, if my intention is to notify others of the time. On the other hand, a constitutive use of the same statement may be used to politely imply to my guests that it is late, and you should leave (Popp-Baier, 2002).

Having established these two models of communicative behaviour, Stromberg adds another dimension to this category: 'canonical language' and 'metaphorical language'. Canonical language, which is referential in nature, refers to 'the most certain and unquestionable of meanings' and the metaphorical language, which is constitutive in nature, refers to 'unfamiliar words with no established meanings' (Stromberg, 1993: 13). According to Stromberg's (1993: 13–14) analysis, when individuals incorporate canonical language into the idiosyncratic details of their lives, these two forms of language blend together: 'the canonical becomes constitutive, while the metaphoric becomes interpretable'. In other words, as the individual learns to anchor the canonical language to the details of their life and experiences, aspects of the religious symbolism come to be real and meaningful for the believer (or constitutive).

Stromberg (1993: 24–25) builds his thesis on the assumption that individuals harbour multiple and often contradictory aims, which can manifest verbally through utterances that are commonly known as slips of a tongue, parapraxes, or 'deniable communications'. Whereas the common-sense view may render these utterances as meaningless or unintentional, Stromberg (1993: 25) posits that they do indeed 'reflect the purposes of a speaker, but these purposes may be unacknowledged ones'.

Stromberg's method of analysis allows him to identify various paradoxes, tensions, and inconsistencies in the converts' narrative.[2] He then proceeds to interpretively link these inconsistencies to certain reoccurring themes in the lives of the converts (as they recount in their narratives). Through this detailed and fascinating analysis, Stromberg illustrates how the conflicts that seem to have animated the original conversion experience do *not* cease to exist after conversion (1993: 36). Instead, he argues (1993: 31), 'They come to be approached in a manner that makes their ongoing resolution possible'.

In the case of Evangelical Christians, Stromberg concludes that the re-enactment of that change or the 'performance' of the conversion narrative itself becomes the tool through which conflicts are brought to the fore and resolved through the use of religious language. According to this view, a sense of self-transformation is achieved once the individual learns to express and *articulate* their unacknowledged and contradictory aims through a given religious language. The religious language then becomes a resource for meaning making.

Using these descriptions as a starting point, I provide a detailed analysis of a key passage in which Elijah narrates about how his first Vipassana course resulted in a 'massive transformation' and 'profound shift' in his self-understanding and perspective. I outline the commonalities between Elijah's depiction of his experience and conversion narratives. This narrative, as I demonstrate in this chapter, is built on three intrinsically linked themes: (1) self-acceptance, (2) agency, and (3) mind-body relationship, which I explore subsequently.

Selected Case Study: Elijah

Elijah was born in New Zealand. His parents divorced when he was a young child, and he lived with his mother during his teenage years. Although he attended a private Catholic school from the age of five to twelve, he noted that his family were not practicing Christians and that this choice of schooling merely reflected his mother's concerns about the quality of the education he received. Elijah did not dwell on his family except to emphasise two

---

[2] Stromberg has a detailed method of analysis which pays attention to linguistic cues such as changes in tone, pauses, slips of tongue, patterns of lexical choices, and so on.

points: first, he described this relationship with them as 'dysfunctional'. Second, on several occasions Elijah mentioned that his mother had always been 'open to alternative stuff' and 'unconventional' enterprises.

In talking about his childhood, Elijah repeatedly emphasised his lack of interest in education and described his experience of school as 'floaty', 'drifty', and stressful. Instead, he depicted himself as a physically active person who, as an adolescent, spent more time outside of school playing rugby, cricket, golf, and swimming. From the beginning of the interview, Elijah quickly structured his narrative around two major events in his life: first, the death of his father, which according to his own words, instigated a 'search, or an exploration of [himself] and life'; second, he spoke about a physical injury, which impinged on his livelihood. These incidents led Elijah to seek reconciliation through various means—from counsellors to acupuncturists, from tarot card readers to chronicle psychotherapists—most of which were ineffective. I must note that whilst Elijah hinged his narrative on these two events, he also briefly highlighted the role of his network in the process of arriving at Vipassana. Specifically, Elijah spoke about his (short-lived) relationship with a young woman for whom Vipassana meditation was a 'catalyst for her to completely change her life around from drugs and alcohol and money and just craziness to more of a soul search'.

Plotting the Narrative

According to his account, Elijah's experience of self-transformation occurred during a group meditation session, on his first ten-day Vipassana course— an experience so 'profound' that it led him to an emotional outburst in the meditation hall. Elijah contextualised this narrative in constant juxtaposition to his previous interests in other spiritual practices, including his affinity for Buddhism, presenting them as ineffective in producing *genuine* transformation.[3] Accordingly, Elijah had been experiencing intense pain whilst meditating cross-legged during the first few days of the course. Noticing that chairs are available to some meditators, he approached his Vipassana teacher

---

[3] Elijah noted, 'vipassana [was] the most profound shift for me . . . to that level, that, had been, ignored! and on the surface level, on the exterior, I've always been quite Passive, or, the peacemaker, or this calm exterior but I've never, Really, Realised, how fucked up my Mind was! or How much turmoil there really was underneath . . . like I think the stuff I've read about Buddhism, the peacefulness and calmness have helped me on this exterior surface layer'.

and requested to use a chair instead of a meditation cushion. The teacher in return encouraged him to 'be strong', by alluding to Elijah's nationality and New Zealand's national rugby team:

E. he said to me 'you're from New Zealand right?' and I said 'yeah' and he said 'the
   All Blacks?' and I said 'yeah!' and he said 'I want you to be Strong' and I thought,
30   'Sure [g] I can be strong!'

According to his story, Elijah took the teacher's remarks to heart and continued to meditate through pain 'without moving a finger'. This approach enabled him to develop sensitivity to his bodily sensations. While depicting this experience, Elijah repeatedly oscillated between four different vocal tones. These included narratorial tone (medium pace; softly spoken); tranquil tone (slow tempo; softly spoken); bewildered tone (slow tempo; low-pitched); and animated tone (fast tempo; high-pitched). In fact, the shift between these tones was so pronounced that I felt compelled to distinguish them in the transcript and explore their functionality in his storytelling. In the following transcript, I have used the symbol [vc:] to indicate instances where his voice changes. It became clear that Elijah's composition and movement through these voices enable him to both depict the situation and express different aspects of himself (Goffman, 1981: 155).

E. I couldn't get up straight away I had to wait like five minutes and then I went to get
   up and, [p] my body was shaking! [p] and I had all these cold spots on my face
S. yeah
E. and I was Really like [vc: bewildered; slow tempo; low-pitched] 'what, is, going,
35   on?' because I was uncontrollably shaking so I went for a walk for five minutes or
   something. [vc: narratorial] and I went and saw the teacher after wards [cough]
   and he was like 'okay [p] [giggle] don't, don't put yourself through [p] this,
   [vc: tranquil; slower tempo; softly spoken] This is not what I meant'
S. [giggle]
40 E. um [p] but his 'stay strong' stuck with me for a few days and I was really Trying, [p]
   really hard!
S. mhm
E. and I was experiencing all sorts of sensations that I've never experienced before and
   I was all kind of like [vc: bewildered; low-pitched] 'wow, crazy stuff', [p] really
45   pushing myself [vc: narratorial] and then one day he [p] said to me, like day five or
   something, he [p] Asked to see me [p] and [p] or something along those lines, or

maybe when I went in and asked one of my hundred questions [vc: animated; faster tempo; high-pitched] I was going to the teacher Everyday asking questions

S. [l]

50 E. like blah blah blah, blah blah blah, what does this mean? what does that mean? one of the first questions was, so if I drink milk. and they're factory farming the cows, does that mean we should all be vegans? just like, I was asking everything [vc: narratorial] and he said 'I want [p] there's something I want to tell you, I want to tell you to [p] [vc: tranquil; slower tempo; softly spoken] I want you to stop trying so hard'

55 S. really?

E. [vc: animated; fast tempo; high-pitched] yeah! and so I was like, you know anything he said, I was just like 'yeah, yeah, yeah, sweet' [giggle]

These four distinguishable tones were marked in ways to reflect both their characteristics and the content that they represented. I distinguished these four voices by the method of constant comparison. The first step involved identifying Elijah's narratorial voice and using its characteristics as the baseline for identifying *outstanding* changes in the tempo of Elijah's speech. The next step involved manually marking the changes to the transcript. The same procedure was done for other dimensions of his voice such as pitch and loudness.[4] Before I proceed further, it is important to make a few comments about Elijah's skillful use of the four distinguishable voices outlined. As Riessman (1993: 19) notes, 'Narrators indicate the terms on which they request to be interpreted by the style of telling they choose'. Thus, it is important to distinguish these stylistic features and incorporate them into the analyses, as it will enrich our understanding and interpretations of the key passages of Elijah's narrative.[5]

In the passage, the first detectable change occurred when Elijah describes his unusual experiences during meditation (on lines 34–35 and 44–45). In these clauses, Elijah's 'bewildered' tone corresponded with and complemented the content of the spoken words, in a way that dramatises the depiction of that experience. For example, by using a lower pitched voice and speaking slower than he usually did (narratorial voice), he re-enacted for himself and the listener a sense of utter confusion. The second shift occurred

---

[4] To be sure, I cross-examined all the manual details against an audio analyser software, which illustrates waveforms, depicting frequency, tempo, and pitch.

[5] My method of analysis and the particular attention I am paying here at the key passage in Elijah's story is heavily influenced by the narrative analysis of Catherine Riessman (1990, 1993, 2008) and Peter Stromberg (1993). I am indebted to both scholars for their stimulating studies and for generously providing me with valuable comments and advice from afar.

when Elijah directly quoted the Vipassana teacher (lines 38 and 54). This 'tranquil' tone, in comparison to his narratorial tone, was dramatically slower in tempo and was spoken with much softer tone. Elijah seemed rather committed to quoting the teacher in this particular tone (in fact, he used the same tone in quoting Goenka elsewhere in the interview). This occurred on both occasions (again, lines 38 and 54) where he deemed it necessary to pause halfway through his delivery and utter those words in a distinctive tone and style. Interestingly, however, when Elijah narrated his encounters with other dhamma servers, he did *not* use this tranquil tone.

And finally, the last movement in Elijah's speech pattern involved the adoption of the 'animated' tone, which is characterised by its higher pitch and faster tempo. This is a tone of voice that Elijah seems to have reserved for depicting aspects of himself that he no longer favours. For example, in the previous passage, the animated tone is used on two separate occasions (lines 48–52 and 56–57), both times involving self-deprecating comments,[6] albeit uttered with a pinch of humour. Thus, the tranquil tone and the animated tone stand on the far ends of this spectrum. Moreover, in the tranquil tone, the utterances were sculpted punctiliously and stood in perfect rhythmic balance against each other (e.g. 'don't put yourself through this; this is not what I meant' lines 37 and 38). While in the animated tone, words flew freely and sentences arrived faster.

The Performance of Conversion Narrative

Having outlined the distinctive tonalities in Elijah's speech, I now return to the key passage of his narrative. As we learnt from the previous excerpt, Elijah had been subjecting himself to extreme pain, to the extent that his teacher felt the necessity to intervene and ask Elijah to be gentler in his approach. According to Elijah, after the teacher advised him to 'stop trying', he lost his ability to concentrate and could no longer observe any sensations.

---

[6] During a meditation course, each student is allocated a slot to visit the teacher and ask questions strictly pertaining to his or her meditative experience. This is to say that students are discouraged from using this time slot for philosophical debates or 'intellectual discussion', since they are rendered useless and irrelevant to one's progress in Goenka's Vipassana tradition. As Goenka notes, '[Dhamma] is not the play of useless intellectual games' (Goenka, 2005: 99 cited in VRI Dhamma, 2014). Thus, Elijah's self-deprecating statement must be understood in light of the movement's attitude towards debates and discussions during a private interview with the teacher.

This led him to a realisation (about himself) that underlines his experience of self-transformation:

E. [Narratorial voice] after he said that, nothing was happening like Nothing. no sensations, I couldn't focus, couldn't concentrate for nearly two days [p] and, my
60   ego was like [p] [vc: bewildered; drop to whisper] what I'm assuming that was going on it started creeping in and it was like [vc: narratorial; rhythmic style] I had been in my Mind, running away with how good I had been doing

S. mhm

E. with all these crazy sensations I was feeling

65 S. yeah

E. [v: narratorial; rhythmic] and then to have nothing! and it was like I'd gone up in this pedestal [p] and then [p] [vc: bewildered; drop to whisper] this is you know, this is what I understand to be all the ego, [vc: narratorial; rhythmic] And then, [p] my reality changed, and it was like, Crushed! I just felt Useless, [vc: tranquil;
70   rhythmic style] to the point where [p] that, [p] Underlying, [p] Feeling [p]

S. mhm

E. came through. [p] and [p] yeah it was just a feeling of [p] lack of self-worth

S. yeah

E. and lack of [p] Self um [p] and [p] I guess I had kind of realised [p] that most of my
75   life, had been that. [p] inside my head, [p] was, [in] all this negativity

S. mhm

E. for At Least twenty years [vc: narratorial; rhythmic] and then after twenty years sort of Flipped itself, went into this positive, side, which again is part of the buddhism, it was like, more positive thinking and, and, Not sort of so much negativity, Stuff

80 S. yeah

Dhamma server: how much longer you guys are gonna be [conversation with dhamma server is omitted]

E. um [long pause] Yeah so, [vc: tranquil; rhythmic] Most of, most of my life had been this negative, [p] thought, [p] patterns, that were going on, about Self, normally,
85   and then [long pause] this whole positive side, tried to come in

S. mhm

E. And that also then [long pause] tried to Boost itself, [vc: bewildered; drop to whisper] so it was either like negativity or Positivity towards self, it was like [p] the ego, what- ever it is playing this [vc: narratorial; rhythmic] Mind game, um and this happened
90   in really, quick succession and the vipassana was like Really good, now really bad

S. ok

E. and then, this Complete [p] like Hopelessness

S. mhm

E. was what I felt [p] and yeah so I was just sitting there [p] and ended up [p] started

95   crying [p] and then [p] I heard a girl about [p] [vc: animated; faster tempo; high-pitched; rhythmic] about three rows back from me started crying [giggle]

S. [laugh]

E. and then [giggle] this guy behind me started crying

S. yeah so you kicked off a

100   E. yeah!

S. a crying domino

E. and then [p] [vc: narratorial; rhythmic] um After that I felt [p] much better

S. yeah

E. but I still Felt [p] kind of hopeless but I, [p] Let [p] it out, and then I came to this

105   realisation that this is where I'm at

S. yeah

E. and I just need to work from this point um [p] [vc: tranquil; rhythmic style] and then, progressively [p] worked, my way, out of that, Really slowly, but I was [p] accepting that, I needed that patience

110   S. mhm

E. and it didn't Matter, if I wasn't [p] doing, [p] the best in the class, or whatever it was

S. yeah

E. um [p] and [p] by the end of it, Felt, [p] much more at peace, with myself, [p] Much [p] Calmer about things, I didn't have this [p] [vc: animated; faster tempo; high-

115   pitched] paranoia running through my head, or about, what someone's thinking or what, that means, or what this means, or how I acted, whether that was good or bad, and all of this Stuff [vc: tranquil; slow tempo; softly spoken] that, was, really conditioned into my, [long pause] the processing that went on in my head [in]

S. yeah

120   E. and [p] And [p] I Really gained much more of an awar[e], of an awareness about that, [p] which [p] yeah then through [in] what I, am, starting to understand, about vipassana is just about [p] acknowledging it, and letting it go and the more that I can do that, the less react to it [p] the better I feel

S. yeah

125   E. and much more at peace, I feel. [the tranquil tone is maintained in a rhythmic style till the end]

The first noticeable pattern that will grasp the attention of a scholar of conversion is biographical reconstruction (e.g. lines 76–79, 83–88, and 113–118), which was explored in considerable depth in the previous chapter.

Therefore, instead of recapitulating the many points that I addressed previously, I will use this space to conduct a structural and thematic analysis, scrutinising how Elijah delivers his narrative and what that means. Accordingly, one important structural feature of this passage is the rhythmic style of Elijah's speech. With the exception of two asides (or evaluations on lines 67–68 and 88), Elijah incorporates a rhythmic speaking style to describe what led him to experience an emotional outburst during his first meditation course. The rhythmic feature of this segment is highly conspicuous, given the composition of the pauses and emphases that are repeated at consistent intervals—to the point that the utterances on the aforementioned lines can be easily read as poetry:

> I had been in my Mind
> Running away with how good I have been doing
> With all these crazy sensations I was feeling
> And then to have Nothing!

This is by no means a unique observation. Both Stromberg (1993) and Harding (1987, 2000: 103) have observed similar poetic features in their analysis of conversion narratives. They considered the rhythmic speech as markers of an oral performance (Harding, 1987: 172) 'of something central to [the narrator's] experience and self-conception' (Stromberg, 1993: 96). From this viewpoint, it could be said that Elijah is performing the role of a serious Vipassana meditator (core member). This interpretation rests on the observation of the changes that occur in Elijah's speech, particularly his extension and adoption of the tranquil tone: whereas he initially used the tranquil voice to quote the Vipassana teacher and hence implicitly attributed its qualities to the teacher, it has now become the dominant tone through which Elijah depicts his experience of self-transformation (e.g. lines 70–77, 107–114, and 117–125). In other words, it could be argued that Elijah is now painting a picture of himself using the same hues that he initially used to depict his teacher in the interview. However, this is an over-simplistic understanding of what is at play. To add another layer of interpretation, I will attend to the structure of the narrative.

From a structural perspective, the most salient aspect of this segment is the peculiar patterning of the 'psychological subjects' (Gee, 1991: 33), or the grammatical subjects of each clause. In particular, I am referring to Elijah's sudden abandonment of the word 'I' from lines 75–94. In this passage,

Elijah makes use of two distinguishable styles to depict two distinctive self-concepts.[7] On the one hand, he uses a passive (grammatical) voice to portray a former sense of self—repeatedly referred to as 'the ego, whatever it is playing this Mind game' (lines 89–90). In doing so, not only is Elijah abstracting his current self-concept from a previous one, but also, he is at once disclaiming a sense of control and agency during this phase of his life. For instance, utterances such as 'positive side tried to come in' (line 85) and 'boost itself' (line 87) perfectly conveys this point.

On the other hand, there seems to be an active (grammatical) voice that represents a new sense of self. This distinction is particularly evident from line 94 onwards, where Elijah reintroduces 'I' into his speech. The new sense of self is now characterised by having an increased 'awareness' (towards his previous 'conditioning'), agency, and a profound sense of self-acceptance (e.g. 'I came to this realisation that this is where I am at'). To emphasise the difference between the former and the current senses of self, not only does Elijah make use of verbs such as 'crushed', but he also speaks of his experience of emotional outburst (line 95).

Experiences of emotional upheavals during a Vipassana course, such as crying, are not unusual. In fact, I had experienced a 'crying spell' during my first Vipassana course in 2006 and witnessed others undergo similar experiences during my participant observation at a ten-day Vipassana course. As other observers have accurately noted, the intensity of the ten-day course coupled with its isolating features (separation from loved ones, inability to communicate, etc.) can often result in emotional experiences such as sadness, desperation, boredom (Pagis, 2008: 203), fear, and anxiety attacks.

The point I want to address is not why these episodes occur, rather my interpretation of why Elijah made a mention of this incident. I posit that by referring to his crying episode, Elijah was implicitly conveying that a genuine transformation had taken place—a message that gains much of its momentum in defying conventional ideas about masculinity. In particular, I am referring to the general norm in most cultures with defined gender roles, including New Zealand (Holmes, 1997), that consider crying inappropriate for men. Thus, when interpreted against this cultural backdrop, Elijah's statement finds its significance.

---

[7] In this chapter, I use the term 'self-concept' in order to include various characteristics of the self (or senses of the self) (Montgomery, 2014: 165) as opposed to the term 'identity', which may limit our understandings of Elijah's case to social structures (i.e. group membership).

In order to make sense of these observations and add another layer of interpretation, it is important to pay attention to the religious content of the narrative, specifically the significance of the concept of sankhara to Elijah's narrative. Briefly, in Goenka's tradition, the concept of sankhara carries negative connotations and is often referred to as the 'habit of blind reactions' (Goenka, 1997: 18). The movement's publication (*VRI*) translates sankhara as 'mental formation; volitional activity; mental reaction; and mental conditioning'—which are some of the terms Goenka interchangeably utilises in his teachings to refer to this Buddhist concept. Goenka's choice of words suggests that sankharas are the actual agents behind actions and influence all volitional activities (Pagis, 2008: 98). Moreover, Goenka's instructions teach the practitioners that every time they emotionally react to any internal or external stimuli, they generate new sankharas or strengthen previous ones. To achieve enlightenment, one must both refrain from generating new sankharas and eradicate all previous ones.

The concept of sankhara sits at the heart of Elijah's narrative of self-transformation (lines 84 and 118). In these instances, the core message of the narrative is about (1) recognising and accepting the conditioned nature of the mind and (2) regaining a sense of agency and control. To dramatise the first point, Elijah does not refer to himself in the first person. Instead, he chooses terms such as 'ego', which enables him to actively disassociate and distance his current self-understanding from his past sense of self. This further enables him to easily allude to a lack of agency without communicating it directly. Elijah's reintroduction of 'I' and his arrangements of active sentences strongly correspond with the second point. Moreover, the sentences uttered in the active voice involve positive and hopeful content (e.g. 'I just need to work from this point'), indicating Elijah's contentedness for the present and optimism for the future. Thus, Elijah's abandonment of the word 'I' from lines 75–94, his oscillation between an active and a passive grammatical voice, and his alternating between different vocal tones can be seen as a performance, a waltz between two conceptions of the self, harmonised to the tone of his voice. On the one hand, the re-enactment of the narrative allows Elijah to strengthen his commitment and emotional investment in Vipassana's religious language; on the other hand, it can be read as an expression of his commitment, conveyed to the interviewer (myself).

Indeed, the thematic analysis of all the interviews conducted in this research reveals that the majority of participants were familiar with the concept of sankhara, incorporated this notion in their narratives, and related it to their own life experiences. However, only few participants referred to this notion in Pali, whereas the vast majority referred to this concept in English using one of Goenka's translations (e.g. conditioned mind, thought patterns). For example, Katrin stated: 'I was conditioned by others, I was trying to please them . . . my hopes were that I would discover my conditioned things, I wanted to unconditional [sic] my mind', and Jazz mentioned that 'I really do feel like it [Vipassana meditation] changed my habit pathways in my brain with how I handled situations and things like that'.

Self-Acceptance and Agency

The search for self-acceptance was also a recurring theme in the narratives of many Vipassana practitioners. In Elijah's case, a desire for self-acceptance exists alongside a desire to gain acceptance and recognition from others. In other words, these two can be seen as contradictory aims.[8] To contextualise this point, I return to the earlier passage in Elijah's narrative in which he reflected upon his interaction with the Vipassana teacher.

There, we learned that in response to the teacher's remarks (be strong like the 'All Blacks'[9]—lines 28–30), Elijah put himself through excruciating pain and meditated diligently. His immediate response to the teacher ('sure, I can be strong') conveys Elijah's desire to gain recognition and acceptance from others (or in this particular instance, the teacher). However, Elijah himself is not immediately aware of this desire—in fact the central point of his narrative is depicting the process that led him to this realisation about himself. To borrow from Stromberg (1993), it could be argued that Elijah's desire to gain acceptance from others is an 'unacknowledged aim'. From this perspective, an important aspect of Elijah's experience of self-transformation is his ability to acknowledge and articulate his unacknowledged aim. This is a plausible interpretation when one considers Elijah's statements such as 'it didn't matter if I wasn't doing the best in the class' (line 111). This is precisely what Stromberg (1993) refers to as a shift from constitutive communicative

---

[8] Generally speaking, however, one can either attempt to please others at the expense of one's desires (e.g. by suppressing or controlling one's behaviour) or develop self-acceptance *in spite of* what others may think.

[9] New Zealand's national rugby union team.

behaviour to referential. Whereas once, Elijah did not explicitly state this desire (to gain acceptance from others), he is now able to articulate this through the movement's language.

Thus, Goenka's teachings (of sankhara and the interplay of this concept with not-self) and its associated terminology, including 'ego', 'conditioning', 'thought patterns', 'lack of self', and so on, becomes rooted in Elijah's narrative and shapes his self-understanding—what Stromberg (1993: 14) referred to as 'the shift between the canonical and the constitutive'. In other words, Vipassana's language gives Elijah the means to both interpret and reconstruct a new sense of self (Beckford, 1978; Griffin, 1990; Harding, 1987). As I have shown, this is the experience in which the significance of the movement's meaning system is confirmed for Elijah in an embodied way. According to Stromberg (1993: 30), for the believer, this profound feeling is most likely responsible for generating a strong emotional commitment to the movement and its canonical language.

Moreover, the content of the narrative alludes to a shift from a self-oppressive behaviour (self-control) to a sense of agency. As mentioned, the desire to gain acceptance from others stands in contradiction with a sense of agency. Since the need to gain recognition from others is interpreted (by Elijah) as an inherited pattern of behaviour (one that is, e.g. 'conditioned' in his mind), any action taken towards that need fundamentally lacks agency. Hence, by learning to observe, recognise, not react to, and, more importantly, to articulate this habitual behaviour, Elijah gains a sense of agency (e.g. 'acknowledging it and letting go'—line 122). Note, however, that the theme of agency and control in relation to meditational practice is often assumed as paradoxical and requires further qualification. By this I am referring to a specific line of reasoning that renders the Buddhist endeavour for self-discipline as oppressive, claiming that 'one deliberately chooses suffering with a hope to eliminate suffering' (Deleanu, 2010: 618). However, in contrast to the conventional sense (i.e. interpreting self-control in terms of passivity or oppression), for the majority of Vipassana practitioners, the outcomes are a feeling of choice and agency. For example, having the option to decide how to react in certain situations without being led by desires (or uncontrolled behaviour). Thus, to avoid the murkiness of the term 'control', I use the term 'agency' to refer to this experience.

Furthermore, the experience described by Elijah involves themes related to both a transformation of self and interpersonal relations. To explain the latter, I draw upon a passage in which Elijah explains why he returned to the organisation to attend his second course:

E. about a Month ago I just started to Feel like I was reacting [vc: animated] to things going on around me. I was noticing that I, Internally I was getting more and more frustrated with things that were out of my control

130 S. mhm

E. and Up to that point I'd been able to just calmly [p] [in] manage them [vc: tranquil] by sitting down by someone, talking with them, having a lot of patience, and Not, not Reacting in my communication [p] which is effective [p] But [p] I felt like internally, that I was [p] Starting to hold on to more and more stuff and Feeling more frustrated

135 S. yeah

E. and I kind of [p] Knew that I, [vc: faster tempo; low-pitched] At some point, something happened and I was like I Know that I need to come back here, [vc: bewildered] because I'm starting to Lose [p]

S. yeah

140 E. Lose it! [g]

This passage is important for two reasons. On the one hand, it shows the extent of Elijah's commitment to the practice, which as I have suggested, is partly due to its efficacy in providing him with a sense of agency (i.e. by not reacting or becoming frustrated with things that 'were out of [his] control'—line 129). On the other hand, it depicts the impact of this experience (of transformation) on his social interactions (e.g. allowing him to behave in a non-reactive manner and consequently to represent himself as a calm and non-reactive person in social situations). Perhaps a more tangible example of this behaviour is reflected in the way Elijah communicated with me during the interview. As I noted in the beginning of this chapter, Elijah executed an incredible amount of control over himself during our conversation. His interaction during the interview closely resembled what he described as an appropriate or effective template or style of communicating with others (lines 131–133). This *style* of communication is by no means unique to Elijah; it is, as I have argued previously, the most salient (and observable) characteristic of old students (or serious Vipassana practitioners). Therefore, it could be argued that by adopting a certain style of communication or intersubjective behaviour, Elijah is performing a particular identity in the context of the interview—in this case, the role of an old Vipassana student.

Mind-Body Relationship

The final theme that appears central to Elijah's narrative of self-transformation involves his new-found understanding of the mind-body relationship. To explore this theme, I will refer to a passage from his narrative and provide my interpretations of it. The following passage was uttered as a side story appearing chronologically prior to the (lengthy) passage analysed earlier, and in response to my question about his crying episode. In many respects, it can be seen as Elijah's evaluation of the narrative that was about to unfold. A striking feature of this passage concerns Elijah's fluency, which suggests that he had narrated this story before:[10]

E. [narratorial voice:] Soo there was a, the first couple of days were tough, Physically,
S. yeah
E. but this is, I now understand that it was [p] Mental! um [c] I asked a guy, [p] before the course started, 'how many course he had done Before?' and he said 'oh I've done

145   seventeen, ten-day courses' and I was like 'Wow' and I said 'what's the most profound thing you've learnt from all of that' and he said [no detectable voice change] 'that if, this is my pain,—say of a scale of a hundred—then [p] the real pain is ten per cent [p] and the other ninety per cent is all mental' and I was like 'ok, that's interesting' [in] I, [p] whatever day it was in, it was day four maybe of the course, I was sitting there

150   and [p] just from Sitting, my backside was [vc: bewildered] So Sore, and [vc: narratorial] I was really trying, you know, this strong determination trying to sit through it and I got to the chanting at the end and then the 'sadhu sadhu sadhu' and I was like [vc: bewildered] 'Fuck thank god', and I leaned forwards and I was like oh that feels [g] So nice, just a bit of relief [vc: narratorial] and I sat back down and there was No Pain!

155 S. mhm
E. All I could do was, all I Felt was me sitting on the cushion and I was like [vc: bewildered] 'woah I've just been sitting here with this intense pain, for At Least the last half an hour'
S. yeah
E. and it's been getting worse and then I like leaned forward, just let the pressure off

160   and I was like 'oh that feels good' [vc: narratorial] and then sat back down Expecting to Feel this, still feel of pain and all I could feel was myself sitting on the cushion
E. and Then [vc: slow tempo and spoken softly] these words rang up from this guy

---

[10] In fact, his readiness to initiate this story is quite outstanding and easily detectable in the audio recording of the interview. For example, he immediately starts narrating this passage without allowing me to finish an utterance. Moreover, in comparison to the rest of the interview, this segment features the minimum number of pauses or slips of the tongue.

As mentioned, this segment of the narrative highlights Elijah's evolving understanding of the relationship between mental and physical phenomena. This theme appears to be significant to Elijah's experience, and it reoccurs at various points throughout his interview. As mentioned earlier in this chapter, from the beginning of the interview, Elijah structured his entire life story around two major events in his life: first, the death of his father, and second, his physical injury. According to his own interpretations, these two incidents led him to seek alternative resolutions since 'nothing conventional was helping' him. However, despite describing both incidents as equally important in prompting a 'search', Elijah did not elaborate on the first incident (the death of his father or his relationship with him). Instead, he provided a substantial amount of material for interpretation and analysis of the latter incident.

The theme related to his physical injury, therefore, must be interpreted in relation to the image Elijah presented of himself as a 'physical' person at the outset of the interview. He mentions that he spent most of his life outdoors, engaging in various physical activities. Later in his life, as the result of this physical injury, Elijah was told that he 'would not be able to do any physical work for the rest of [his] life' and that he would be forever 'bound behind the desk'. Despite this diagnosis, Elijah managed to recover to return to work. However, the physical injury remained a part of his life ever since:

E. and so over the years I started to think that no one was able to tell me what was
        wrong with my [body part], or [p] fix it, that I started thinking Maybe there's
165   something else going on. Maybe it's some sort of psychological, emotional thing,
        but never Really [p] settled on it but was just open to that fact.

When this aspect of his life is brought to light, Elijah's new-found perspective on the relationship between mind and body finds its significance. This understanding is precisely the 'fact' he alludes to on line 166. Thus, in the weakest interpretation, it can be argued that Elijah learns the means to interpret and, to an extent, tolerate his physical problem by understanding it primarily as a mental condition. This theme runs parallel to self-acceptance and agency: by interpreting his pain primarily as a psychological condition, he is bringing the phenomenon into the realm of his control. Moreover, this account is not significant simply because it reveals Elijah's new-found perspective. It is important because, as the narrative suggests, he came to adopt this perspective in an embodied way through a direct experience.[11]

Concluding Summary

This chapter has emphasised an interpretive approach that is sensitive to both content and the delivery of language. My analysis has demonstrated that even though the language of conversion was absent from Elijah's story—and therefore may not identically fit a normative understanding of conversion narratives—it nonetheless fitted its major contours. For instance, following Stromberg (1993), I have demonstrated the ways in which the movement's canonical language came to inform Elijah's interpretation of himself and his interaction with the surrounding world; by isolating the different tone of his voice, I attempted to resurrect his performance and his movement between two self-concepts, as he dramatically depicted them, and, to an extent, re-lived them in his narrative.

These analyses were undertaken despite that the language of conversion was entirely absent from his narrative; for the passages in this chapter clearly suggest that Elijah prefers the language of transformation. However, as reflected in the excerpt cited at the outset of this chapter, when the participants are posed with questions about categories (conversion, religion, etc.), not only do they exhibit ambivalence, but they also resolve these through the use of the movement's rhetorical strategies. Hence, to a large extent, the adoption of the movement's rhetoric, such as its emphasis on the pragmatic aspects of the practice (tool), marginalised the movement's religious elements such as its strict regulations, code of conduct, and even gender segregation laws, and therefore concealed any religious character. Indeed, other studies of this movement have confirmed that almost all Vipassana practitioners reject religious Buddhist identities (Loss, 2010; Pagis, 2008) and often self-identify as nones or even atheists. Therefore, it could be argued that in addition to a transformation in self-understanding and language, conversion to this

---

[11] Although, in this particular case, it could be argued that what he had experienced was, to an extent, a rehearsal process of internalising the received doctrines (Deleanu, 2010: 616; Griffiths, 1981: 613)—which was the result of his dialogue with an old student, and due to Goenka's instructions which are replete with references to Buddhist doctrines, including impermanence (anicca) and sankhara. However, any issue regarding the legitimacy of meditational experience is not the concern of this book. Rather my objective was to show that part of Elijah's aim in providing a detailed narrative was to convey that his experience led him to a new self-understanding.

movement entails a change in religious identity; it just happens to be that the new claimed identity is understood to be a non-religious one. Therefore, presenting Elijah's story under the comparative umbrella of conversion and conversion narrative is useful for expanding our understanding of conversion particularly in new religious movements and spiritual movements with blurred religious/secular boundaries. More importantly, the concept of tacit conversion enables the linguistic examination of disaffiliated individuals who display ongoing commitment to this movement, its language, and to its perspective on the world.

3

Pragmatic Leaving

This chapter presents an exploration of the narratives of pragmatic leavers—a term that describes those individuals who disengaged prior to developing a commitment to the movement (see figure 3.1). In this chapter, I assert that the disengagement narratives of pragmatic leavers are distinguished by a dynamic combination of three interrelated linguistic features: (1) pragmatism, (2) dualistic discourse (inner/outer, mind/body, immanent/transcendent, etc.), and (3) ambivalence caused by a dissonance between culturally/institutionally informed expectations of meditation and the participants' inability to meet them. While ambivalence was a common characteristic of almost all disengagement narratives (including disaffiliates), I argue that the other two linguistic features enable the pragmatic leavers to negotiate inactivity through a cost-benefit rationalisation without questioning the efficacy of the practice, jeopardising the value of their spiritual seekership or rendering their spiritual growth stalled.

Note, despite the exponential growth of academic interest in meditation, no study to date (to the best of my knowledge) has explored the *cause* of disengagement from meditational practices. This is in spite of the high disengagement rates of people who, regardless of their good intentions, do not return to the centre for a second course. According to Pagis's (2008: 21) estimation, only 30 per cent of course attendees are likely to return for another course, while 10 per cent drop out during the first course. The remaining 60 per cent never return. In this regard, this chapter offers a unique perspective on both meditational studies and disengagement literature, particularly as it examines religious inactivity/disengagement prior to the advanced levels of religious involvement/commitment. Hence, in the absence of reliable theoretical frameworks—the exit literature is primarily built upon the experience of those who leave after longer and intense commitment—I have prioritised a *descriptive* approach to both adequately depict this phenomenon and open a window for future comparative research on this topic. Therefore, I provide a broad overview of the linguistic features of the narratives of these

Drifting Through Samsara. Masoumeh Rahmani, Oxford University Press. © Oxford University Press 2022.
DOI: 10.1093/oso/9780197579961.003.0004

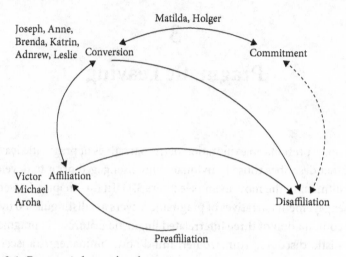

Figure 3.1 Pragmatic leavers' pathways

This diagram solely includes individuals who have completed at least one standard course and who have disengaged prior to developing commitment.

participants coupled with detailed analyses that outline a variety of prototypical narrative structures and plots.

In the following pages, I briefly introduce these linguistic features and subsequently demonstrate (through examples) how they manifest in pragmatic leavers' narratives by systematically exploring disengagement across the axis of meditative experience: (1) negative experiences, (2) frustrations, and (3) loss of positive experiences. As becomes clear in the following chapters (4, 5, and 6), there is a degree of continuity between the themes explored in this chapter and that of disaffiliation narratives. The difference, however, lies in the intensity and depth of these themes, which have significant implications for the experience of disengagement and its narrative plots.

(1) Pragmatism

The first noteworthy characteristic of these disengagement plots was the pragmatic language in which all these stories were formulated (e.g. 'not seeing results', 'losing the meditation high', or 'being distracted by life'). By pragmatic language, I refer to a kind of language that is practical, rational, and non-spiritual. This feature applied to the narratives of all participants in this group regardless of the fact that in describing their attraction to the movement (i.e. retrospective accounts of their approaches to meditation, motivations for joining, and their experiences with the practice), their accounts were anchored on the idea of *spiritual development* and *spiritual search*. As noted, these participants frequently conceptualised their religious development as a 'journey' and framed their motivations for attending a Vipassana course as a quest for meaning and purpose (e.g. 'a search for truth' and 'finding answers for big questions in life'). The point is that the goal of spiritual development was never left behind even for those individuals who equally emphasised the more practical aspects of Vipassana (e.g. the popular discourse on meditation and well-being: that Vipassana meditation offered them a practical solution to their emotional suffering, etc.). Against this backdrop, in forming the plot of the disengagement process and experience, some narratives indicated a *sudden* shift in language: between a spiritual discourse and a pragmatic one. Hence, irrespective of how attraction/approach to the movement was framed, all participants adopted a pragmatic language and rationalised their disengagement in the same fashion.

(2) Dualistic Discourse

The second noteworthy characteristic of the pragmatic leavers' narratives is the dualistic discourse; a distinction is constantly enforced between internal realms and external realities, mind and body, as well as the immanent and the transcendent frameworks. For instance, some of the individuals in this group commonly rationalised disengagement by strategically negotiating, and effectively *prioritising*, the mundane dimension of their lives over and above a transcendental one, while others rationalised their disengagement in terms of bridging a perceived disconnect between mind and body. The choice of the term 'pragmatic leavers' is intended to capture both linguistic features discussed so far. Pragmatic leavers were the only group (compared to old students and disaffiliates) that overwhelmingly utilised this form of discourse in their narratives. I do not, however, intend to make any assumptions about the phenomenological experience of this duality (i.e. how they experience self and world), nor am I interested in asserting value judgements.

Generally speaking, pragmatic leavers are individuals tied to family and/ or career commitments. Hence, regardless of their needs, desire, or even fantasies about spirituality and spiritual development, they are tightly bound to the responsibilities associated with living a conventional life. Thus, I must stress that in approaching this linguistic feature (dualism) in the narratives of pragmatic leavers, my intention is not to trivialise or de-emphasise this element of the everyday reality of these participants. Rather, my aim in this chapter is to simply explore the *function* of this discourse and propose my preliminary suggestions about its meaning and its implications for understanding the cause of disengagement from Vipassana movement.

(3) Ambivalence

The final characteristic of pragmatic leavers' narratives is grounded in a dissonance between cultural/institutional structures and personal experience. In short, the individuals in this research (including pragmatic leavers) are influenced by cultural structures that shape their values and their imagination about the efficacy of meditation. For instance, these individuals describe how the Western cultural world informs them that happiness is a worthy goal; that each person is responsible for their own happiness and well-being; that self-discovery and self-transformation are necessary; and that meditation is an effective resolution for these concerns. Not only do these values shape the participants' imaginations, expectations, and their experiences of meditation, but they also influence how the participants experience, rationalise, and negotiate disengagement. That is, a self-imposed obligation to continue meditation was ubiquitous in all these narratives. In fact, in the vast majority of cases, it prompted a sense of guilt, anger, and self-resentment when participants discontinued their practice.

The institutional structures leading to a sense of ambivalence and even impatience were amplified by deep-seated dichotomies in the movement's teachings (Goenka's discourses about progress are explored in chapter 4 and 5) and, more relevantly, by their marketing strategies which implicitly promotes Vipassana meditation as a low-cost practice that delivers a high-value product. This is seen, for instance, in the ways the movement represents itself to the outside world or to potential students as a 'universal remedy'; an 'easy' and straightforward path to 'real happiness'; a 'practical' practice attuned to the demands of the conventional life, the 'art of living' (Dhamma Medini, 2017). However, the purpose of the practice shifts towards other-worldly concerns (enlightenment) for individuals operating from within the movement, whilst the path to real happiness is gradually stretched and demands higher levels of commitment (e.g. complete observance of the moral codes, including celibacy for single students).

Indeed, the narratives of pragmatic leavers were contingent on other factors such as the types of experiences individuals undergo during meditation. In short, positive meditative experiences cemented, validated, and strengthened these structures in the imagination of the participant, whereas negative experiences created a vacuum for reflection and interrogation. The most noteworthy examples of the latter scenario are taken from Andrew's narrative and Leslie's follow-up interview in which both individuals reflect and renegotiate their culturally inherited ideas (e.g. the efficacy of meditation or the universal applicability of this practice) due to unexpected meditative experiences. However, even these narratives have traces of ambivalence arising from the conflict between experience and culturally informed expectations.

Experience Seekers

The category of 'experience' is tightly tangled with various dimensions of the participants' narratives (as noted previously), but it is mostly valued as a method of acquiring knowledge about the self and the surrounding world. Earlier in this book, I demonstrated how the theme of experience manifested as a rhetorical strategy in the narrative of those who had developed commitment to this movement (old students and disaffiliates). In this section, I aim to show that, while, like other participants, the pragmatic leavers valued experience for the insights and knowledge they gained about themselves, others, and the world, they also desired experience for the sake of experiencing something different, extraordinary, and transcendental.

In other words, I argue that pragmatic leavers are to some extent experience seekers—they typically interlaced their seekership plot with an experiential approach to the movement (Lofland and Skonovd, 1981). Most pragmatic leavers framed their first course participation as partly motivated by 'curiosity' (e.g. 'go and do it and have the full experience'). This perhaps explains why the narratives of pragmatic leavers were some of the most colourful and detailed depictions of meditative experiences, even though in some instances the temporal distance from the original experience exceeds two decades. Moreover, all pragmatic leavers exhibited a sense of accomplishment for successfully completing a ten-day course (e.g. 'Vipassana was like running a marathon, now I know I can do it').[1] Moreover, not only did the pragmatic leavers passionately narrate their meditative experience, but they also often voluntarily launched into these stories and described extraordinary episodes without the question being directly raised in the interview.

This unequivocal emphasis on, and desire for, experience brings to mind the remarks of Woodhead and Heelas (2000: 112) that rendered 'experiential religions' as suppliers of a high-demand 'product—namely experience', and their adherents as consumers. By saying this, I have no intention of advocating market or economic theories of religion tightly entwined with rational choice theory (Stark and Finke, 2000).[2] Rather, I intend to highlight the weight that these participants allocated to meditative experience, presumably as a tangible measure for evaluating efficacy and gains. More relevantly, I want to stress the implication of different types of meditative experience (as well as the loss of it) for the narratives of pragmatic leavers.

My exploration of pragmatic leavers' disengagement narrative plots proceeds in the following order: (1) traumatic meditative experiences (a case study of depersonalisation) and unpleasant experiences (a case study of disconnection from the external world); (2) frustrations and lack of extraordinary experiences; (3) the loss of extraordinary (transcendental) meditative experiences. It is important to note that these categorisations are not mutually exclusive; the themes explored in each section have relevance to others. For instance, some of the participants who anchored their

---

[1] Another participant, Brenda, noted: 'in the Strange way it was sort of Ego boost I think, or that it was self-confidence boost in that you sort of think "wow I did that"', I'm silent for ten days and you know I kept to the rules'.

[2] In short, rational choice theory—closely associated with Rodney Stark—is fundamentally anchored in the assumption that religious institutions are providers of social 'goods'—ranging from immediate (belonging, peace) to ultimate goods (salvation, eternal life, enlightenment) and people are consumers with 'subjective efforts to weigh the anticipated rewards against the anticipated costs, although these efforts usually are inexact and somewhat casual' (Stark and Finke, 2000: 37). Accordingly, the success of a given religious organisation is dependent upon its ability to produce (and sell) the desired product. On the whole, this theory has been widely controversial and subject to criticisms on various grounds. For example, for its lack of generalisability (beyond the US model) as it neglects the diversity of perception of 'cost and benefits' both at micro and macro levels (Spickard, 1998); its presupposition that individuals make rational choices (Veer, 2012); and, more profoundly, for its psychological assumptions and its discourse of compensators and rewards (Bruce, 1999). However, the most baffling claim set forth by the rational choice theorists, Stark and Finke (2002: 135), is their passive conceptualisation of religious actors at the expense of emphasising network influences—stating, 'conversion is really a matter of resocialisation, rather than choice, and in that sense, converts are more or less passive victims of social processes beyond their grasp and control'.

narrative on unpleasant experiences had also expressed frustration with private meditation; some of the participants who framed their disengagement as a result of frustration also shared concerns about feeling disconnected from the external world. Likewise, some of those participants who emphasised frustration or traumatic experiences shared similar concerns with those who framed disengagement as a result of the loss of positive experiences. This most commonly involved a shared aversion to commitment and/or rendering Vipassana impractical in everyday life, for example, by indicating that one's progress in this tradition requires a 'full commitment' and the abandonment of 'any recognisable form of regular human life and interaction'. Therefore, there are various overlaps between these categories, even though I have separated them in order to systematically analyse the narratives.

Traumatic Meditative Experiences

Traumatic experiences are neither unusual to the process of meditation nor to the process of disengagement from the meditative practices. Among the twenty-six participants in this study, four individuals provided first-hand reports of unpleasant and negative meditative experiences such as disorientation, depression, and suicidal states that often lingered for several months after their participation in a Vipassana course. Additionally, two other participants reported second-hand narratives based on witnessing their friend(s) undergo disorienting experiences—they all considered these experiences to be a direct result of course participation. However, as becomes clear (in this chapter and in chapter 6), only three individuals plotted their exit narratives in terms of a direct response to or resolution of traumatic experiences, whereas other participants indicated their efforts to look beyond these unsettling experiences in the attempt to resolve doubts.

Framing disengagement as a resolution, those individuals with first-hand traumatic experiences used adjectives such as 'scary', 'crazy', 'dense', 'heavy', and 'flat' to describe those experiences. They also strongly emphasised the 'realness' of their experiences. Although I am unfit to apply a psychological diagnosis to these incidents, a thematic exploration of these accounts suggests that the participants often connected these incidents to the imbalance between practice and theoretical understanding of certain concepts such as not-self, impermanence, and detachment.

Insufficient Balance Between Theory and Practice

To illustrate how a disconnection between theory and practice can lead to disorienting experiences and consequently disengagement, I explore two excerpts from my interview with Andrew. Note, as a result of his traumatic meditative experience, Andrew does not wish to return to the centre and holds a firm view that intense meditation retreats are not 'healthy' environments for him. In fact, Andrew's meditative experiences led him to conclude that the ten-day Vipassana course and the state of mind that arises from it are impractical for a person leading a 'daily life'. Instead, he argued that it belongs to 'monks' with 'very little responsibility outside [who] got the space to be crazy'. In spite of these opinions, what is of particular importance in this narrative is that Andrew continues to interpret aspects of himself and his experiences in the light of the movement's meaning system. Therefore, while his traumatic experience led him to disengage without looking back, it has not resulted in deconversion:

A. my whole physical experience was really changing and, and Until, Until then in my life I've been so physically rooted you know

S. mhm

A. I'm like [p] Farming, growing up, sports like rugby, [p] building you know I'm a really Practical, physical sort of person so to sit, have a complete different physical experience was really um, it started to, [p] [in] effect, My, yk mental sort of physical Balance . . . Taste would started going crazy yk like stuff, food just did not taste like it had, or good, or, just, [p] pff yk I could barely eat food after a while . . . it was, it was pretty, and totally upset my mental balance I think

S. yeah

A. cause all of those [p] um I guess when I <u>say</u> <u>'I'm strongly physical' I'm probably</u> <u>saying 'I'm strongly attached to that physical</u> <u>experience'</u>

S. mhm

A. yk and that was completely changed and so I was like fuck [g] if I can't feel any, if I can't feel emotions, yk how do I have a human experience. it was, that was the hard thing . . . I basically was, [p] going into a place, going into a place where I did Not know what that place was. you know, I didn't have guidance . . . the Experience was Soo intense that I was like 'I actually can't live like this, yk [p] if this is in fact where I am at now [vc: drops to whisper] I'll last two weeks and I'll kill myself basically', that's what I felt. yeah

[Later in the interview Andrew described another incident that occurred weeks after his initial Vipassana course]

A. the realisation of that, in that experience was that 'I'm completely alone' and all
   of those attachments to love and [p] um my family and all these things are really
   just [p] not Real . . . I felt myself, if I'm to visualise it, it was like this black hole that
   I found myself sliding into

S. mhm

A. and I was like 'I'm not ready to go there', I could feel that and I was like the only way
   that I could stop going there, was, I just had this image of my sister, yk and I really
   just [g] just held on to that really strongly and that was all I had, so I didn't, I didn't
   go down that path [g] But I won't yk, [p] I don't I don't regret doing that, and um
   but I Wonder, yk whether that was, [p] [p] heading in that direction of just letting
   go of all attachment . . . I felt like I was gonna wake up and have Nothing, Nothing!

The main theme of the first excerpt is Andrew's inability to readjust to a
normal life outside the centre. The source of discomfort as Andrew described here is caused by a radical shift and a reorientation in his sense of self
and perception of reality. To convey this, Andrew begins by presenting his
prior-to-the-course self as a 'practical physical person', whose sense of selfhood is strongly anchored in an embodied experience of the world where
he acts and draws meaning from (farming, rugby, building). Meditation for
him carried an intense process of depersonalisation of his physical experiences, which, without the appropriate theoretical knowledge and guidance,
resulted in a state akin to what Pollio et al. (1997: 171) describe as alienation from the self and estrangement from feelings and desires. It could be
said that the retreat had rendered meaningless the emotional vocabulary by
which Andrew made sense of himself and the world. This is reflected in the
questions he posed: 'how do I have a human experience' when I feel completely 'flat'?

The second segment, on the other hand, rests on Andrew's confused
understanding of detachment. This excerpt describes the fragmentation of
a sense of self that is anchored in relation to others (especially family). Here,
Andrew speaks about attachment to family, love, and the profound sense of
existential loneliness that accompanied the idea of a self detached from all
the social and emotional ties that gave meaning to and a sense of belonging in
his life. The fear of losing these were expressed through the image of sliding
into a 'black hole' and waking up to 'nothing'. What Andrew describes in this
segment resembles Gaev's concept of 'spiritual loneliness' or Sadler's concept
of the 'cosmic dimension of loneliness', which phenomenologically is characterised by a sense of profound isolation that occurs when one is unable to
find meaning in life (cited in Pollio et al., 1997: 172).

In both instances, Andrew depicts experiences reminiscent of what has been traditionally identified by Buddhist meditation masters as 'meditation sickness'—a state where the practitioner loses touch with the socioculturally constructed world that he/she lives in and draws meaning from (Sharf, 2015: 479). Indeed, a similar observation has been noted in Tim Lomas et al.'s (2014) qualitative research on thirty male meditators. Amongst the many examples, Lomas et al. (2014: 855) quote from a participant, who, similar to Andrew, had disorienting experiences due to practicing intense meditation techniques (the Six Element) without training: 'It felt like I'd disappeared into some ethereal sort of realm . . . You just feel like you don't exist, you're nothing, there's nothing really there. It's nihilistic, pretty terrifying'. The point is that without the appropriate guidance (from a teacher) and training, the deconstruction of self and reality (which is the goal of both techniques) was experienced as traumatic rather than liberating (Lomas et al., 2014).

According to Sharf (2015), Andrew's meditation sickness may be a consequence of an insufficient balance between doctrine and practice, suggesting what may be a more general pattern for these dramatic types of disengagement. In support of this hypothesis, Sharf (2015) explored early forms of Chinese Zen (Chan) and Tibetan Dzogchen and argues that, similar to modern Burmese teachers, the masters and advocates of these practices were commonly under fire from critics for 'dumbing down the tradition, for devaluing ethical training, for misconstruing or devaluing the role of wisdom, and for their crassly "instrumental" approach to practice' (2015: 476). According to Sharf's (2015: 476) review, one common criticism directed at those techniques, which were taught and practiced unbalanced by a critical engagement with Buddhist doctrine and scripture, was that they could lead to paralysing states described as 'falling into emptiness' or 'meditation sickness'.

Thus, such experiences are not unusual; rather, there have been centuries-old warnings against the forms of practices that emphasise quick results as opposed to gradual transformation balanced with intellectual engagement with scripture (Sharf, 2015). However, individuals who attend Vipassana courses are rarely informed about the range of possible meditation-related experiences that could accompany the practice. This is partly due to the fact that scientific research that informs and directs public knowledge of meditation has almost exclusively focused on reporting positive and beneficial effects of meditational practices (Lindahl et al., 2014).

There are a few exceptions to this trend. In addition to Lomas et al.'s (2014) study, a study by Lindhal and colleagues (2017) offers a taxonomy of fifty-nine meditative-related challenges which they categorised into seven domains of *cognitive* (changes to mental functioning), *perceptual* (changes to any of the five senses), *affective* (changes in the type, intensity, or frequency of the emotions), *somatic* (observable changes to bodily functioning), *conative* (changes in motivations), *sense of self*, and *social* (changes in interpersonal activities). These interrelated categories emerged from their analysis of sixty interviews with long-term Western meditators from Theravada, Zen, and Tibetan Buddhism. From this perspective, Andrew's narrative, at the very least, features four of the abovementioned categories: perceptual, affective, sense of self, and social.

Moreover, Miguel Farias and Catherine Wikholm's (2015) *The Buddha Pill*—which has gained substantial media coverage since its publication—is amongst the first books to dedicate a chapter to reporting the 'dark side of meditation' in a format accessible to a wider non-academic audience. Interestingly enough, Leslie (as discussed, a participant in this research) introduced me to an article that referred to Farias and Wikholm's book. Additionally, Willoughby Britton and her team at Brown University have also shifted attention from exclusively reporting the positive effects to attempting to map traumatic experiences, which she calls 'The Dark Side of Dharma'. [3] That said, the field that explores unusual and adverse effects of meditation remains underdeveloped and in dire need of scholarly attention.

The frequent occurrence of disorienting meditative experiences such as Andrew's has forced the movement to consider cautionary measures, such as rejecting the application of those who indicate a history of 'mental health problems'. [4] According to a Vipassana assistant teacher I interviewed, the organisation is selective in accepting applications from individuals with a history of mental health issues to prevent negative incidents. She noted, 'people who get plagued by panic attacks or something which is a very difficult thing to deal with and we're very careful about checking in people who have

---

[3] Willoughby Britton has not yet published her findings but has addressed them in a number of interviews (Britton, 2011; Stone, 2013). https://journals.sagepub.com/doi/10.1177/2167702621996340 https://www.oxfordhandbooks.com/view/10.1093/oxfordhb/9780198808640.001.0001/oxfordhb-9780198808640-e-51

[4] Prior to attending a Vipassana course, all practitioners (new and old students) are required to complete a course application form. One of the mandatory questions on this form concerns the participants' psychological health: 'Do you have, or have you ever had, any mental health problems such as significant depression or anxiety, panic attacks, manic depression, schizophrenia, etc.? If yes, please give details (dates, symptoms, duration, hospitalization, treatment, and present condition)'.

a History of panic attack'. Nevertheless, the movement has little to offer in support of those who do undergo these experiences. As a result, individuals such as Andrew are abandoned in a state of bewilderment, which potentially puts them at risk of being misdiagnosed for serious psychological disorders (Lindahl et al., 2014). Consequently, it could be said that the movement's cautionary measures to prevent these incidents function to protect the organisation itself (from potential negative publicity) rather than the well-being of its practitioners.

Having explored the significance of traumatic meditative experiences for disengagement narratives, I now draw attention to a similar, but less severe, case study from Leslie's disengagement narrative: a disconnection from the external/physical world, which was also relevant to several other participants, including Andrew.

Disconnection from the External World

Disengagement narrative plots that hinged on the theme of isolation and disconnection from external reality are not exclusive to individuals who embarked on the process of conversion. Such a plot was relevant to the narrative of Michael, who did not even contemplate the idea of private meditation, and who rejected the 'philosophy of sitting still', arguing 'the body is meant to move and . . . I'm more interested to live life as a meditation than sitting and meditating'. This theme is important, as a similar but more advanced version of this plot manifests in some of the disaffiliation narratives (i.e. the pursuers of the gateless gate). I elaborate on the theme of disconnection from the world in the following pages and argue that disengagement in the context of both traumatic and unpleasant meditative experiences brings about a reconceptualisation of the purpose of meditation which in turn is used to negotiate disengagement (e.g. that Vipassana aims for enlightenment and therefore it is impractical for my immediate worldly concerns).

To demonstrate these points, I refer to a follow-up interview with Leslie, conducted one year after her first course attendance in which she explains why she had completely stopped her practice. A noteworthy characteristic of Leslie's language is the sense of authority it encapsulates. In her initial interview, which took place two weeks after her first course, Leslie noted that she had 'made an executive decision' to reduce the two-hour recommended sitting meditation to an hour of meditating whilst lying down in bed. As becomes clear later, this quality in negotiating disengaging distinguishes Leslie's approach from other participants who indicated a degree of guilt for discontinuating their practice:

L. when other people would talk about, [p] needing three days to quiet their mind down from all the rushing around, I've never been like . . . that's not my head. My head is quiet a lot of the time. So I found the meditation [p] made me . . . it almost made me a little depressed more than anything . . . it's more, it doesn't necessarily bring me to [p] a quiet happy peaceful place. [p] and it doesn't bring me to a dark horrible place either. Some of it I just felt like either it didn't bring me anywhere . . . and that a lot of that [p][p] wasn't [p] interesting enough. um so, I wasn't finding [p][p] Hugely useful things about myself, to pay attention to, or to work on, or, great insight . . . I don't know if that's terrible, probably a failed meditator . . . I think I find I get, Nourish by the natural world so much

S. mhm

L. that, [p] [p] yeah putting in, so much in my own world, does feel like it's cutting off, a big part of the bigger world that we inhabit . . . I just felt that there were things, that, at least to who I am, I was gonna get into a deeper place by being in a natural world.

The themes that initially standout in Leslie's narrative are loneliness, isolation, and disconnection from the external world. While there is no way of knowing whether Leslie's (or other participants') depression is related to or triggered by Vipassana, the fact that these individuals highlight this theme and directly link it to their disengagement tells us a great deal about how they negotiate disengagement. More importantly, as these examples demonstrate, the mind/body dualism was the prominent characteristic of the disengagement narratives of both Andrew and Leslie. Unlike Andrew, who portrayed himself as a physically rooted person, hence linking his traumatic experience and disengagement to a perturbation of that strongly embodied self, Leslie's self-concept (according to her own understanding) is grounded in the mind/intellect. For instance, elsewhere in the interview Leslie self-categorised herself as a 'head-oriented' person, for whom 'the body is a foreign country'. However, similar to Andrew, Leslie used this dualism to negotiate disengagement by emphasising a disconnection between the self and the external/natural world and the sense of loneliness resulting from it. She argued that the act of introspection isolated her from the external world because it was 'too embodied', and she proposed, 'what I need is to go walk and actually feel my body for a while instead'. Hence, in both instances, disengagement was rationalised as a solution to restore a functional self-concept fostered from an indexical relationship to the world. Since meditation had disturbed the balance of anchoring their self-concept in relation to mind/body, these participants hinged their narratives on a dualistic discourse (mind/body, inner world/external world).

Here, it is important to remember that the theme of mind/body split was one of the important themes by which Leslie had reconstructed her biography in the initial interview.[5] According to Stromberg's (1993: 31) theory, Leslie's struggle with the mind/body split can be seen as an ongoing emotional conflict between contradictory aims. For instance, she at once desires to 'protect her heart' and to 'feel all her feelings'. However, while Leslie was partially able to articulate this conflict in her initial interview, this was not done to the *extent* that we witnessed in Elijah's narrative (in chapter 2). Rather, unlike the other notions she took from Vipassana such as sankhara, or conditioning, Leslie translated the concept of mind/body into her own vocabulary. In fact, she spoke about the struggle she faced in maintaining Vipassana's conceptualisation in this regard:

L. I'm still struggling with that whole question around embodiment and knowing your body so well . . . it's actually far more frightening . . . parts of me aren't ready to say 'it's okay to just let things go' . . . my mind isn't gonna give up really easily . . . I get a glimpse of times that observing mind is just watching, but my kind of day-to-day mind is, Pretty much fighting like a cat, being thrown into a sink full of water.

The insufficiency of the movement's language to resolve this tension led Leslie to resort to yet another universe of discourse, which provided her with a system of meaning with which to come to terms with these persisting ambivalences and conflicts (mind/body split). Instead of maintaining Vipassana's explanation and ideas on the links between mind and body, Leslie's follow-up interview drew heavily from psychological theories.[6] These theories were instrumental to her purposes; they prompted self-acceptance

---

[5] Refer to the passage cited earlier under 'Biographical Reconstruction' section in chapter 1.

[6] As noted in the conversion career chapter, Leslie drew from certain psychological theories of personality types: mind-oriented people vs. body-oriented people, introverts vs. extroverts, and so on. These ideas provided her with a clear dualistic framework that explained why meditation was ineffective because of her personality type and that other practices (such as walking) were more appropriate tools to bridge the mind/body split.

and helped her reason why Vipassana meditation had produced a sense of loneliness, isolation, and possibly depression. Hence, in this instance, Leslie's disengagement from Vipassana involved a search for a new interpretative framework to resolve certain conflicts. Nevertheless, in both cases (Andrew and Leslie), disengagement was motivated by de-stabilisation of the self, which resulted in unpleasant and traumatic experiences.

As noted, the second overarching characteristic of the pragmatic leavers' narrative is the pragmatic language in which disengagement is negotiated. This feature is explicit in the selected excerpt from Leslie's narrative, although it is also relevant to all other narratives categorised in this chapter. For instance, Leslie argued that observing sensations was not 'interesting enough' and that private meditation did not reveal 'hugely useful things' for her to explore. This linguistic feature finds its significance once juxtaposed with the participant's initial interview (as well as other participants' narratives) in which Vipassana meditation was praised for enabling insight and facilitating spiritual development. That said, this kind of pragmatic language connects to assumptions that these individuals had about meditation as an undemanding, painless, universally applicable relaxation technique that aims to calm the mind and drift the practitioner to a 'quiet, happy, peaceful place'.

As is clear in both instances, Leslie's and Andrew's unpleasant meditative experiences prompted a new conceptualisation of Vipassana meditation: Vipassana meditation was not suitable for them as individuals; the practice is irrelevant to their immediate needs; and it is impractical in an everyday context. Instead, they proposed that Vipassana meditation was suitable for those ('monks') who seek the ultimate goal of enlightenment. Hence, while neither of these participants had *explicitly* disclaimed their desire for spiritual development, their adoption of this pragmatic language enabled them to implicitly disqualify Vipassana for their immediate needs without rendering the practice ineffective. Consequently, we encounter moments of ambivalence in their narratives such as 'I do feel it's the most sensible, logical, best system I've ever come across . . . [I'm] probably a failed meditator'. However, these instances of ambivalence (Andrew and Leslie) were far less pronounced than in the narratives of those who articulated disengagement in the context of experiencing frustrations during meditation (discussed in the next section).

Finally, upon disengagement, both individuals reoriented towards *physical* activities that resumed a kind of connection to the world through direct experience. While disengagement did not lead Leslie to seek other practices at the time of the second interview (as she approached walking in nature as a tool to reconnect to the world), her language and discourse indicated a slight reorientation towards psychological/scientific explanations of self, mind, and body relationships. On the other hand, Andrew's language remained comparably confined within the movement's universe of discourse, although he integrated Vipassana meditation with Tai Chi, which he described as a 'grounding' practice that bridged the previously felt disconnection between the self and the external world.

Frustrating Experiences

As briefly mentioned, in instances where disengagements were not linked directly to unpleasant or negative meditative experiences, the narratives were accompanied by a sense of guilt, remorse, and even anger, which are benched in the participants' response to culturally and institutionally moulded (self-)expectations. In short, these involved a sense of obligation to maintain a meditation routine (two hours per day) for the sake of one's happiness, well-being, and progress on this path, and/or expectations to experience extraordinary sensations (such as a free flow, dissolution, etc.). Once again, a more dramatic demonstration of this theme (doubt about one's progress) is relevant to the narrative of disaffiliates. In the meantime, however, I aim to illustrate how frustrations and lack of extraordinary experiences result in disengagement and reorientation towards less demanding and easily accomplished practices. This, to an extent, qualifies my earlier claim that the pragmatic leavers are experience seekers.

To contextualise these points, I draw from my interviews with Katrin. At the time of her initial interview, Katrin was committed to a daily routine despite feeling frustrated by an inability to achieve a 'free flow' and the physical pain she endured during sits. She noted, 'I'm torn between oh this is a bit frustrating and oh I'm really sure that this technique has benefits for me'. During her first interview, Katrin spoke about developing a tolerance towards her physical pain and took this as an indication of strength and progress in 'non-reactivity'. [7] However, within the span of one year, Katrin discontinued her

---

[7] Katrin noted, 'I was quite amazed, how much pain I can suffer and not react to it, I thought it really made me strong, I felt it made me quite strong . . . I don't get a free flow, but after a while I think I could let it go and just be with the pain again and just sit there and have a smile on my face'.

private practice and moved to another meditation. She rationalised her disengagement in the following terms:

K. I guess that's probably not the right attitude when you do meditation, but I kind of wanted to see outcomes [g] 'alright I'm doing this now so afterwards I want to feel better?' really, like instrumentalised it. and I did enjoy Vipassana, but I couldn't really see outcomes that much . . . I guess the reason why I kept doing it was I've been reading so much about it for my research in my PhD that always told me meditation is great for you and um very beneficial and hundreds of reasons why I should do it and I thought Alright! so it was more like a um a rational decision . . . and I assumed having these expectations of an outcome [hah] were actually defeating the purpose of making it work probably . . . now that I reflect back on the last year, [p] I don't know if my life has changed, maybe because I'm pregnant [g] I'm just happy in general, but I feel that I've got a good life, [p] and I guess, [p] I'm less desperate than I was maybe a year before, so I think that meditation must have had, an impact on my life, a good one . . . I know that I am not perfect yet, but yeah I feel like I've made a lot of progress towards being happy with who I am without being, without achieving certain things all the time.

This passage envelops Katrin's ambivalence about the efficacy of Vipassana meditation. On the one hand, with a language drenched in self-deprecation, Katrin suggests that she had stopped meditation because she could not 'see outcomes'; on the other hand, she concludes that meditation 'must have had an impact' because she now feels content with herself (self-acceptance) and her life. Once again, these ambivalences are responses to both broader cultural and even scientific influences (e.g. meditation is great and effective; the happiness she feels must be the result of meditation), as well as institutional (e.g. having expectations counteracts one's progress: Goenka encourages his meditators to not measure their progress based on specific physical sensations, although they are bound to come if one is practicing appropriately). Comparably, while a similar sense of ambivalence prevailed in those narratives that emphasised frustrations due to the inability to concentrate in private practice, the participants' emotional responses were often shaded with guilt, sorrow, and anger. For instance, Anne noted:

A. I felt incredibly guilty . . . I felt there were so much pressure that 'if you don't continue it won't have effects' . . . yeah that's probably a negative side, I mean it's probably good [l] um [p] that there is so much pressure to practice . . . we are way too busy and, and, that our everyday life's focus [p] should be at some stage to a certain degree on a meditative practice . . . it would be really, really nice if someone from the modern world would take the idea of Vipassana and transform it into something that can be used everyday.

These frustrations are common to many meditational practices. For instance, this theme strongly surfaced among participants of mindfulness meditation in Lomas et al.'s (2014) research. Similar to the participants in this research, Lomas et al.'s (2014: 852) interviewees highlighted the pressures of mundane life such as 'demands from relationships, work and financial concerns, and stress from living in a busy city', impeding the quality of their practice. However, unlike the analysis I have offered in this chapter, Lomas et al.'s study did not concentrate on disengagement narratives or the broader cultural structures influencing these experiences; rather, being grounded in the field of psychology, their research aimed for a thematic exploration of challenges associated with meditation and issues around safeguarding meditators in therapeutic settings.

Upon disengagement, individuals who reported frustrations during meditation reoriented towards practices that (1) involved easily accomplished goals, (2) provided more tangible benefits, and (3) answered questions that Vipassana meditation did not adequately address. For instance, Katrin replaced her regular routine of Vipassana meditation with the Presence Process, which, according to her own account, 'is more for beginners who have no idea what Vipassana is and it makes it easier for you to keep your attention to the breath', and 'the book that you read when you're doing this explains a lot of psychological processes that makes me understand how I sometimes react and how I'm creating my own reality'. Joseph, meanwhile, advocated a practice called the 'Journey', which according to his account 'was like, Vipassana's ten-days condensed into two hours, with more Added!' Once again, another appealing element of the Journey was its ability to explain idiosyncratic details of the participant's life that Vipassana meditation did not necessarily address (or, indeed, discouraged the students from seeking causal explanations).

Finally, the language of those three participants who framed disengagement in face of frustrations, indicated an amalgamation of Vipassana's universe of discourse and that of other traditions. These individuals essentially integrated Vipassana meditation with other practices that complemented their needs. In a sense, their narratives resembled a conversion pattern that

Manning (1996: 299–311) identified as 'combinatory conversion'. Manning developed this concept in the context of religious syncretism to account for the 'possibility of equal multiple allegiances' he encountered in the narratives of Neo-Pagans who also believed in the 'truth of the gospels'. This framework explains the mixed identities that these participants preferred, such as 'Buddhist-Pagan' and 'Buddhist-Christian' (see appendix 2).

Loss of Experience

This section explores the narratives of those pragmatic leavers who passionately reported positive meditative experiences, which they often construed as 'glimpses of enlightenment', 'entering nirvana', or 'transcending the self'. I argue that these individuals also demonstrate signs of ambivalence in their language. However, in these particular cases, the ambivalence is mainly anchored on (1) a conflict between mundane and spiritual motives, aims, and desires, and (2) the idea that the practice is unsuitable for the everyday environment and its 'distractions'. These individuals commonly fantasised about deferring their desires for spiritual development/attainment to an unforeseen future—a later phase in life, when they have fulfilled their conventional responsibilities in the present—and linked their disengagement with their inability to recreate these unique experiences in the everyday environment. In other words, participants with positive/extraordinary experiences presented narratives of conflicted selves torn between the inescapable mundane and the irresistible transcendence.

Note, while these accounts are worthy of consideration in their own terms, for the purpose of the present chapter, I do not get into the specific details of these experiences. Rather, I intend to focus on the ways in which these anecdotes influenced the disengagement narratives. Suffice to note that the pragmatic leavers who retrospectively narrated their extraordinary experiences commonly structured these narrative asides according to three consecutive developments: (1) *discomfort,* which was usually depicted as an intense physical pain during meditation; (2) *revelation,* which framed a moment of 'bliss', composed in juxtaposition to the previous clause. Participants commonly described this clause in the following terms: 'the dissolving of physical pain', 'cessation of mental thought', 'transcending the self', 'weightlessness', 'floating', 'hovering in space', 'blinding light', 'euphoric', and 'otherworldly'; and (3) *evaluation,* or the participants' interpretations of the experience, which they commonly labelled as 'nirvana' or 'enlightenment'.

As mentioned, an important characteristic of pragmatic leavers' narratives is echoed in the participants' dualistic discourse through which they express a sense of self and determine the self's position in relation to the world. I also argued that the pragmatic leavers use this form of language to negotiate disengagement. However, whereas Andrew and Leslie used the mind/body and inner/external dualism, the prevalent theme in the narratives of these individuals concerned the duality of the immanent/transcendent. For example, by prioritising their 'this-worldly' needs above a spiritual one.

When I began a thematic exploration of my interviews with old students and Vipassana teachers, it soon became clear that these individuals commonly conceptualised other practitioners' disengagement in terms of priorities in life. For instance, Carole framed new students' disengagement in terms of becoming 'swamped by worldly life and losing sight of the priority of purifying your mind'. Initially, I was captivated by the old students' (and Vipassana teachers') choice of words, particularly their terminology of 'worldly life' that implicitly asserted a value-laden categorisation. I was surprised to find that this language and reasoning was not restricted to old students; pragmatic leavers who had gradually discontinued their private meditation rationalised their disengagement within the same framework.

Matilda is one of the four pragmatic leavers who enthusiastically narrated about having 'glimpses of enlightenment' through practising Vipassana meditation. In accounting for her disengagement, Matilda highlighted two elements in her narrative: (1) the loss of experience, arguing that private meditation is 'less rewarding' in comparison to a ten-day course and that the felt benefits were 'not so radical'; and (2) a felt conflict in priorities, specifically between prosaic and spiritual goals. Take, for instance, the following passage from my conversation with Matilda:

M. I have observed myself and I agree with the, what they do at the course . . . not
   eating meat . . . I have this funny thing where I kind of belie[ve] that for a spiritual
   journey that definitely no meat, is a really good idea but then for my, for, but it's a
   funny contrast because I feel like for, growing and my daughter and when I was
   pregnant, da-da-da-da, that the meat was kind of essential. So I have this total
   conflict in my head where my body wants one thing [g] my mind wants the other
   one so, I would now. so where I was in total agreement before, I'm not like, like

kind of agree with my head, or maybe I agree with my heart but I think I couldn't do a one hundred per cent vegan, vegetarian

S. this conflict that you're feeling, [are you] making a distinction between spiritual life?

M. yeah, yeah

S. and life basically

M. worldly life

S. worldly life ... do you think there's a distinction?

M. um, [p] maybe it's more like priorities ... some take priority over others, at different parts of life ... so again I feel like perhaps later in my life I might be able to withdraw slightly from, other part, aspects of life and put more time and effort into a spiritual path.

From the structuralists' perspective, there is nothing out of the ordinary in this passage. In fact, Lorne Dawson's (1999, cited in Chryssides, 2016) concept of 'structural availability'[8] provides a reasonable explanation why participants, such as Matilda, disengage or do not fully commit to Vipassana. According to this theory, there are a number of factors that must be in place to make conversion—or more appropriately, *commitment*—possible. For instance, the convert's life, career, and relationships need to be structured in such a way that allows the individual the freedom to leave his/her conventional lifestyle and meet the demands of the movement if need be. This theory supports conversion patterns to 'controversial' New Religious Movements (NRMs) of the 1960s and 1970s that typically involved 'communal living apart from mainstream society' such as the Family, the Unification Church, and ISKCON (Chryssides, 2016: 29). In these specific contexts, George Chryssides (2016: 29) argues that NRMs tended to mainly attract the youth 'because they were more readily available for the NRM's lifestyle, having few commitments, perhaps being in a gap year, or being willing to interrupt or abandon their education'.

Thus, in one sense, the fact that pragmatic leavers did not develop commitment and disengaged from Vipassana due to their other obligations is both comprehensible and indisputable. Without denying this evidential condition of the pragmatic leavers' everyday life, I want to explore what else could be learned from the participants' language and the conditions of their spirituality in these instances.

[8] Dawson has borrowed this term from Snow et al., 1980.

Generally speaking, the majority of pragmatic leavers are professional adults, mothers or fathers whose responsibilities in 'this life' mean they have less time to 'daydream' about what may or may not be beyond 'this' realm. In simple terms, these individuals see themselves strained within a mundane frame, yet at the same time nostalgically desire the transcendent. This sense of nostalgia is partly reflected in the ways in which the pragmatic leavers described spirituality or narrate about extraordinary experiences they have had as adults (typically during a Vipassana course) or in their childhood.

More specifically, however, this desire to invest in and (re)connect to that which some of these individuals consider to be the transcendent can be seen in the pragmatic leavers' optimistic approach that does not abandon all hope but rather postpones a fully engrossed spiritual life to an unforeseen future. This discourse was common among householders, such as Matilda (as well as a number of disaffiliates), who claimed that they have given up the fantasy of becoming a monk in their old age. Take, for instance, the following statements in which Matilda explains why she is unable to fully commit to Vipassana:

M. I feel like I would be, sacrificing other things in my life, for example my, relationship, so my husband. um, my relationship with my daughter, so my role as a parent to a certain degree. um and also sort of like, Myyy, my passions, so in art practice my painting . . . I kind of take stock from what I understand in the Hindu religion they consider difference phases of lives . . . something appeals to me in the idea that later in my life being able to engross myself more fully in a spiritual, spiritual life style [smile] [. . .] you know I might hit sixty or eighty or who knows and be like, Yeah! [clapping hands] now I'm ready. Bye to my daughter [hand gesture: waving goodbye], I'll see you once a year. I'm gonna be in the Vipassana. Bless. see you later!

S. [l]

M. Or perhaps, perhaps if for example, I got a terminal cancer or something, which was, pulling the world away from me anyway.

Several points can be made here. First, Matilda's statement raises serious questions about the relevance of this laicised version of Vipassana meditation propagated by Goenka and marketed for individuals living a conventional/domestic life in an increasingly secularised society. Once again, these ideas are *not* expressed in explicit terms.[9] Instead, Matilda draws from a dualistic language to convey them implicitly. Here, the dualist discourse enables Matilda to compartmentalise her world, her goals, her needs, and aspects of her self-concept into categories ordered in importance (her identity and role as a mother, wife, and artist, come before the idea of a spiritually oriented self).

Second, disengagement in the context of positive meditative experiences did not result in active seekership post-disengagement, nor did the participants emphasise a need for another practice. Instead, they enthusiastically anticipated their return to the Vipassana centre, which they perceived as a spiritual haven. However, similar to other pragmatic leavers, most individuals (with the exception of Holger) tended to integrate the insights gained from Vipassana (e.g. awareness) with other practices, most typically yoga. Hence, because Vipassana meditation had induced 'glimpses of enlightenment', these individuals did not doubt or reject the transformative effects of the practice, and, in fact, they tended to accentuate the practical benefits of the technique whenever necessary (such as relief from stress, physical pain, and as a cure for insomnia). Finally, their language and self-understandings were constructed and fixed within the movement's universe of discourse, even in cases where the temporal distance from the last course attended was over five years. Therefore, it is more appropriate to speak of this group of pragmatic leavers as inactive Vipassana practitioners.

As demonstrated, experience was a highly desired commodity for all pragmatic leavers; those who did not achieve extraordinary experiences, felt unaccomplished; those who could not recreate it outside the course environment, gave up trying. Even Andrew, whose course attendance resulted in a disorienting state, revealed mixed sentiments and used arrays of adjectives such as 'crazy', 'cool,', and 'amazing' to describe his bewildering, yet remarkably insightful, experiences as a 'framework for understanding [his] human experience'. More importantly, based on the limited number of narratives (eleven) in this chapter, it seems that those individuals who had some sort of intense experience (whether positive or negative) represented selves and constructed narratives that remained close to the movement's universe of

---

[9] In fact, when I proposed this question (whether the practice is practical, if she is unable to achieve a certain outcome at home), Matilda emphasised the issue of commitment, claiming that it is possible to reproduce or achieve the same experience (and outcomes) if one makes 'intentional changes' in life.

discourse. This points to the significance of embodied experiences in the process of conversion and its role in leaving a deeper imprint of the movement's language on these participants' self-concepts and worldviews.

Loss of Experience in Disengagement Literature

Amid the scholarly research on religious disengagement, Streib's (2011, 2014) studies are among the few to consider 'loss of a specific religious experience'—or indeed, an individual's attraction to a *new* kind of religious experience—as an important element of the deconversion process. Hence, in their comprehensive account of 'deconversion', Streib and his colleagues (2011) added this dimension to the criteria initially set out by Barbour (1994: 2) that outlined four characteristics of deconversion narrative: intellectual doubt, moral criticism, emotional suffering, and disaffiliation (I return to this study in chapters 4 and 6). Streib et al.'s (2011: 22) rationale for considering loss of religious experience as a facet of deconversion was due to the frequent occurrence of this theme in their qualitative data. Interestingly, however, in almost all the examples provided by Streib et al. (2011: 134–152), the loss of religious experience is accompanied by another deconversion element, most notably 'intellectual doubt' surrounding the doctrinal aspect of the given religion. That said, the pragmatic leavers rarely harboured intellectual doubt (or moral criticism) to the extent presented in the disaffiliation or deconversion literature (Barbour, 1994).

This is not to say that all pragmatic leavers were immune to doubt or did not experience some sort of conflict with the institutional or doctrinal aspect of the movement. Rather, those few who did mention some sort of conflict considered it irrelevant to their disengagement. In fact, even in instances where Leslie expressed an ambivalence about the efficacy of the practice, she did not doubt its doctrines or its teachings—unlike deconverts (such as Luke) whose sources of doubt and conflict was comparably severe and fundamental to their exit narrative. More importantly, the pragmatic leavers considered these conflicts 'minor' and generally presented issues or conflicts by quoting from other meditators (e.g. 'I remember people saying . . . '), thus effectively distancing themselves from this topic. Briefly, these minor conflicts were commonly experienced with the organisational aspects of the movement. For instance, its regulations prohibiting amalgamation of Vipassana with other practice; inconsistencies in the behaviour of dhamma servers;[10] the movement's strict code of conduct, such as certain elements of the Noble Silence, which effectively discourages participants from acknowledging one another or from practicing kindness to one another.[11] Last but not least, the lack of a meaningful relationship between students and teachers (disciple-master relations), the absence of support from the teachers, and a lack of a (relaxed) social community.[12]

The collection of these 'minor' conflicts brings to mind Gooren's (2010) critique of Stark and Finke's (2000) rational choice theory. Gooren rejects the authors' version of rational choice theory on several grounds (such as their passive conceptualisation of the religious actor, their disproportionate emphasis on network in conversion, or their assumption that converts make goal-oriented actions), and instead of 'rational actors', he (2010: 67) speaks of 'rationalist actors'. Gooren (2010: 135) argues that potential members always make 'implicit or explicit cost-benefit analyses of the groups they visit, and he outlines several requirements that visitors may have on their list. These include (in order of decreasing importance) whether the new members 'got along well with other members and leaders'; whether they 'felt that they received sufficient attention and support'; whether they 'liked the group's code of conduct' and 'essential beliefs and doctrines'; and whether they generally 'appreciated being asked to perform special tasks as a volunteer' (Gooren, 2010: 136).

While the resemblances between the participants' list of minor conflicts and the list provided by Gooren are indisputable, several important questions emerge: If the participants' disengagement are linked to one or more of the abovementioned factors, why did they render them irrelevant to their disengagement? Why did only a few speak about a conflict in their narratives? If a social network or a teacher-student relationship is essential in the development of commitment in Vipassana, why did most of the participants de-emphasise the

[10] For instance, Holger argued, 'people who keep serving, they have . . . very strong difficulties in real life [and] that's what they bring into the Vipassana centre . . . Not that I'm saying that the centre would owe me that if I serve it would make me happy'.

[11] For instance, Leslie noted, 'I did mind not being able to acknowledge one another, and like when you and I sat on the deck, I hated not being able to gesture and say "can I get you a cup of tea?" or not being able to smile at you'.

[12] For instance, Andrew compared Goenka's movement with the Insight Meditation community and pointed out that 'the Goenka one is a big international organisation, [p] feels more impersonal . . . the, insight group is international as well but it's smaller, it feels smaller, you feel like when you become involved you're part of a community of people who are meditating and, so it feels like more of a family I guess and you feel more supported in that'.

network factor in their narratives? Finally, if Stark and Finke's (2000) rational choice theory is 'moot', as Gooren (2010: 131) suggests, why did the category of experience—or the lack/loss of it—play an essential role in these narratives, and why did these participants adopt a pragmatic language to mould their disengagement stories?

Based on a thematic and structural analysis of eleven narratives, I suggest that an underlying commonality among these narratives is a desire to exercise, uphold, and exhibit their value of autonomous spiritual seekership. Both the pragmatic language and the dualistic discourse allowed the participants to explain their disengagement through a cost-benefit language in ways that avoid transmitting the impression that they have abandoned spiritual growth as a goal and/or renounced their individual responsibility towards this end. I argue that these forms of language warrant the continuity of their spiritual search/development without implying that the search is stalled or the individual is completely idle.

Thus, even though the language of the pragmatic leavers were replete with phrases that alluded to a cost-benefit rationalisation—such as Leslie who claimed Vipassana meditation no longer provided her with 'useful information', Katrin who rendered her previous commitment as a 'rational decision', and Matilda who did not commit to Vipassana because she was not done with 'shopping around' or was unwilling to 'sacrifice' her other responsibilities—it is possible that they were forced to think about their disengagement and construct some kind of rational explanation for their actions or inactions—one that made sense to a researcher. Perceived this way, Stark and Finke's (2000) rational actor or Gooren's (2010) rationalist actor can be reconceptualised as rationalising actors or, more accurately, as 'rationalising seekers'.[13]

Upon disengagement, the vast majority of the pragmatic leavers (nine of eleven) integrated elements of the Vipassana (e.g. awareness and observing bodily sensation from moment to moment) with other supplementary

---

[13] Note, however, that Stark and Finke's (2010) concept of 'rational actor' and Gooren's (2010) concept of 'rationalist actor' both designate the situation prior to any change in religious affiliation taking place. On the other hand, my concept of 'rationalising actor/seeker' signifies the linguistic dimension of the participants' narratives and designates a post-hoc rationalisation after a change in religious affiliation has taken place. The concept I offer here is grounded in empirical data. In fact, I suggest that these authors' concepts remain abstract and they are methodologically problematic for three interrelated reasons: (1) the difficulty of recruiting participants at their preaffiliation stage, (2) the problem of retrospective account giving, and (3) overlooking the simple fact that when a researcher proposes a (rational) question to a participant, he/she will try to rationalise and articulate an answer that makes sense to the researcher.

practices in one way or another. This means that disengagement led most participants to seek out other practices. The analysis presented in this chapter shows the participants purposefully sought practices that provided some kind of resolution to their *immediate* felt needs. Hence, their post-involvement seekerships were not haphazard; rather, it was focused and involved a reflective identification of what was needed and a creative amalgamation of techniques to suit that need. Clearly, then, the pragmatic leavers' de-emphasis of (minor) conflicts is linked with the fact that they are actively engaged in assembling their own outlook and approach through a kind of bricolage.

Concluding Summary

At the outset of this chapter, I proposed three overarching characteristics of pragmatic leavers' narratives: pragmatic language, dualistic discourse, and ambivalence. I argued that each disengagement narrative is composed of a particular dynamic of these features. I subsequently contextualised these themes by a systematic exploration of pragmatic leavers' narratives, based on various meditative experiences such as a depersonalisation (Andrew's narrative), disconnection from reality (Leslie's account), frustration (Katrin's case study) and the loss of experience (Matilda's account).

In short, (1) those who indicated unfavourable experiences appropriated pragmatic and dualistic language and revealed (relatively) fewer indicators of ambivalence in their narratives. Seeing their discomfort as a result of Vipassana meditation, they commonly framed their new adopted practices (or activities) as a *resolution* to the felt unease. (2) Individuals who experienced frustration were more likely to form ambivalent narratives and utilise a pragmatic language in framing their disengagement. These individuals indicated impatience and tended to gravitate towards, or actively seek out, practices with (relatively) easily accomplished goals and practices that offered more tangible and comprehensible outcomes. And finally, (3) the language of those who disclosed positive meditative experiences in their narratives featured all three characteristics outlined, although the dualistic discourse seemed to be the dominant feature. While these individuals integrated Vipassana meditation with other practices, they did not understand their actions to be heretical and nor did they consider Vipassana meditation inadequate.

As demonstrated, while pragmatic leavers often romantically conceptualised Vipassana meditation as an effective tool—through which, for instance, they could bridge the boundary between the self and the transcendent[14]—their narratives, to an extent, contradicted this idea. Clearly, both the pragmatic language and the dualistic discourse enabled the participant to negotiate and rationalise disengagement *without* directly questioning certain cultural or institutional structures that shaped their expectations. Both linguistic features were also instrumental in enabling the participants to avoid rendering their spiritual search/development as stalled. As will become clear, there is continuity between certain themes outlined in this chapter and those that manifest in the disaffiliation narratives in the next chapter.

---

[14] For instance, Anne argued: 'it [Vipassana] gives me a feeling of um [p] [p] it makes me trust that there is something else out there, that there is an answer to every question that I have and if I go deep enough inside myself, I will find the answer and that's what Vipassana, for me that's what Vipassana is about'.

4

Disaffiliation

This chapter explores the narratives of eight participants who disaffiliated after years of intense commitment to Goenka's Vipassana organisation (see figure 4.1). They had typically attended between a minimum of three to a maximum of ten, ten-day courses and exhibited less or no inclination to return to a Vipassana centre in the future. I see 'disaffiliation narratives' as a cluster of stories about leaving Goenka's Vipassana movement and its community—it does *not* mean that the participant has entirely rejected the movement's universe of discourse, teachings, and truth claims.[1]

Unlike the pragmatic leavers, who accentuated the worldly benefits of Vipassana meditation, the narratives of the disaffiliates suggest that these individuals primarily pursued the ultimate goal of enlightenment—even though they exhibited a considerable amount of hesitancy in disclosing this information. However, similar to the narratives of the pragmatic leavers, the disaffiliation narratives were characterised by ambivalent language. Yet, the sense of ambivalence undergirding the disaffiliation narratives was entangled with the movement's linguistic and institutional structures as opposed to having roots primarily in cultural structures (which was the case with the pragmatic leavers). Hence, whereas most pragmatic leavers indicated uncertainties about the practicality of the technique, ambivalence in disaffiliation narratives involved the participants' unequivocal trust in the transformative efficacy of the technique, but there was a certain doubt about their own abilities to achieve the propagated goals.

The theme of 'self-doubt' was shared across the vast majority of disaffiliation narratives, and it appeared to have been prompted by the movement's ambiguous discourse surrounding progress and enlightenment. Despite this characteristic, many facets of Vipassana disaffiliation narratives corresponded

---

[1] Hence, what I perceive as the conceptual difference between disaffiliation and deconversion is the form of language and the extent to which the participants' (current) self-concept and narratives are shaped by the movement's universe of discourse. Including whether they made a strategic use of any of the four rhetorics explored in chapter 1 as the linguistic markers of commitment: (1) the rhetoric of experience, (2) rhetoric of 'here and now', (3) Vipassana as an instrumental practice or a 'tool', and (4) 'pure teachings of the Buddha'.

Drifting Through Samsara. Masoumeh Rahmani, Oxford University Press. © Oxford University Press 2022.
DOI: 10.1093/oso/9780197579961.003.0005

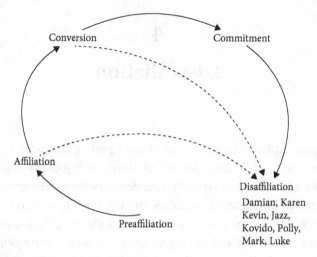

Figure 4.1 Disaffiliated participants' pathway

This diagram solely includes the names of individuals who disengaged after years of commitment.

with the existing literature on religious disengagement (Bromley, 2004; Coates, 2013; Wright, 1984), even though the process of conversion was *tacit* for these individuals. I contextualise these points through a detailed reading of Damian's narrative as a typical example of a Vipassana disaffiliation narratives. Evidently, the personal details of Damian's narrative are unique to him. In this chapter I primarily focus on, as well as quote from, segments of his narrative I considered to be common to the other participants' disaffiliation narratives.

Religious Disaffiliation

Scholarly literature suggests that religious disengagement is a gradual and multidimensional process (Bromley, 2006), which according to Wright and Ebaugh (1993: 119), at the very least involves three components: '(1) affection (disaffection), (2) cognitive (disillusionment), and (3) social organizational (disaffiliation)'. According to this categorisation, the term 'disaffection' refers to emotional withdrawal from the group, which may result in the deterioration of members' commitment. Several sociological studies (Bromley and Shupe, 1979; Lofland and Stark, 1965) have emphasised the importance of interpersonal ties in sustaining commitment, even in cases where the converts exhibit little evidence of their theological understanding. Wright and Ebaugh (1993: 120) note, 'Feelings of oneness, solidarity, communion, love, and shared religious experience serve to enhance loyalty to the group' and therefore disaffection may arise when interpersonal relationships decrease in value and come to be perceived as indifferent or uncaring. This dimension of religious disengagement has received attention mostly from the field of sociology.

Wright and Ebaugh (1993: 120) reserved the term 'disillusionment' to refer to 'disbelief and doubts that arise from cognitive dissonance'. This dimension of disengagement attempts to reflect on the dissonance in the interpretive framework the convert/member defines, orders, and interprets the self and the world. Hence, a disillusioned New Religious Movement (NRM) member questions 'the truth value of the movement's ideology or doctrine' and discards 'the moral authority of the organization and its leaders' (Wright and Ebaugh, 1993: 120). Experiences of disillusionment may not immediately result in exit but rather motivate the member to re-evaluate his/her faith and membership and to seek alternative interpretive frameworks. This dimension of disengagement has received considerable attention in the field of psychology and is occasionally framed as 'intellectual doubt' in the disengagement literature (Barbour, 1994; Streib et al., 2011; Streib, 2014).

While disaffected and disillusioned members may choose to remain affiliated with the movement, disaffiliation exclusively refers to severance of organisational ties (Wright and Ebaugh, 1993: 120). Thus, in addition to accounting for the forms of language used by the participant, this book adopts the term 'disaffiliation' because it is neutral to the cognitive or affective dimension of the exit process and it encompasses the narratives of all eight participants who departed after years of intense involvement with the movement. Finally, irrespective of which of the abovementioned components sets the process of exit in motion (or whether all three occur in tandem), it is widely assumed that exit is often negotiated by members, or jointly with the organisation, when doubts and conflicts become irresolvable.[2]

Doubt is therefore considered an integral element of religious disengagement and is acknowledged consistently by a wide range of scholarship in this field. From apostasy (Brinkerhoff and Mackie, 1993; Hunsberger and Brown, 1984; Skonovd, 1981) and deconversion (Barbour, 1994; Jacobs, 1989; Streib

---

[2] Except in cases of expulsion, in which the decision to exit is imposed by the group rather than a personal decision made by the member (Wright, 2014: 710).

et al., 2011; Streib, 2014) to NRM disaffiliation (Bromley, 2006; Coates, 2013; Healy, 2011), from causal process models (Skonovd, 1981; Wright, 1991) to role exit theories (Bromley, 1998a, 1998b; Ebaugh, 1988), from first gener-ation to second generation NRM disaffiliates (Shoenberger and Grayburn, 2016), all studies consensually recognise the significance of doubt in this process.

According to these literatures, doubt does not immediately result in dis-affiliation. In most cases, members (or believers) may adopt various coping strategies, such as denial, to defer exit until an alternative identity and social network become available (Healy, 2011; Coates, 2013; Wright, 1984). In other cases, members may continue to reconcile doubts until avoidance strategies become ineffective and dissonances culminate in a 'crisis' event (Bromley, 2004; Wright, 1991).

Damian's narrative is one of such instances where doubt was ignored (for several years) until it proved irresolvable, ultimately resulting in his disaffili-ation. Damian was involved with Goenka's Vipassana movement for six con-secutive years, during which he participated in ten, ten-day courses, served at an equal number of ten-day courses, and participated at one Satipatthana Sutta course and one twenty-day course. Therefore, he had not only invested a considerable amount of time in Goenka's movement, but he had, arguably, also developed a strong sense of belonging to the movement and embraced the role of a Vipassana meditator (see chapter 1).[3]

According to his account, Damian's disaffiliation was triggered by a 'ser-ies of disillusioning events', which involved the recognition of inconsist-encies between how the movement propagated itself as 'open teaching' and how it functioned. For instance, he spoke of 'hidden stories that were not publicly acknowledged' and his experience with the implicit politics within the movement's hierarchical system. Damian's narrative was heavily infused with 'moral criticism' (Barbour, 1994), and the basic layout of his narrative plot resembled what scholars call the 'crisis' model (Bromley, 2004; Coates, 2013; Wright, 1991).

These salient features of Damian's narrative, coupled with his depiction of the exit process as emotionally 'painful', correspond with the existing litera-ture (Coates, 2013). However, in spite of these similarities, a close inspec-tion of Damian's narrative suggests that the sense of doubt underlying his

---

[3] In our initial interview, Damian noted, 'I centred my whole life around Vipassana certainly the first three years I lived around meditation centres I spent a lot of my spare time there and all the people I associated with were pretty much involved'.

(and other participants') disaffiliation narrative is primarily *self-doubt*, which appears to stem from his ongoing convictions about the movement's truth claims, as opposed to an intellectual doubt about the truth of a doctrine, as the exit literature often suggests, or that his disaffiliation was solely the result of an interpersonal discord, as a shallow reading of his narrative might indicate.

Selected Case Study: Damian

Damian is a New Zealander in his mid-forties. He has been working as a tradesman in the building industry for the nearly twenty years. Damian struck me as a serious, articulate, and delightfully sarcastic man with a small John Waters type moustache and a complex personality. Similar to most of my interviewees, Damian possesses a creative mind and made use of various art forms as an outlet to express his emotions. From showcasing paintings of erect phalluses on rustic wooden doors to self-publishing poetry collections, social commentaries, and 'metaphysical reviews', Damian's undertakings alluded to a sense that he had no insecurities about opening up to others, and, he seemed to enjoy publicly playing with controversial topics such as male sexuality.

Damian noted that his family was not strictly religious, although Christianity was strongly imbued in the small farming town where he grew up. He attended Sunday school from the age of nine to eleven and described his voluntary withdrawal as the 'end of [his] Christian experience'. In speaking about his childhood, Damian described this period as 'conventional', 'uneventful', 'boring', with 'no major traumas'. Nevertheless, he portrayed an image of himself in adolescence as a 'confrontational', outspoken, and 'rebellious' person who began experiencing various signs of 'personal difficulty', which propelled him to 'seek' remedy in spiritual teachings.

I was introduced to Damian through the method of snowball sampling. From our initial encounter, I developed the impression that Damian was eager to be heard and perhaps even enjoyed being a subject of inquiry, and it seemed he wanted to preserve this impression. On the evening of 19 April 2015, and after several email exchanges, we met for the first time in a café in Dunedin. The aim of this introductory meeting was to elucidate the objectives of the research and to explain the treatment of the collected material, which seemed to have been a concern to Damian. Despite this, he turned up with copies of his lengthy correspondence with Vipassana teachers for me to 'take away and digest' before we proceeded with the formal interview.

According to Damian, these exchanges of letters (that extended over a period of two years) captured the nature of his conflicts with the 'teaching body' of the organisation; they involved a series of critical comments challenging the power dynamics between the old students and the assistant teachers. In order to protect the anonymity of the other parties involved in these documents and to maintain a methodological coherence (given that my analysis is geared oral narrative and not textual material), I refrain from directly quoting them. Instead, I draw upon my initial interview with Damian in which he accounts for his experience:

S. because I can't use this [pointing to the documents] can you just tell me briefly, what happened and how that process, how you Felt during that process of moving away, that two years that you were talking about.

D. what happened! Well fundamentally the structure of the organisation is set up so that
5   teachers have all of the power and everyone else has none, so teachers are the last word, the last authority on everything on every issue. and they have the backing of the 'Protecting the purity of the teaching' as the kind of Leverage or credibility which, um [p] which sort of Empowers them I guess, to, to you know, certainly with the students. the students are like [vc: silly mechanical accent] 'Ah, the purity of the teaching! Cannot,
10   question, the teacher' [vc: narratorial] you know and I Guess I saw there were moments of injustice, there were, there were situations and decisions that were made by these teachers that showed they were fallible but the Whole structure of the teaching meant that you, it was very [in] you were encouraged not to question them. encouraged not to, not to, to, doubt their judgement and umm so finally I did um [in] question their
15   authority and their judgement and Confront them and the letters that I wrote sort of started to compile a kind of series of issues, um [p] Around the Structure of their power
S. mhm
D. and I started questioning and [p] [ntch] it was actually, [vc: softer tone] it was quite a painful process, because I think I was very idealistic and it was kind of um breaking
20   of my idealism of, of, um putting these people and this teaching on a pedestal and [in] it was hard to let that go, it was like a safety net it was like a crutch of all sorts for my Faith, it was um, that it was hard for me to admit to myself that there was problems with this teaching [p] um or the people involved um [p] [in] And perhaps the inevitable [ex] happened that, that, that, as I queried the, the structure of
25   the power that the teachers wielded, um in what I felt was an entirely unjust way

towards me, it only extenuated my problems [hah] <u>with their power</u> and [p] um But there was nowhere for me to Go to. and this is something I detailed in my letters, there was nowhere for me to go to Talk, Discuss, debate, Analyse, [p] plead or Beg anyone else, to to, to [in] take my side, Or um offer another opinion about the situation, [vc: narratorial] Essentially <u>if I didn't</u> like the teachers' authority and the decisions they made, the only choice <u>you have</u> is to leave.

30

My first comment here concerns a structural observation that will significantly enhance the analysis of Damian's narrative as well as help elucidate the context of the interview—most notably the relationship Damian construed to me. Accordingly, the most outstanding feature of Damian's linguistic style is his oscillation between 'I' and a generalised 'you' (lines 10–13, and 30–31) through which he signals the self as commonly like others in that situation (O'Connor, 2000: 77, cited in Shuman, 2011: 132). This arrangement of the grammatical subjects—when the narrator switches from 'I' to 'you', yet indexes the self—repeatedly emerges in Damian's narrative. The effect of this switching is twofold for Damian. On the one hand, this switching draws in and involves the listener (myself). On the other hand, it implies that others, including the targeted audience, would have acted the same way had they been in that situation. In a sense, he is implicitly seeking the empathy of the listener and tries to develop a rapport about the ideas he is discussing. Interestingly, however, Damian completely resigns from this style of speech in segments where the content of the narrative becomes sensitive, expressive, and arguably painful (such as lines 18–29). Due to Damian's frequent use of this form of speech, I will refrain from repetitive mention of it and instead <u>underline</u> the clauses in which this switching occurs in the transcripts cited henceforth.

Despite not revealing any detailed information, Damian's plot emphasised events that disturbed his taken-for-granted assumptions and uncritical faith in the teachers and the organisation, paving the way to heightened doubts and ultimately to his withdrawal from the movement (Wright, 2007: 198). In other words, the stress was primarily on *events* that ultimately led to crisis and disengagement. This is the same model that Damian consistently followed in plotting his disaffiliation narrative(s). As becomes clear, the structure of his narratives was hinged almost entirely on *moral criticism* and involved signs of emotional upheavals (apparent both in the content and the verbal depiction of the experiences, lines 24–29 and 47–52). For example, in a follow-up interview conducted ten months after the initial one, Damian elaborated on what he regarded as a 'pivotal' incident, which set a 'series of disillusioning events' in motion:[4]

D. I was a devout practitioner, doing two hours every day, and I had a desire, <u>maybe it was an egotistic desire,</u> I can't even remember now, I wanted a group sit! where I lived and I knew there was certain conditions around that,

35   S. yeah

D. you had to have no alcohol around the house, there was a series of injunctions that I knew fairly Well, um [p] but one thing that I didn't know, but was advised by someone who was another old student and it came out, out of a conversation, sort of tangentially that there was a problem with um [p] masturbating. that masturbation

40   was a breakage of sila

S. yeah

D. which I never previously heard, from any shape or forms, I mean none of the courses said you shouldn't masturbate ... this was News to me and, and I sort of queried ... I asked the teacher, 'is this True? is, is, is, are you meant to abstain from All sexual

45   activity, even masturbation if you want to have a group sit' and he said 'yeah that's true' [in] and I said 'ok', and I didn't say anything more to him then, but this was a key disillusioning event [vc: rhythmic] because part of what, I had, found very, [p] positive and, [p] I guess [p] alluring,

S. mhm

50   D. about vipassana was that goenka constantly said this is all, open teaching, there's no hidden teaching, there's no esoteric especial thing, for, um select students, or um yk It's totally open, But that wasn't the truth about it.

S. mhm

D. and then I ran into other students who, started telling me stories about this sort of Sexual

55   politics within Vipassana and [p] How they dealt with sexuality and [p] that got me pretty aggravated and annoyed. but it didn't stop me from remaining a practitioner, but then I just gave up on the idea of a group sit. but it was the whole reason I moved to a flat by myself. Cause I felt very sincerely and, and, and, I was very, I was very Zealous when I was meditating that if I've been told that you should not masturbate I

60   would've stopped, I would've not masturbated. yk I would've taken that very seriously

S. mhm

---

[4] The initiative for a second interview came from Damian himself who expressed a desire to share more detail about his experience of leaving the movement. In fact, this study was originally designed to only conduct follow-up interviews with 'new students' approximately a year after their first ten-day course.

D. but there were no such public announcement to that [...] somehow it quite hit me quite hard that I felt there was a deception going on that I haven't felt before.

As the passage suggests, Damian interprets this precipitating incident— which may seem trivial to an outside observer (Bromley, 2006: 55)—as a catalyst for doubt, which instigated his disengagement process. The narrative emphasises a sense of deception as the result of the unravelling discrepancies between how the movement symbolically represented itself from the outset (as an open teaching) and the 'hidden' structures within it. Consequently, similar to the previous excerpt, moral criticism is the framework within which Damian plots his narratives, and it is the lens through which he invites us to grasp it. In the first instance, this criticism was directed at the teachers, and in the second instance, it was directed at the movement's institutional structure.

Barbour (1994: 51) suggests that this use of a crisis model in disengagement narratives provides the narrator with a coherent way to present and apprehend a transition between two different views, even though events may have been experienced as 'unconnected, confusing or inconclusive'. According to Barbour (1994: 51), the threefold pattern of tension, climax, and resolution warrants the dramatic traits of the narrative 'as increasing doubt and internal conflict come to sudden crisis and climax, and culminate in new belief and commitment'.

This pattern is not unique to Damian's narrative. Other participants categorised in this group reported similar stories and morally condemned certain structural elements and/or the behaviour of the movement's authoritative figures (e.g. Kovido and Luke). Disillusionment with leadership, which generally may occur as a result of the movement's authoritative figures contradicting the movement's ideology and/or result from them claiming more power, has been consistently addressed in disaffiliation literature (Bromley, 2004; Robinson et al., 1997; Shoenberger and Grayburn, 2016; Skonovd, 1981; Wright, 1984). According to the same literature, another highly reported facet of disaffiliation involves the members' doubt about their movement's doctrine and ideology, which was overwhelmingly absent in the disaffiliation narratives in the present study (with the exception of Luke's story).

As already noted, from the beginning of our correspondence and, indeed, during each encounter, Damian insisted that his disaffiliation from Vipassana was primarily due to his conflict with the 'organisational' aspect of the movement and that elements of the teaching were 'still part of [his] consciousness'. In narrating his disaffiliation experience, however, Damian occasionally vacillated between these two separate ideas and at times conflated the two, associating his conflict with (1) the movement's leadership/ authority ('the people involved', lines 4–6 and 20) and (2) the movement's doctrine and practice ('this teaching', line 23). As the interview progressed, the separation between these two elements became blurred which inspired me to ask the following question:

S. what did you think about the teachings? I mean um [p] cause you said, you tried to
65   distinguish that your conflict was with the organisation
D. uhum uhum
S. so what was your perspective on the teaching, during [the time] that conflict was happening?
D. [in] Well I had some, [p] doubts about the teachings not that, it, it, it had no, that it
70   didn't work, but that the, there was, that there was a propaganda element within the, the, teaching of retreats that [p] made you Believe [p] you were near to a breakthrough
S. mhm
D. you know that if you just try hard enough you would, you would get, you would have a big breakthrough pretty much it was kind of like [p] um you know Goenka's
75   discourses would exhort you to, to, you know [vc: accent imitating Goenka] 'Work hard, work hard and be Diligent and persevere' and, and you thought [vc: faster tempo] 'oh really, I'm gonna, I'm gonna get there, I'm gonna' like um [p] get enlightened [loud laugh] and at the end of the retreat! and then on the last day he says [vc: imitating Goenka] 'well it is a long Path' and you know [banging mug on
80   the table] 'you have to work, maybe a lifetime path', da da da and he sort of excuses himself out of that propaganda element. So I had some conflicts with the idea that, that, that of, [p] mmm Progress, within the retreat
S. mhm
D. and I think I raised (?*) that in one of my letters that, that 'was there really a
85   relationship between, meditating a certain amount and becoming happier?'
S. yeah
D. and doing one retreat a year and two hours a day, and all that, was that really umm [long pause] did that Equate to you progressing?
S. hmmm
90 D. [vc: softer] cause I had doubt about my progress, I guess [l] anyway in Fact the first two years I was Terribly wracked with doubt about my progress. I felt, I was not progressing

I felt, I felt that in fact I was going backwards [in] I was becoming more mentally unstable [hah] and more unhappy but then, [vf>] things shifted, so it became better. [ntch] um [p] so expand on your question because I think I've lost The thread.

95   S. yes if you had a conflict with the teaching and if you still believe in the teaching. or the meditation?

D. [long pause] [ntch] [p] yeah um [p] anyway it seems like primarily my, my, my problems for with the organisation with the people and the hierarchy, with the processes behind organising retreats and, and, and propagating the teaching. um [p] [ntch] [p]

100   But I guess I felt, umm that I could go away and practice by myself and did I really need to be attached to this tradition [. . .] um in the end pulling away from it, um [p] while it was difficult it didn't seem, um [p] like I was gonna completely lose, the teaching and, and [p] [in] and still remains sort of a bit of sort of a bit of a touchstone in my life, actually the teaching, still. still element of the practices that

105   are still part of my consciousness and, and [p] Awareness, Now. But when I first got involved with vipassana I felt I Had to Stay with this tradition

S. mmm

D. I was very, like, and I think that's another element of sort of propaganda, goenka sort of encourages you, not he doesn't say 'this is the best tradition' but, [p] like I was

110   saying it, it, it implies that it's pure and he encourages you to not to go and dabble with other traditions, you know he says 'if you dig a well you must dig in one spot and don't dig here and other places' you know he has all these stories and analogies and I think I took that to heart . . .

S. yeah. so these are the things you associate with the organisation and not with the

115   teaching, that's essentially my question

D. Yeah, well I think, I, I, I, I still, I felt [past tense] that the teaching, Did [p] offer me um [p] [ntch] [tapping fingers on the table] um resolution to things within myself, myself and I did not [past tense] feel that the teaching had Stopped doing that um [p] the Technique perhaps, cause perhaps you have to slightly um separate, the intellectual

120   component the, the, the, spoken and written instructions [p] About the teaching versus the, the bare bones of what the technique is Which is yk um [vc: softer] observing your breath and observing your body sensations with the idea of impermanence

S. mm

D. Which is quite a simplistic [tapping fingers on table] thing, you know it's not, I

125   don't think you can have much ideological conflict with the idea of [tapping fingers on the table] observing your breath or observing your body sensations there doesn't seem to be um [p] a massive um political conspiracy within that, you know, [tapping fingers on the table] seems like it's quite, it's um an Elegant Idea.

The most striking theme in this excerpt concerns Damian's self-doubt about his progress in this tradition (lines 84–93). However, before I present my argument about the significance of self-doubt in Vipassana disaffiliation narratives, it is important that I first make a comment regarding my role as the interviewer and the effect my questions may have unwittingly had on shaping Damian's responses, particularly from line 114 onwards. In reviewing the transcript, I realised that prior to my questions, Damian had already expressed cues regarding his ongoing appreciation/conviction and approval of the technique (suggesting not that the technique didn't work, and by recapitulating his main argument on lines 97–99). Despite this, I reinforced my question twice and overlooked Damian's remarks and his unwillingness to address it directly. Admittedly, my insensitivity in this interaction was because I had not met a single person who had rejected the technique of Vipassana meditation on *theoretical* grounds. Hence, this idea not only turned into a fascination that preoccupied my thoughts, but I also felt it was crucial to pinpoint Damian's position, particularly because Damian's statements, such as 'the practice is still part of my consciousness', seemed opaque and did not explicitly divulge his position.

That said, Damian's ongoing appreciation of certain aspects of the movement is echoed in his attempt to selectively separate Vipassana's teachings on the grounds of its discursive or 'intellectual component' and the embodied or 'bare bones' of the technique (lines 119–122), implying that he continues to appreciate the latter element of the teachings, which he conceived to be 'elegant' and 'universal'. Damian is not the only disaffiliate who distinguished Vipassana on three levels of (1) the organisation, (2) the teachings, and (3) the 'bare bones' of the technique. One of the other interviewees, Karen,[5] had raised the same point in her narrative and effectively distinguished the 'essence' of the technique from its institutional and traditional features. For both participants, this separation accompanies a hierarchical value, explicit in the participants' choice of words (e.g. 'essence', versus 'what to do what not

---

[5] Karen offered the following statement in response to an intentionally vague question that asked the participant to reflect on the 'most meaningful thing' she had learnt from Vipassana. Correspondingly, we observe that the participant separates various layers of the term Vipassana in order to establish a common vocabulary and respond to the interviewer's question:

K. I'm mindful that when we say Vipassana there might be a few different interpretations [. . .] there's Vipassana as in the tradition of what is taught by Goenka, and there's, which includes what to do what not to do all that sort of thing um [p] and the essence, kind of the essence of what it is, the technique itself and then the lineage and then Goenka [p] um, definition of it, so I kind of see three when we use, when we use the word Vipassana I kind of see three possible interpretations, so, can you ask me the question again and I'd be more specific as to which application [l].

to do'). Understandably, this discursive strategy enabled the participant to avoid conflating the movement's positive features (which they continued to have emotional attachments) with its unfavourable ones. Wright (1984: 180) points to similar observations in his study of defectors, noting that former NRM members engaged in a 'sifting process in which favourable events or experiences are separated out from what is later perceived as wrong, immoral or theologically adrift'. However, in Wright's (1984) research, these ambiva-lences were exposed in relation to the ex-members' positive recollections of certain events or their intersubjective experiences with other members; in the case of Vipassana disaffiliates, they are primarily attached to the movement's core ideas and practices (i.e. the 'essence' or 'bare bones' of the technique). Lastly, while almost all disaffiliation studies consider doubt as the main in-gredient in this process, doubt regarding the core ideas and practices of the movement was lacking in all disaffiliation narratives. In the following sec-tion, I scrutinise the existing scholarship on disengagement in order to create a niche for highlighting the significance of self-doubt in Vipassana disaffili-ation narratives.

Doubt and Religious Disengagement

The centrality of doubt to disengagement narratives and the diversity of the-ories and methodological perspectives in studies of religious disengagement have produced typologies of religious doubt (Ebaugh, 1988; Hunsberger et al., 1994). Accordingly, the sources of doubt could fall within two artifi-cial categories of 'intellectual' and 'interpersonal'. Intellectual or cognitive doubt typically refers to doubt, uncertainty, or scepticism about the truth of a system of belief (Barbour, 1994: 2), whereas interpersonal discord refers to feelings of alienation (Bromley, 2006) or perceived hypocrisy among church members (Brinkerhoff and Mackie, 1993). That said, not all scholars discern these two facets of doubt in religious disengagement.[6] In fact, there seems to be considerable bias in coalescing all forms of doubt under the banner of 'in-tellectual doubt' (Streib et al., 2011), which may be related to the theological features of the traditions in which these studies were commonly grounded.

---

[6] However, not all studies differentiate religious doubt according to these two dichotomous aspects of doubt, namely cognitive and interpersonal aspects. Hoge's study of Roman Catholics (1988, cited in Brinkerhoff and Mackie, 1993), for example, emphasises an emotional and interpersonal compo-nent of doubt overriding cognitive factors.

Barbour's (1994: 12) readings of the *Confessions* reminds us of the role intellectual doubt played in Augustine's migration from Manicheism to Christianity; doubts that primarily emerged from the discrepancies Augustine recognised between Manichee doctrines and the known astronomical facts of his time. Seventeen centuries later, the same concept appears in an interview excerpt cited by Lori Fazzino (2014: 256) in her study of Evangelical deconverts: 'everything that we know about geology and the formation of the Earth completely contradicted everything I was hearing in church'. Niklas Foxeus (2020) exploration of deconversion from traditional Theravada Buddhism in Myanmar also considers (intellectual) doubt an integral element in the narratives of Burmese Buddhists.

While admittedly the abovementioned studies are focused primarily on deconversion, the element of doubt is not confined to this dimension of religious disengagement. 'I thought, What am I doing here? I am worshipping some dude', were the utterances of a 'disenchanted' Siddha yoga devotee cited in Healy's research (2008: 160). Similar statements, such as 'Looking at it now I realise how stupid all of it is, but at the time these explanations seemed entirely acceptable', can be found in Coates's (2013: 7) research on disaffiliates from Eastern meditation who struggled with the conception of karma as a justification for the movement's ill treatment of members with mental health problems.

Examples in which doubt leads to disillusionment and results in disengagement are many (Streib et al., 2011). The point is that, in the majority of the examples, doubt is expressed and articulated in relation to an external element—either a philosophical theory, a doctrine, or a disagreement with other members over certain principles (Bromley, 2006: 54)—and is *not* articulated in regard to the self. This could be partly due to that most of the published studies on religious disengagement are channelled from the field of sociology, where, arguably, less attention is paid to psychological and/or detailed linguistic analyses. Indeed, a recent psychological study of disengagement from ideological social groups (e.g. one-percenter motorcyclist club, white supremacy, fundamental religious/political groups, etc.) identified self-doubt and loss in self-esteem among a multiplicity of variables related to post-exit psychological experiences, particularly in post-exit grief responses (Harris, 2015).

In terms of NRM disaffiliation, however, very few studies have qualitatively distinguished self-doubt from other forms of doubt (intellectual). This does not mean that self-doubt is entirely unique to Vipassana disaffiliates and ex-members of ideological groups. Take, for example, the following excerpt from an interview with a 'voluntary defector' from the Unification Church cited in one of Stuart Wright's (interview #31 in 1984: 176) earliest works:

> I think a lot of people . . . left for personal reasons of frustration, like myself. I felt like I wasn't able to accomplish anything and I wasn't bringing in more people and that simply paying rent on a building wasn't actually changing the world. We weren't growing and no one was really taking an interest in us and there was such a tremendous amount of bad publicity at that point. I think there were a lot of people who just got frustrated and said, 'This isn't working', and left. Not so much that these people have taken advantage of me, or what-are-they-doing-to-my-life type of thing. I think a lot of people left out of frustration more than anything else.

Wright (1984: 176; italics added) presents this quote as an example of a 'typical voluntary defector who left out of frustration with the *movement's inability* to realise its claims and objectives'. From the same set of data, Wright (1983: 109, 1984: 176) classifies this passage as a 'perceived lack of success in achieving world transformation' as one of the organizational or 'social psychological factors' that set the process of disengagement and disaffiliation in motion.[7] Although I do not disagree with Wright's coding of the quote,[8] nevertheless, I would argue that this categorisation falls short of providing adequate explanation as to the nature of this dissonance. In other words, it is unclear whether the source of this 'frustration' that presumably led interviewee #31 to re-evaluate his/her membership and leave was due to a lack of self-confidence (self-doubt), a lack of confidence in the movement's world-transformative claims, or both. Admirably, however, the pinnacle of Wright's (1983, 1984) work was to challenge the rubric under which members' commitment to NRMs was perceived as 'coercive persuasion' and ex-members portrayed as victims of 'brainwashing'.

---

[7] The factors outlined by Wright (1984: 176) include '(1) the breakdown of members' insulation from the outside world, (2) unregulated development of dyadic relationships within the communal context, (3) perceived lack of success in achieving world transformation, and (4) inconsistencies between the actions of leaders and the ideals they symbolically represent'.

[8] Certainly, Wright's (1983, 1984) interviewees belonged to movements that he labelled as, 'world-transforming' (i.e. claiming the status of the agents of imminent and total change), whereas through the same interpretive lens, Goenka's Vipassana movement can be seen as a self-transforming' movement (i.e. claiming to provide its practitioners the appropriate tool for achieving self-change). Therefore, it is understandable when Wright proceeds to interpret this passage as a perceived lack of success in achieving world transformation.

Yet, in comparison to the abovementioned studies, Damian's sense of doubt is articulated differently. By this, I do not suggest that self-doubt and doubt in a theory or interpersonal relationships are watertight categories. Rather, unlike previous studies, I want to attend to the intrapersonal dimension of doubt: I argue that the source of self-doubt in Damian's narrative stems from his ongoing commitment to the movement's language and his convictions about the efficacy of the technique in providing self-transformation (as opposed to examples of doubt in other studies which mainly involve a rejection of a doctrine). As a result, one can see moments of ambiguity in Damian's narrative. For example, on the one hand, Damian is determined to show his approval of the technique (lines 69–70: 'not that it didn't work', and lines 116–118: 'teaching did offer me resolutions . . . '); on the other hand, Damian indicates a certain scepticism about the efficacy of it through utterances such as 'doubt about my progress', 'going backwards', and 'becoming more mentally unstable'. Yet, the weight of his conviction and commitment to a *particular form* of language seem to take precedence over his experiences.

Ambivalent Language in Disaffiliation Narratives

To elucidate my point regarding the significance of self-doubt in Damian's disaffiliation narrative, I return to a structural analysis of the main clauses in which this theme manifests (lines 64 to 128). In the first segment of this excerpt, the structure of Damian's speech is consistent with his overall plot (framing disaffiliation as the result of a conflict with the movement's structure). Accordingly, in this segment Damian primarily adopted a critical position against Goenka and sought to maintain a certain distance (linguistically) from the ideas he was criticising (i.e. the element of propaganda in Goenka's teachings). The first observable feature of this segment is Damian's discomfort when uttering the word 'enlightenment', referring to his doubt and conflict with the idea of progress (lines 73–78); instead, he opts for the term 'breakthrough '.[9] Despite this reluctance, Damian finally utters the term (line 78) followed by a loud nervous laugh, yet, in an attempt to regain some distance from this topic, he reframes his criticism in relation to the retreats.

[9] Another indication of this occurs on line 73 where it is clear that Damian is trying to describe this idea (enlightenment) and gets as far as uttering ('you would get',), yet resigns to use the same alternative as before.

Clearly, Damian exhibits a certain amount of unwillingness to position himself in relation to this doctrine.

This reaction was commonly shared across disaffiliation narratives. In fact, almost all participants in this category exhibited various signs of discomfort—most notably sarcastic laughter—in accounting for, and discussing, their former pursuit of enlightenment. However, while this discomfort manifested in the form of lapses (in speech) in Damian's case, others adopted a humorous or self-deprecating tone in reporting their past. Take, for example, the following statement from Karen:

K. at that time of meditating four or five hours a day I was thinking, that's what, that's
130   what gets you to nirvana, that's what gets you enlightened
S. mhm
K. it's, you sit on your bum until I don't know what happens I don't know, [p] someone
       pops a party cracker it's done, I don't know what actually, I don't know what
       I thought it was going to happen [l] I didn't really analyse that terribly but I had
135   people who I trusted who said sit and meditate so I went 'alright I'll meditate!'

In another instance, after departing from Goenka's movement, Kovido's desire for enlightenment took him on a journey across the globe: he ordained, disrobed, went ashram to ashram, from Swami Ram Dass to Father Bede Griffiths, from laughing and crying at Osho's mystic rose course to queuing for Ammaji's hug and Sai Baba's miracles. In narrating this aspect of his biography, Kovido sarcastically laughed almost every single time he spoke of his previous urge to become enlightened and/or whenever he uttered the word enlightenment. In my view, this communicative behaviour among the disaffiliates indicates their attempt to 'shake off' or de-emphasise certain aspects of their previous identity and establish new ones in the process of retelling the story—a pattern that Ebaugh (1988: 156–174) defines as 'hangover identity'. Overall, the types of communicative behaviour that accompanied disaffiliates' divulgence of their former pursuance of enlightenment was characterised by a profound sense of ambivalence involving both embarrassment and nostalgia.

Interestingly, however, disaffiliates were not the only group that showed hesitancy in using the term enlightenment or nibbana. This pattern was also commonly shared among old students and Vipassana teachers who tend to draw from a rich pool of substitutive language, identical to the way the movement describes its ultimate goals: 'this path will lead to full liberation', 'my sole motivation in life is to ... purify the mind ... free myself from all attachment to craving and aversion, trying to develop wisdom, completely transform my old habit patterns of how to live into new habit patterns'. Yet, as discussed in chapter 1, the old students avoided these terms for its religious/ Buddhist connotations. Having detailed the participants' normative behaviours in relation to accounting for their previous desire for enlightenment, I will now return to my analysis of Damian's narrative.

The next segment (lines 84–94) of Damian's passage not only contains a noteworthy change in Damian's tone of voice (becoming softer and significantly quieter), but it also includes a very important stance marker—'I guess' (line 90)—which appears immediately after the utterance, 'cause I had doubts about my progress' (again, followed by nervous laughter on the same line). This use of 'I guess', as the linguistic scholar, Elise Kärkkäinen (2007) has argued, reveals two interrelated insights. First and foremost, it displays the reasoning process of the speaker, indicating 'a special meaning of making an inferential discovery', 'coming to a realization', or 'drawing a conclusion" (Kärkkäinen, 2007: 184). On another level, when one considers the implication of this marker in relation to the direction of the speech (i.e. the preceding and following sequence of statements or stance-taking actions using the linguistic terminology), 'I guess' may indicate the speaker is about to insert a new and *relevant* side to the story. Thus, in relation to the overall excerpt, 'I guess', as Kärkkäinen (2007: 206) suggests, reveals that the speaker is 'recognizing the similarity of import of the prior story as well as the present story-so-far'.

In other words, Damian's use of 'I guess' in this excerpt can be taken as a realisation about the significance of self-doubt to his internal conflict. This reading of Damian's narrative becomes a conceivable interpretation when one reflects on the content of his following statements (various evidential examples such as 'I was terribly wracked', 'more unhappy'—lines 91–93). Interestingly, however, the pattern of evidential examples suddenly culminates in a vague statement uttered in a very quiet and almost inaudible tone: 'but then things shifted, so it became better' (lines 93–94). These observations left me with the impression that Damian had either lost his train of thought, which could potentially imply that he was taken aback by his own words, or it was simply the case that he did not wish to expatiate this subject. This is perhaps why Damian chose to redirect the conversation from this topic, and after a long pause (lines 97–99), reiterated the main points of his argument and retrieved his 'narrative anchors' (Johnson, 1998, cited in

Wright, 2014: 719), insisting that his conflict was related to the movement's power structure, yet this time, with a sense of uncertainty ('anyway it *seems* like primarily my problem . . . '—line 97).

In saying that Damian was taken aback by articulating his self-doubt, I do not mean to imply that he was unaware of it, nor do I intend to undermine the overall plot of his disaffiliation narrative (i.e. power conflict with the teachers). Rather, I suggest that Damian did not consider self-doubt as an intrinsic aspect of his disaffiliation. Hence, the role of self-doubt was not integrated into Damian's rationale for disaffiliation. This is evident in the structure of the narrative where we encounter considerably higher levels of articulation in Damian's delivery of segments where he criticised Goenka and spoke of his power conflict with the movement (e.g. lines 4–16). This indicates that Damian's preferred narrative plot (conflict with Goenka, etc.) has been the subject of rehearsals. Alternatively, it could be simply the case that he was not comfortable discussing this topic.

Nonetheless, Damian was not alone in this ordeal. Take, for example, the following excerpt from my interview with Kevin, who regarded Vipassana as a 'set-up to failure kind-of-thing'. According to his story, Kevin later opted for mindful yoga, which he considered to be a 'much more achievable' practice:

K. there is Perhaps fear around [p] around ever being able to go that deep and Doubt, like doubting myself, I spent a lot of time doubting whether, I'd ever be able to, [p] [in] um Correctly perform the technique, yk [. . .] this is where I'm still, [p] um just thinking it's gonna happen reasonably, magically and naturally, [p] yk, in ten
140 days [p] [in] you're bound to be seeing some results, and Really it's quite, [p] quite subtle, so [p] I didn't yk I was still [p] um mooching around, stuck on gross sensations [. . .] But, intellectually from that very first, encounter with vipassana [in] I had a, an ideal that [p] um [p] this was perhaps the, The authentic technique um and [p] I didn't want to be a dilettante about it and try lots of other things until
145 I found the one I liked, so I thought I'd try and stick with it, even though I had these huge doubts and by The Third time [. . .] I kind of realised that yeah, I need to, to um [long pause] not lacking in conviction but just disorganised perhaps.

Thus, Kevin's account complements my reading of Damian's narrative: both passages encapsulate a certain ambiguous language that involves (1) a sense of self-doubt or cynicism about their abilities to progress and (2) the practitioners' unequivocal trust and conviction in the capacities of the technique.

These characteristics are evident in both narratives. For instance, in Kevin's segment, he negotiated: even though results may be 'quite subtle', they 'are bound to come' (lines 140–142). Additionally, this passage discloses another important, yet comparatively less common, pattern of doubt that concerns not the self but the legitimacy of the technique (lines 141–143). Interestingly, questions about the authenticity of the technique are not addressed in this passage; rather, they are represented implicitly as a former 'ideal', using past-tense verbs and ultimately downplayed by the gravitational field of self-doubt and Kevin's conviction.

Clearly then, there are continuities between the narratives of pragmatic leavers' and disaffiliates' narratives. As demonstrated, uncertainties with progress are common across the majority (if not all) of the Vipassana disaf-filiation narratives. The theme of progress itself (in context of disaffiliation) is entangled with the concept of enlightenment, as understood and taught by Goenka. Thus, before I proceed any further with the analysis of Damian's narrative, it is important to first expound the issues surrounding the idea of progress and enlightenment within Goenka's teachings. This will elucidate the institutional source of self-doubt in disaffiliates' narratives and allow for a better conceptual understanding of disaffiliation and the trajectories that some of these individuals embarked on after departing the movement.

In the following section, I will first depict the ambiguous discourse on progress that is inherent to Goenka's teachings to illustrate how and why some Vipassana practitioners (such as Damian and Kevin) developed doubt and uncertainties about their own progress. This will further cement the themes explored in the previous chapter, particularly in reference to prag-matic leavers, such as Katrin, who gave up their practices as a result of frus-trations and impatience. Thereafter, I will demonstrate that the source of this conflict (and self-doubt) lies in disaffiliates' continuing commitment to the movement's language and discourse, even when they report inconsistencies between the movement's ideas/theory and their lived experiences—which I see as the indication of tacit conversion.

Chasing Enlightenment

Even though Goenka adopts a world-affirming and scientific language to transmit the 'teachings of the Buddha' to his non-Buddhist audience, the ultimate goal of nibbana is never left behind in his discourses. In fact, Goenka (1997: 1) constantly vacillates between emphasising the practical (this-worldly) benefits of Vipassana meditation and its instrumentality to achieve the final goal of enlightenment or full liberation. This constant movement between this-worldly and otherworldly goals of the meditational technique has created confusion among many Vipassana participants. Andrew, a pragmatic leaver, spontaneously raised this issue at the end of our interview when he was asked to provide any additional comments that he deemed important and related to his experience of disengagement:

A. the whole question of enlightenment

S. yeah, what about that?

A. I mean that's a kind of a massive, thing which isn't, it's like [p] What is it?!

S. [giggle]

A. [laugh] yk it's kind of like this, and, and, and how do you get there? [. . .] and you kind of go there and there's this kind of Thing of like, it's almost like a [in] a Goal out there or something, or it can be

S. yeah

A. and it's like, how does that, How does that, [p] it's like a parameter almost, how does that fit within people's experience [. . .] it's like um [long pause] what are we doing here, are we trying to become enlightened or are we trying to have a daily experience

S. yeah

A. or how do we, how does that, and How does even the idea of enlightenment Effect, the experience that we're having, do we, [p] does it feel like an unattainable goal [. . .] cause I think you go to Kaukapakapa and it's up there

S. yeah yeah

A. you know, 'you do this, and this is where you're heading' yk

Surprisingly, this confusion around the idea of enlightenment and/or the goal of Vipassana meditation is not limited to disengagers. 'Where is enlightenment, I don't know if I want it if it's going to take me away from earth' were the utterances of an old student with several years of involvement in this movement. Thus, participants not only exhibit uncertainties as to the purpose of the technique (as Andrew's excerpt suggests), but they also seem significantly intimidated by the idea of enlightenment, often lacking a theoretical understanding of the doctrine. However, such characteristics are not unique to Western Vipassana practitioners; Spiro's (1982 [1970]: 59) study shows that most Burmese (both laymen and monks) interpreted nibbana as a state of 'total annihilation' and 'extinction' and did not consider it a desirable goal.

In fact, the only participants that conveyed an understanding of the theoretical aspect of the practice beyond a rudimentary level were from the category of disaffiliates.[10] This could be due to that, for many, the process of disaffiliation involved an intense engagement with both insider (VRI) and outsider (academic) literature on Buddhism. This sudden appetite for intellectual knowledge for some participants such as Luke (chapter 6) was motivated by a need to reconstruct a sense of self, as well as a desire to confirm doubts and strengthen the grounds upon which he critiqued the movement both in terms of theory and ethics. For others, however, this turn to literature was inspired by a desire to validate their experiences, evaluate Goenka's claims (of the technique being *the* correct way to practice, and the movement's claims that the lineage went back to the Buddha), and to locate the movement within its historical Buddhist context. Kevin, for example, had enrolled in an introductory course on Buddhism at the tertiary level to find out 'whether or not [g] there was any mention of Vipassana [in both Buddhist and academic literature] and if it was actually, really a thing'.

During their involvement, however, many practitioners commonly face uncertainties including doubts about their progress. This is because meditators are given no solid criteria to assess their development on this path, as the discourses surrounding the idea of progress are kept intentionally vague. For example, during a standard ten-day course, students are repeatedly told that their progress cannot be measured by the types of sensations they experience (subtle or gross); rather, it is measured by the sense of equanimity they develop in response to their sensations (i.e. how they handle their cravings and aversions)—which is difficult to measure (Pagis, 2008: 174).

Despite this, there are various descriptions in Goenka's instructions that are taken by the practitioners as yardsticks. For instance, students are told that by maintaining their equanimity, they shall soon find out that the 'gross, solidified and unpleasant sensations begin to dissolve into subtle vibrations.

[10] For instance, the theoretical underpinning of the practice within the framework of the Four Noble Truths; the Eight Noble Paths; and in relation to the three Buddhist tenets of dukkha, anicca, and anatta.

One starts to experience a very pleasant *flow* of energy throughout the body'
(Goenka, 1997: 35). Similar descriptions are provided for the experience of
bhanga during both a standard ten-day course and the more advanced meditation courses (such as the Satipathhana Sutta course).[11]

Yet, at the same time, the instructions also remind the practitioners that
it is normal to experience blind areas and gross sensations after one has experienced a free flow.[12] According to Goenka (1997: 35–36), this is *not* to be
interpreted as a sign of regression, but rather a sign of progress. Accordingly,
the gross and unpleasant sensations are associated with the 'deep-rooted
sankharas' and 'complexes' that arise on the surface, as one 'penetrates deeper
into the unconscious mind, and uncovers impurities hidden there' (Goenka,
1997: 35).

Thus, on a Vipassana course, students are constantly discouraged from
developing expectations, yet constantly reassured that 'results are bound to
come' and they will experience some sort of change if they understand and
practice the technique 'properly' (Goenka, 1997: 33). As a result, it is not surprising to see that the disaffiliated participants in this research indicated a
great deal of frustration and self-doubt about their progress.

Additionally, it must be noted that beyond these ambiguous descriptions
in Goenka's instructions and evening discourses, the teachers provide no detailed feedback that could help the meditators evaluate their progress and/
or validate their experiences. In fact, almost *all* participants in this research
(except for the teachers themselves) complained, one way or another, about
the lack of valuable feedback on behalf of Vipassana teachers and commonly
(mis-)interpreted this as the teachers' lack of support. This occurs because
the teachers respond with short, vague, and generic answers, which encourage the practitioners to *observe* the experience rather than seek an explanation for it. I had similar experiences during fieldwork and witnessed
multiple interactions of this nature between the teachers and the new students. Contrary to the practitioners' views, the aim of this vagueness, as Pagis
(2008: 175) has argued, is to detach the practitioner from external measurements and anchor the meditator's self-knowledge into an embodied experience. However, in the absence of a clear-cut response from the teachers,

---

[11] Bhanga is considered an important stage in the practice of Vipassana. It refers to the experience of total dissolution of the apparent solidity of the body into waves of pleasant sensations, which
emphasises the embodied experience of the doctrine of not-self.

[12] Blind area refers to part(s) of the body where the mind is not, yet, able to detect and observe the
sensations of that area.

students are often forced to use each other's experience to assess their own progress:[13]

> K. I've heard people talking about it yk, 'oh I've experience the bhanga or dissolution' [p] Not Me! [hah] Plus, yk I was never really going for that, I knew I was a plonker. I didn't like the fact that I didn't got there and other people did, dada-dada-da [in] [p] but I kind of [yawn] accepted it [long pause] and now it doesn't bother me at all, fuck all.

150

This passage from Kevin's interview encapsulates a profound sense of disappointment resulting from both uncertainties about his own progress and the lack of clear guidelines from the movement/teachers. As he represents in this passage, Kevin's self-doubt was instigated when he subjected himself to comparisons with other students, which consequentially led to a perceived inability to achieve extraordinary experiences such as bhanga. This particular expression of self-doubt (i.e. framed in terms of comparisons with others) was rather uncommon among disaffiliation narratives. Instead, the participants' self-doubt about their progress seemed to involve ideas concerning a perceived inability to eradicate sankharas or eliminate patterns of craving (such as sexual passion)—this was indeed central to Damian's self-doubt, which I will be exploring shortly when addressing his disaffiliation trajectory.

Thus far, and through the examples of Damian and other disaffiliates, I have sought to demonstrate that the theme of self-doubt and its associated frustrations were extremely common across the narratives of disaffiliates (as well as the pragmatic leavers, explored in the previous chapter). I have traced the institutional source of this doubt and linked it with the ambiguities enclosed within the discourse of progress in Goenka's teachings. Through a structural reading of Damian's narrative, I have proposed that Damian himself was, arguably, oblivious to the significance of self-doubt to his disaffiliation process and/or that this was a sentimental topic that he was not comfortable with. Moreover, I have illustrated that disaffiliates were somewhat resistant to openly discuss (with me) their desire for achieving enlightenment and their ongoing convictions about certain aspects of the practice that Damian referred to as the 'bare bones' of the technique. In the context of Damian's case study, I interpreted this as being an indication of dissonance

---

[13] However, advanced students rarely compare experiences with one another; rather they discuss their experiences and remark on the benefits gained with less experienced practitioners (as we learnt from Elijah's narrative and his interaction with an old student).

and disconformity with the role he had adopted as an ex-member/disaffiliate in the context of the interview. These understandings and interpretations are essential for contextualising participants' disaffiliation trajectory; that is, how disaffiliated participants resolved their uncertainties and the different trajectories they took after departing from the movement.

Concluding Summary

This chapter explored Damian's disaffiliation narrative as a representative of individuals who departed from Goenka's movement after years of intensive commitment. While Vipassana disaffiliation narratives shared many similarities with the existing literature, they also centred on the element of self-doubt. Using this theme as a marker, in the following chapter I examine common disaffiliation trajectories based on how the participants dealt with their uncertainties and how they (re)orientated towards the concept of enlightenment. These include (1) drifters in samsara, (2) pursuers of the gateless gate, and (3) deconversion. The first two trajectories represent those narratives that continued to be influenced by the movement's language and therefore will be scrutinised comparatively in the next chapter. Conversely, the final trajectory, deconversion, will be scrutinised in a separate chapter for it exemplifies a case where the participant presented a narrative that was almost entirely constructed outside the movement's language.

5

Disaffiliation Trajectories

In this chapter, I explore (1) drifters in samsara and (2) pursuers of the gateless gate as two common Vipassana disaffiliation trajectories and argue that deconversion or migration outside of the movement's universe of discourse is a rare exit pattern in this movement. I show that in the vast majority of cases, the participants' search for an alternative universe of discourse post-exit did *not* land them outside the Buddhist tradition; that, in fact, the language and reasoning of most participants remained close to that of the movement. I contextualise this claim by borrowing from Bromley's (1998a, 1998b) tripartite typology, which asserts that organisations that occupy a low-tension position in their host environment are likely to exert control over the exit process and its narrative, and, consequently, departing members tend to reaffirm the goals and values of the group. I argue that the Vipassana movement's linguistic strategies warrant its placement in a low-tension niche within New Zealand's cultural environment which itself values similar dispositions. As a result of this harmony, deconversion becomes a rare possibility for individuals who exhibited an *intellectual commitment* to the movement's language and rhetorical strategies (outlined in chapter 1).

The previous chapter highlighted self-doubt in one's ability to progress towards enlightenment as a shared characteristic of all disaffiliation narratives. Disaffiliation trajectories were thus distinguished based on the way participants had plotted their narratives, dealt with their uncertainties and self-doubt, and how they (re)orientated towards the concept of enlightenment. According to the analysis of eight narratives, the participants who disaffiliated after intense involvement in Goenka's movement embarked on three distinct paths (see figure 5.1): (1) three of these individuals (Damian, Kevin, and Jazz) illustrated a more traditional understanding of enlightenment, considering the ultimate goal essentially beyond their reach and/or agenda for this life and, therefore, abandoned hopes for achieving that in this life-time; (2) whereas others (Kovido, Karen, Mark, and Polly) had moved towards a different understanding of the concept by shifting from a transcendental framework to an immanent one. The participants in the latter group

Drifting Through Samsara. Masoumeh Rahmani, Oxford University Press. © Oxford University Press 2022.
DOI: 10.1093/oso/9780197579961.003.0006

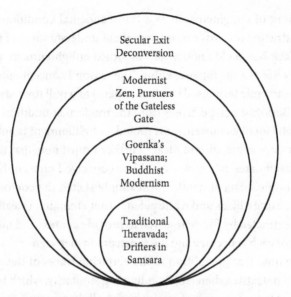

Figure 5.1 Disaffiliation trajectories and narrative plots

Drifters in samsara moved towards the traditional Theravadin discourse, whereas the pursuers of the gateless gate moved towards the modernist Zen discourse.

essentially argued that the practice of private meditation is 'counterproduct-ive'. They conceptualised the discontinuation of their private practice not in terms of a complete disengagement but rather as an integration of the insight gained from Vipassana in every moment of their lives. In their own words, they claim to be living Vipassana 'off the cushion'. Having said that, despite these differences, all the individuals in these two groups continued to sub-scribe to the movement's language and reasoning. On the contrary, as a single representative of the final trajectory—(3) deconversion—Luke had migrated outside the movement's universe of discourse towards a secular/humanistic worldview (see chapter 6). In the following pages, I explore the first two tra-jectories by drawing upon relevant passages from their narratives.

Trajectory (1): Drifters in Samsara

The distinction between these trajectories is primarily anchored in the ways the practitioners dealt with self-doubt and responded to the concept of en-lightenment: those who were pulled towards the more traditional Theravada understanding of enlightenment as a transcendental condition, and those who were attracted towards a more immanent understanding of the concept similar to Jack Kornfield's notion of 'embodied enlightenment' that affirms the ordinary life as a site for awakening. The reason I conceptualised 'drifters in samsara' (an emic term used by a participant) as a pull towards traditional Theravada Buddhist perspective is from the modernist Buddhist viewpoint, within which Goenka's movement is rooted; enlightenment is not conceptualised as an impossible, distant ideal.[1] Further I must note that this categorisation of disaffiliates' narratives should be conceived on a continuum. Yet, due to the limited data at hand,[2] I will simply sketch the contours of these trajectories, using a black and white palette. There remains a wealth of knowledge to be extracted by future research to provide context and nuance to the complexity of each trajectory and the spectrum in-between.

Suffice to note that in addition to the enduring traces of the movement's language, all narratives shared one underlying similarity, which involved the giving up and letting go of an obsession with enlightenment.

I must note that in almost every instance, the participants brought up the topic of enlightenment themselves. Hence, due to its significance, I incorporated more specific questions on this topic in a follow-up interview conducted with Damian:

D. I have to say that in my current life, there's an element of resignation, an element of
    [p] um um [p] even you can say capitulations perhaps, to [p] feeling that, [p] [p]
    [p] not much, can change for me, um [p] in the rest of my life, I mean when I was
    young, when I was nineteen, [p] I was Very [p] [p] [hah] dynamically, um [p]
    pulled to the idea that I can radically transform myself and my life and . . . I was
    looking for something um [c] And I found something and it, it, it did, help me,
    and it did, benefit me, [p] but What it showed me, what Vipassana showed me
    was that the process of transformation is very, very slow
S. mhm

---

[1] In fact, the distinct features of the teachings of Mahasi Sayadaw, a renowned teacher in the modernist Buddhist lineage, was that he provided lay meditators with (1) a direct entry into the path of Vipassana without any training in concentration and mastery of jhanas and (2) the promise of quick result. As Mahasi has famously noted, 'It will not take long to achieve the object, but possibly in a month, or twenty days, or fifteen days; or on rare occasions even in seven days for a selected few with extraordinary Perfection' (Mahasi Sayadaw 1971, preface cited in Sharf, 1995: 256).

[2] These categories emerged from a thematic and structural analysis of the narratives, after the data collection came to an end. They were neither anticipated, nor any explicit questions regarding enlightenment were incorporated in the interviews (except Damian's follow-up interview).

D. like Very slow. and um the Karmic, [p] [p] load and the karmic History of each
consciousness [p] in general is quite vast . . . so I feel a bit resigned to, the Shit
parts of me that I think there's sort of, be here [hah]

S. mhm

D. I guess [p] Which in a funny way, you could almost say that that was, that was,
[p] [p] a sort of a logical outcome of Vipassana, because it's all about acceptance . . . have you heard of Ram Dass? . . . he'd been in India, where he went exten-
sively and he'd come back and he was on a bus and he saw some woman and he
though [vc] 'hmm, she's pretty attractive' and then he had this self-reflection and
he, he felt like after All of |this|

S. |mhm|

D. how come I haven't managed to, why haven't I been able to get past this? yk, why
am I, still got this sort of sexual interest. um [p] [p] [p] and, and, and it kind of
echoes what I'm trying to say is that, yk you can do realms and realms of spiritual
practice but, yk you still Str[uggle] can be wind up struggling with the same old
[p] junk, that you were struggling when you were a teenager, I mean [in] The
only difference to me now, is that, um [p] [p] I'm not tormented [p] by it, I'm still
Bothered by it, but I'm not tormented by it.

This passage invokes two related themes. The main theme involves
abandoning the hope for a 'quick fix', the realisation that transformation is
a long and slow process, and ultimately, giving up the idea that enlightenment can be achieved in this life. This excerpt is also indicative of Damian's
position on morality. Clearly, from Damian's perspective, the path to enlightenment is tied to the mastery of emotions and cravings, particularly
sexual passion.[3] Recall how the theme of sexuality was highlighted earlier
(in the previous chapter) as a catalyst to his disengagement process. When
this theme was evoked initially, it culminated in a series of moral criticisms
about Goenka on accounts of deception. In fact, the movement was not ques-
tioned or rejected for its position on sexuality. This led me to construe that
in the passage, and through the retelling of Ram Dass's story, Damian depicted sexual passion as 'junk', a life-long 'struggle', and a sin (using Christian
terminology).

[3] As noted earlier, Goenka suggests that one way of measuring progress on this path (towards enlightenment) is reflected in how the meditator handles craving and aversion in his everyday life. In
other words, progress towards nibbana requires one's mastery of emotions and cravings. This is the
context within which Damian's struggle with sexuality, 'self-doubt', and his 'capitulations' from the
goal of spiritual liberation must be interpreted.

This facet of Damian's narrative, coupled with his perception of enlightenment as a distant ideal, closely aligns his position to a widely endorsed perspective among Theravada Buddhists in Asia (Sharf, 1995). This outlook condemns sexual desire and activity both metaphorically and literally; it generally renders sexual passion as a harmful reaction that limits people's ability to progress towards enlightenment (Gombrich, 2006: 106). This is because sexual passion is understood as a self-centred emotion that produces craving and attachment to this world—a perspective, which has led to debates as to the possibility of enlightenment for non-monks (Pagis, 2008: 222). Except for disaffiliation narratives categorised in this group, very few participants (mostly representing Vipassana teachers and serious meditators) shared Damian's view on morality. In fact, the majority (but not all) of participants considered the movement's moral code of conduct, particularly its guidelines on sexual passion, irrelevant to one's attainment of enlightenment.

Clearly, as has been hinted at before, these are not the official teachings of Vipassana (i.e. they are not addressed during a standard ten-day course); rather, they are reserved for advanced meditators. It must be noted that even though Goenka's movement orients itself towards the laity—sexual relations are not discouraged within permanent relationships—sexual guidelines are much stricter for serious meditators.[4] Hence, single assistant teachers, serious students, and long-term dhamma workers must maintain a strong code of conduct, including celibacy. In fact, in a series of letters addressed to old students, Goenka renders sexual passion as the worst impurity or the 'pus of the mind'. In the same light, during my participant observation at Dhamma Medini, I was required to listen to a special discourse tailored to dhamma workers in which Goenka (1985, cited in VRI Dhamma, 2014) justifies the movement's strict positions on sex segregation in terms of preventing 'Mara [from] stimulating the seed of passion'.

However, the main and most relevant point in this passage is that even though the desire of enlightenment has exhausted these participants' enthusiasm, they nevertheless continue idealising it as a transcendent reality. For instance, Kevin, who consciously revealed his bias in favour of the Theravada understanding of the concept coupled with prejudice towards a Zen understanding, also spoke of his long-lasting desire to renounce the world and

---

[4] Despite this consideration for married couples, Goenka notes, 'By practising Dhamma, both husband and wife will ultimately reach the stage where they naturally live a life of celibacy' (Goenka, 1998: 137, cited in VRI Dhamma, 2014).

become a monk. However, he also renders this desire 'romantic' and imprac-tical.[5] Thus, while in one sense, these participants had lost hopes for achieving radical change due to self-doubt in their ability to progress and a perceived lack of self-mastery, they continue to desire enlightenment as an ideal. It is just that the goal has been postponed to *another life*. This narrative feature of drifters in samsara closely resembles the tendencies of pragmatic leavers who enthusiastically postponed the idea of a spiritually oriented lifestyle to a later phase in life, for instance, when they have fulfilled their mundane responsi-bilities such as parenting. The difference rests in the commitment of drifters in samsara to certain theological concepts, such as reincarnation and karma, as well as their use of these ideas to rationalise the giving up and letting go of the much-desired goal of enlightenment in the present life.

Having said this, in the content of their disaffiliation narratives, both Damian and Kevin note that they have arrived at a sense of acceptance—a claim which is at dissonance with the *structure*, the language, and the com-municative behaviour in which they disclaim self-acceptance (Damian's pas-sage 'struggling the same old junk...' and Kevin's passage noted in the previous chapter: 'I was never really going for that, I knew I was a plonker'). Moreover, those participants whose narratives rested on the spectrum between the drifters in samsara and pursuers of the gateless gate tended both to exhibit an understanding of enlightenment as an unreachable transcendental reality and indicated that attaining such a state is not an agenda for their present life.[6]

Finally, exit literature (Bromley, 1998b; Coates, 2013; Wright, 1987) com-monly assumes that because disaffiliation results in a sudden 'loss of identity', the process of disengagement requires a resource or an 'identity solution' to assist the transition away from the movement (Coates, 2013). Accordingly, this alternative resource can take the form of an 'alternate discursive re-source' or an alternative 'other' (i.e. significant other, new social networks) enabling the New Religious Movement member to overcome doubts and re-construct a sense of self, post-exit. I will address this in considerable detail in the next chapter ("Deconversion"). While participants tended to shy away

---

[5] Kevin: 'I still think that [becoming a monk] would be nice but I couldn't do it, because you can't run off and leave your family, and [p] by the time my kids were out of the house I would be probably decrepit enough whereas if I took off and tried to hang around Burma or Thailand or somewhere like that I'll just probably get sick and die'.

[6] Jazz: 'I could say I am not at a level yet where I feel like I have to strive to be my highest self in this life, for the sake of my next life, existence. I guess I'm more of more on my own agenda enjoying this life [l] with what I've got you know, but I'm not doing it for the sake of a better next life, maybe I'm selfish [l] I don't know'.

from or de-emphasise the role of an alternative other in the process of their disaffiliation, their narratives revealed the participants' need for an alternative perspective to deal with doubts and reconstruct selves. Accordingly, the drifters in samsara and those who occupied the middle ground commonly framed their attempt to reach out for an alternative universe of discourse through the narrative plot of unsettling post-disaffiliation experiences such as ghost visitations.

Ghosts Visitations and Past-Life Memories

Dreams have always played a notable role in religious conversion. Scholars have frequently utilised accounts of dreams in their analyses of conversion narratives (Stromberg, 1993) or used the common features of dreams to map the diversity of conversion experiences across cultural and historical boundaries—to the point where 'dreaming' (Bulkeley, 2014) has secured itself a niche in the *Oxford Handbook of Religious Conversion*. Indeed, many participants in this research, including pragmatic leavers and old students such as Elijah, have incorporated dreams (and visions of religious figures) into their narratives. Although dreams are more regularly reported in conversion narratives, they are not unusual in disengagement stories. For example, Ebaugh (1988: 179) notes that approximately one-fifth of the 106 individuals she interviewed indicated recurrent dreams and occasional 'nightmares', whereas Harris (2015: 196) recounted her participants' dreams/ 'flashbacks' and interpretively linked them to the anxiety, distress, and emotional instability associated with the process of exit.

That said, on the one hand, dreams were not significant to disaffiliation narratives in the current research; enigmatic accounts of 'ghost visitations', 'dark energies',[7] and/or 'past-life experiences', on the other hand, occupied a significant share of the accounts categorised in this chapter (four out of eight disaffiliates[8]). What is of particular importance, however, is that in every instance the participants narrated these incidents of their own volition. No question was asked either concerning 'ghosts' or the specifics of 'past-life memories', rather these stories were more commonly shaped in response

---

[7] E.g. Jazz's disaffiliation narrative involved experiences of 'dark energies' that 'almost felt like a demon... it was something I needed to "renounce" clean myself of in a spiritual way'.

[8] The same number of cases (four) appeared in the narratives of pragmatic leavers, which collectively comprised nearly 30 per cent of the entire sample size (eight out of twenty-six).

to the question of whether they have engaged in any other practices after Vipassana.

Causal explanations of this phenomenon are beyond my disciplinary scope; these findings could merit further investigation from the field of psychology. However, due to the weight of these accounts in disaffiliation narratives, particularly since these incidents and experiences are said to have taken place after disengagement, I explore them in the context of conversion/disaffiliation. Hence, I focus on the language of these narratives and their relevance for the trajectories outlined in this section.

According to these narratives, experiences of 'ghost visitations' and past-life memories (that surfaced after disaffiliation) led participants to seek new frameworks to understand the self and hence achieve a sense of self-acceptance.[9] For instance, Damian noted, 'often when I felt negative, I realised that there's been some sort of psychic presence around me' and 'some of my feelings are coloured by visitations by ghosts and other psychic entities'. As a result of interpreting his experiences in such a manner, Damian argued, he had grown to *question* the idea that 'everything you feel is absolutely your responsibility'. In another instance, Polly's past-life experiences allowed her to reconceptualise the *cause* of trauma in her life and consequently arrive at a 'place of forgiveness'. Overall, these side stories revealed disaffiliates' need for an alternative framework within which they could interpret self and experiences post-exit. However, even though these individuals engaged in what would be discouraged by Goenka (e.g. looking for causal explanations, or rejecting individual responsibility), in most instances, the participants' search for alternative frameworks did not land them far outside the Buddhist tradition. In fact, participants who shared these narratives tended to draw from the Jatakas; they argued that such perspectives do not necessarily contradict Vipassana's views and that they are in perfect harmony with traditional Theravada conventions. As demonstrated, these narratives indicate a shift away from Goenka's modernist position which values individualism and a rational and instrumental approach to Buddhist teachings devoid of its supernatural content.

---

[9] In reference to past-life experience, Damian argued, 'it seemed to bring a little bit of peacefulness . . . made me feel like I could accept myself better because I felt like I understood myself better, because it seemed like "oh this is why I like this," "this is what is going on"'.

Trajectory: (2) Pursuers of the Gateless Gate

Contrary to the previous group (drifters in samsara), the disaffiliation narrative of the participants in the present group signifies a different understanding of enlightenment that leaps outside the purview of Goenka's Vipassana or the traditional Theravada Buddhism and dissipates within the wider subculture of western Buddhism. It consists of interpretations set forth by modernist Zen (i.e. D.T. Suzuki's legacy) and the West Coast American interpretations of Vipassana meditation (i.e. views pioneered by Kornfield).

In short, the participants in this category *no longer* conceive enlightenment as a transcendental reality; rather, they aim to find meaning in the concrete experiences of the everyday such as eating, walking, and parenting.[10] They no longer see the technique of Vipassana meditation as a vehicle carrying them across the ocean of samsara to the distant shore of nibbana, but rather as an exercise to induce the extraordinary attention necessary for observing the ordinary in an undistorted way. This position is not to be confused with the perspectives shared by some of the pragmatic leavers (whose narratives were predominantly characterised by a dualistic language, e.g. immanence vs. transcendence). As mentioned in the previous chapters, the pragmatic leavers resented the mundane and nostalgically desired transcendence; they also yearned for an effortless and spontaneous experience of enlightenment.

Another prevalent characteristic of the narratives in this group is the theme of Perennialism—the idea that there is a shared essence, a mystical core, or an ultimate reality behind the plurality of religious and philosophical traditions, often conceived as a non-dual absolute consciousness (Sharf, 2015: 477). Comparatively, the participants categorised in the previous group either explicitly[11] or implicitly[12] indicated their commitment to the Theravada Buddhist perspective and, in almost in all cases, tended to use popular psychological categories to rationalise their preference (e.g.

---

[10] Take, for instance, the following statement Kovido made about his children: 'They've been extraordinary teachers, I'm not sure if I've learnt the lessons yet, but they are still teaching. yk in the monastery yk I was the peaceful, I was the most peaceful monk there and if anybody was in conflict with something they would send me there. I never used to get angry but yk apparently part of that was repression, but whereas with my kids, yk they can get me Enraged, yk in ten seconds [g]'.

[11] Damian, e.g. readily presented himself as being 'biased' towards Theravada and 'prejudice' towards Tibetan Mahayana traditions, which he considered 'loose' for its moral codes, and 'circus-like' for its rituals.

[12] On the other hand, Kevin, e.g. would convey his tendencies towards Theravada more implicitly by labelling other groups' meditational routine 'wishy-washy' or their understanding of enlightenment fantasy-like: 'look at the Zen stuff and you realise that there is enlightenment in every moment [l] everyone is a Buddha and that kind of thing'.

introversion, seriousness, and dry personality). Alternatively, participants in the present category insist on presenting selves that are open and appreciative of religious diversity, knowing that they all teach and preach the same underlying essence. To explore these themes in detail, I draw from my interview with Karen, whose narrative encapsulates the overall perspectives and themes apparent in the stories of other participants (Kovido, Mark, and Polly) categorised in this group.

Selected Case Study: Karen

Karen is a joyful, articulate, and dynamic young woman in her mid-thirties. Her enthusiasm for discussing abstract concepts, such as reality, coupled with her ability to communicate them not only efficiently but also rather poetically, are some of the characteristics that made Karen an ideal informant for in-depth dialogues (and the task of interview transcription unexpectedly pleasant). A central theme by which Karen reconstructed her biographical narrative was the idea of a 'spiritual search' or a 'journey' to understand the 'nature of reality'. Of course, similar to most of the participants in this chapter (including Damian) the road to this search ends for Karen with the *technique* of Vipassana, which she unapologetically regards as 'utterly sacred' and 'incredibly on the ball' for enabling an understanding of reality as it is.

In spite of embracing what the technique can offer, Karen's story was not without criticism. These were, of course, directed towards the institutional aspects of Goenka's movement and the murkiness of his teachings, particularly about enlightenment, as well as its emphasis on morality.[13] Before exploring Karen's perspectives on these matters, I should first note that (similar to all disaffiliates in this chapter) the quest of enlightenment had become Karen's prime motive for meditation during her involvement with the movement. She stressed, 'To me, there was nothing else, there was no other point in living and it got to this stage [where] if I had to Die to find out what life was, then I was happy to do it'. According to her account, this phase of 'truth

---

[13] Contrary to Damian's position, the participants whose narratives explored herein illustrate a relaxed understanding of morality, and some (Karen, similar to most of the pragmatic leavers) go as far to consider the observance of sila irrelevant to enlightenment: 'to me there wasn't enough clarity between "this is the technique of Vipassana that will make you wake up" and "this is just stuff that will make your life better and more fulfilling and happier." There wasn't enough clarity between the two. So I feel like it's really jumbled that people think that they Have to restrain from sexual activity or not eat this or not do that or, or follow these rules in Order to see the nature of reality'.

or die' involved her intense devotion to the practice and an extensive daily routine of meditation, due to which she developed resentment towards mundane aspects of life such as earning a living. In this respect, Karen's narrative is not distinct from the rest of the participants in this category. In the most extreme instance, after leaving Goenka's movement, Kovido embarked on a quest to become enlightened and joined the Thai Forest tradition of Ajahn Chah in an attempt to make this goal a full-time career.[14]

Having said this, the pinnacle of both narratives (Karen and Kovido) is the abandonment of the pursuit of enlightenment, as it is understood within the Goenka's movement and the Theravada tradition, and a reorientation in perspective and practice. This involved taking the practice 'off the cushion', embracing life and its mundaneness, and implementing the insights gained from the practice into every aspect of life:

> I think I found that actually being able to observe things like my judgement for not meditating enough. or observe things like [p] um that it wasn't about being on the cushion but it was about navigating the day to day life with a different perspective . . . so the four or five hour meditation thing kind of turned into a twenty-four hour [l] observe feast really but it was, it was beyond desperate it was, I have some friends who have gone through something similar as well . . . and it's just one of these, [p] Choiceless, you don't really have a choice in it, it's kind of like life [l] it's like Life just Dying to burst through and you get to a point where it's too extraordinary painful to try and stop it . . . so it started off as I want to be enlightened and I want to know what it is
>
> S. mhm
>
> K. to the point where I kind of realised what needed to happen to actually make that happen, and that's when it went from the cushion to actually just allowing life to do whatever it needed to do, really.

One of the outstanding linguistic features of Karen's narrative (and those of other participants in this group) is the positive context within which life is spoken of. This characteristic stands in juxtaposition to the language of pragmatic leavers who commonly referred to life (i.e. the everyday concerns) as an obstacle to maintaining a regular practice. Comparatively, participants in

---

[14] Kovido: 'what most people who helped at the centre did was to help for a few months and then go home and earn money and then come back again and work at the centre. and I thought why do that, why not be a monk then I can do that full-time'.

the present group (such as Karen) assert that the act of sitting 'on the cushion' progressively became counterproductive and a barrier to living life 'fully' and having a 'pulsate experience' of it. Hence, their narratives emphasised the affirmation and reconnection to the prosaic, the rejection of the idealism encountered in the previous group, and the purely instrumental approach of the pragmatic leavers.

Whereas the narratives of the drifters in samsara were structured in the framework that rendered the search through the metaphor of 'crossing the ocean of samsara'—indicating the quest as an ongoing and slow movement towards a very distant shore—the 'quest' plots in this group are commonly reconstructed within the framework of the proverbial Zen metaphor, 'gateless gate'.[15] This is an emic term, which appeared in the narrative of Karen, although other disaffiliates in this group conveyed the same message. In short, the metaphor has developed from the idea that koans are set up as barriers which are impossible for an ordinary person to pass through unless he/she has realised the true nature of self and reality. When one has attained self-realisation or enlightenment (*satori* or *kensho* in Japanese), these barriers disappear as though they were nothing but illusions, and one finds that from the very beginning one has always been placed within a world where there is neither inside nor outside (Yamada, 2005 [1979])— hence, gateless. Participants in the present category use this metaphor to reconstruct and represent their previous quest of enlightenment as an impediment to appreciating enlightenment as something intrinsic and already existing (as opposed to an unattainable transcendental reality). As Karen passionately put it:

K. from my understanding and my experience it's a total pile of [p] bullshit sales pitch
   that is . . . enticing people to sit their asses on the cushion and donate their money
   to different corporations and [l] institutions, nirvana, nirvana like waaah daaaah
   there's nothing other than this. there's nothing other than this. and once we step
   out of the way and actually allow ourselves to let go of the things we hold dear the
   perspectives that we hold dear and let it go for the possibility of actually seeing
   it as it is and once that's gone [p] there only is, there's only nirvana even the even

---

[15] Gateless gate (or gateless barrier) is primarily known from a classic collection of Zen koans, which are paradoxical riddles or dialogues between a Zen master and disciples. They are commonly structured in the form of a question and an answer that have no clear relation to each other (McMahan, 2008: 124). E.g. 'what is the sound of one hand clapping?' Koans are designed to disturb the sequence of dualistic, logical thinking and enable awakening.

the not seeing nirvana is nirvana . . . it drives me crazy because [p] having been through the whole thing and then still falling into its traps from time to time, in the more subtle traps it's just that [p] [in; ex] it's so sad, it's so sad because it makes people think 'I'm not good enough', 'I'm not there yet', 'there's always something outside of me I need to reach, I need to get to' It's Not, it's Not True.

This passage requires no detailed comments except to draw parallels with the theme of self-acceptance, which was innately desired by all participants in this research, yet distinctively valorised in each instance. Contrary to the nuances of self-acceptance encountered in Damian's (and Kevin's) narrative, which were predicated under the hegemony of Theravada Buddhism (emphasising self-mastery and ascetic renunciation as ideal), the participants in the present category rehearse narratives that are reconstructed within what Gleig (2010) refers to as a 'feminine' approach to Buddhism. Such an approach, according to Gleig (2010: 120), is the characteristic of many contemporary western Buddhist traditions that 'reconfigured dharma as a practice of relationship to the body, community and the earth', and promote 'feminine-associated appreciation of self-acceptance, interdependence and healing'.

These shifts are most notably evident in Kornfield's innovations, which openly condemn Western practitioners' tendencies to misuse Buddhist ideals to feed their harsh and unhealthy 'inner-critic' (Gleig, 2010: 119–121), call for a 'mature spirituality' or 'embodied enlightenment' that forsake unrealistic goals (fantasies of full enlightenment), and aim to develop awareness. In short, this view pushes for a metaphorical reading of the Buddhist path to enlightenment rather than a literal state to be attained. According to Kornfield (2001: 123, cited in Gleig, 2010: 121), it is not possible to completely transcend the 'pain of human life', as Mara always returns to pay a visit to the Buddha. Hence, instead of lamenting Mara's return, Kornfield suggests that we should embrace human vulnerability 'because the real problem is not our humanity, but our denial of it' (Gleig, 2010: 121). In other words, Kornfield's ideal of 'embodied enlightenment' aims not to transcend human, but to acknowledge and develop increasing awareness, and to embody human wholeness in everyday life. Such interpretations resonated seamlessly with the narratives of participants in this category, such as Kovido:

K. as I said I spent years trying to get enlightened. yk and went through various teachers, there's other teachers I haven't told you about yk [p] in New Zealand

and [in] various courses and all that sort of stuff and then kind of actually then coming back to this, the teaching of that, Actually we're ok as we are. yk. that actually, what the Buddha Realised was that it's something that is already here, it's already existing, which is, it's kind of me, yk, or, I don't even know if it's me or something, but it's kind of like, and something to do with living fully yk, I'm a human being.

Thus, as demonstrated, the participants in this group resolved their uncertainties by effectively *replanting* enlightenment in an immanent framework— a reconceptualisation which all of these participants considered 'highly liberating'. Nevertheless, all participants consensually supported the efficacy of Vipassana meditation's technique in allowing one to observe the 'true nature of reality', while some even imagined that it would be impossible to dismiss such an understanding (of self and reality) and turn to other truth claims after disengagement. Hence, beyond these fundamental differences, the language of the drifters in samsara and the pursuers of the gateless gate shared various borders with Goenka's movement, particularly how beliefs in Buddhist doctrine were articulated, the terminologies used, and how the movement's non-religious status was defended. Finally, regardless of their positionality, both the drifters in samsara and the pursuers of the gateless gate highly valued their previous membership and considered it essential to their 'growth'.

Remnants of the Movement's Language

At the outset of this chapter, I suggested that disaffiliation narratives featured the same rhetorical strategies that old students used to distinguish Goenka's movement from religion, hence overlooking the process of conversion. In the following pages, I argue that (except for Luke) disaffiliates' ambivalent narratives and their ongoing conviction in 'certain elements of the practice' is intertwined with their ongoing intellectual commitment to the rhetorical strategies explored in chapter 1. In other words, I argue that since the movement's language is well adjusted to the Western, modern (and postmodern) climate, deconversion from this movement is a rare exit pattern.

To substantiate this claim, I return to examine Damian's persistent use of language and reasoning that he himself seeks to reject by frequently labelling it as 'propaganda'. One obvious example manifested in the passage (previous chapter) where Damian implicitly suggests that his commitment to the movement was, at least partly, influenced by the strategies used by Goenka in his stories and analogies (e.g. 'dig a well in one spot'). Not surprisingly, the same reasoning occurs in Kevin's narrative where he stated, 'I didn't want to be a dilettante about it' (previous chapter). However, by saying this, I do not attempt to make any assumptions about the validity of these statements or to imply that Damian's (and other practitioners') commitment and membership was the result of some sort of brainwashing technique. Rather, my aim is to illustrate how the same rhetorical strategies that Damian finds problematic (propaganda) continue to influence much of his language and reasoning.

The disaffiliates' commitment to the movement's rhetorical strategies persists despite that a substantial number of disaffiliates (five out of eight) retrospectively acknowledged tacit conversion, once the vocabulary and the language were presented to them. Nevertheless, most participants defended the movement's non-sectarian status and thus their retrospective acknowledgement of conversion often involved a reflection on the institutional structures of the movement rather than on its system of beliefs. For instance, conversion was linked with stages of socialisation and integration within the movement such as the fact that one's advancement to longer courses (e.g. thirty day, sixty day, etc.) is dependent on one's adherence to certain protocols (e.g. observing sila, regular meditation, and regular course attendance).

To demonstrate the remnants of the movement's language in disaffiliates' narratives, I reference a segment of Damian's narrative in which he indicates an appreciation for the movement's teaching, arguing that 'the truth that seems to be espoused within it [the practice] are compelling . . . elegantly simple, and indisputable'. As becomes evident, similar to other disaffiliates, Damian's narrative features the same rhetorical strategies outlined previously (chapter 1) as linguistic mechanisms that conceal conversion. These include the rhetoric of meditative experience, Vipassana meditation as a 'tool',[16] and the movement's claims of 'universality'. Moreover, despite his position as a disaffiliate, Damian had the tendency to draw from Goenka's analogies and stories to defend his position considerably more than any of the old students in this research. Take, for example, the following excerpt in which Damian

---

[16] D. 'because I felt that the teaching had actually given me the tools to discriminate and look at the teaching um [p] so was not Wholly useless'.

accounts for Vipassana's appeal and the reasons why people, including him, tend not to reject elements of the teachings and/or the technique:

D. So there's Aspects of the teaching [in] the teachings that Goenka gives that, that certainly [p] um, you know and, and, and he gives a beautiful story . . . about [p] the patient who goes to the doctor and gets a prescription |and|

S. |yup, yup| and you have to go and [g]

D. yeah in the morning he sits in front of the picture of the doctor and yk this is exactly a perfect analogy of, of religions [ntch]

S. yeah

D. you know, they're not practicing anything, they just Blindly believing that this piece of paper is, the truth . . . so things like that, even if you end up hating Goenka and hating the teachings you still like stories and bits within it that are kind of, hard to, [p] they really get into you, they sink into your consciousness

S. mhm

D. and you, you even [p] without wanting to, you might repeat the story years later.
   [The next passage is taken from the follow-up interview.]

D. rationality is inherently something that you're kind of stuck with, um [p] language based, sort of [noise] is something you'll never escape but in terms of understanding truth, um if you could incorporate some elements of the experiential which is very much Vipassana kind of idea, um [ntch] you're quite likely to [vf>] gain greater level of knowledge I would suspect . . . I believed some elements of it are non-sectarian, are not religious, they are not biased, according to um [p] [ntch] just the, the historical, fancies of, of, of, yk, some god creator in that story, um [p] according to a certain cultural background they seemed to be [p] um [p] universal!

S. mhm

D. so, [p] that, [p] Apparent universality, um makes me feel like, Those elements are worth hanging on to.

These examples clearly illustrate that Damian continues to subscribe to the same rhetorical strategies that were recognised in the conversion career chapter as facilitators of tacit conversion. In simple terms, if one subtracts the sections in which Damian explicitly narrates his disengagement and/or heavily incorporates moral criticism in his story, it is rather difficult to differentiate his narrative from that of a committed old student. There are, however, subtle differences to be noted. For example, the narratives of old students (such as Elijah) tended to emphasise and embody self-transformation rather than ratify elements of the practice, as Damian has done in the excerpt. It should be noted, however, that while remnants of Vipassana's language are apparent in the narrative of all participants who have disaffiliated from this movement (except Luke), Damian's language represents the extreme case.

To explain disaffiliates' commitment to the movement's language, the significance of self-doubt in their narratives, the absence of serious intellectual disputes about the movement's beliefs and doctrine in their narratives, and the infrequency of deconversion as an exit pattern, I draw on Bromley's (1998a, 1998b) theory which links exit-role types and organisational structures. Bromley (1998b) argues that the way one leaves an NRM is largely determined by the level of tension between the organisation and the context of the host society. While these typologies are not deterministic, Bromley (1998b: 146) offers three ideal types of exit (I defectors, II whistle-blowers, and III apostates) based on three types of organisations (I allegiant, II contestant, and III subversive) that vary in the levels of legitimacy they receive from the mainstream social context. The logic behind Bromley's (1998b: 146) argument is that 'organizations in the low-tension positions are most likely to be able to control the exit process so as to prevent public dispute while organizations in a high-tension position are much less likely to be able to do so'.

Seen through the prism of Bromley's (1998b) typology, the typical exit pattern from Goenka's Vipassana organisation could be considered to align with that of *defectors,* who represent the individuals who leave allegiant organisations. Allegiant organisations are groups that have high levels of legitimacy and 'whose interests coincide to a high degree with other organizations in their environment' (1998b: 147). Mainstream churches, medical/therapeutic institutions, universities, and professional associations are examples of this category. Bromley (1998b: 147) posits that allegiance organisations sustain their legitimacy by 'aligning organizational structure with external organizations, engaging in service activities commensurate with trustee status, and assuming responsibility for appropriately resolving disputes'. As a result, disputes made against these organisations are usually contained and few become publicly aired. Finally, because the organisation is seen by both the outsiders and insiders to possesses legitimacy within its host environment, the 'burden of proof [is placed] squarely on claimsmakers' (1998b: 147). The defector, according to Bromley (1998b: 148), does not pose a major threat to his or her former group and tends to continue to respect and reaffirm the organisation's values and goals after exit—as has been the case for most disaffiliates. This is due to the fact that allegiance organisations yield control over the process of exit and the interpretive narrative, and, consequently, the defector may be left incapable of articulating grievances or validating claims without meaningful alternative resources (1998b: 147). In other words: 'The high level of legitimacy and moral rectitude attributed to allegiant organisations allows them to translate problems into organisational terms and categories that place primary responsibility for failure on the member' (1998b: 148)—the significance of self-doubt in disaffiliation narratives embodies this point.

In contrast, subversive organisations (in high-tension with the sociocultural environment) are those that 'posit an alternative version of social order' to the status quo. The fundamental difference between subversive organisations and other types (allegiant and contested) is that in face of disputes, there are numerous external agencies and oppositional groups, such as anti-cult movements, which come to the support of the exiting member, and therefore the organisation has limited capacity to control the exit process and exit narrative (Bromley, 1998b: 153). The apostate exit role is born out of this polarised situation, where an exiting member undertakes a total change in positionality in moving from the NRM to an anti-cult movement. Since anti-cult movements justify their existence by subscribing to the brainwashing ideology, the apostates' exit narratives are typically formulated as 'captivity narratives' (1998b: 155). Finally, apostates tend to construct a professional career from their experience, for instance, by providing counselling and even seeking credentials as therapists 'with a specialization in what they define as cult-precipitated disorder' (Hassan, 1988, cited in Bromley, 1998b: 156).

The contestant organisations are situated in-between the abovementioned poles. With moderate levels of tension, these organisations pursue their defined 'self-interest and therefore inhabit an environment populated with both allies and opponents'—hence they are constantly involved in patterns of dispute. According to Bromley (1998b: 150) examples of this category include profit-making economic organisations and political lobbying groups, which typically follow the cultural mottos of 'freedom' and 'success'. Moreover, matters of dispute in contestant organisations are usually resolved through the involvement of third-party agencies (regulatory agencies) that bring their own agenda and tend to translate disputes into their own categories. Noting that whistle-blowing in the context of religious organisation is relatively uncommon, Bromley points out that whistle-blowers are ex-members who tend to produce testimonies about their experience, which are in turn used against the organisation. Moreover, Bromley (1998b: 151–152) adds that whistle-blowers tend to briefly join networks of individuals who are critical of the group, in which case their narrative often depicts the whistle-blower as 'motivated by personal conscience', as occupying the moral high ground, and their involvement with the organisation as a 'result of ignorance, deception, or pressure'. Finally, in the case of religious organisations, the regulatory agencies tend to impose a 'standard of theological truth' and therefore attract whistle-blowers who base their dispute on the rejection of theological beliefs or practices associated with the NRM (1998b: 152). I argue in the next chapter that Luke's exit role can be labelled as that of a whistle-blower.

Even though Bromley (1998a; 1998b) approaches religious exit from a strictly sociological perspective, the findings of this research nevertheless support his tripartite typology. I posit that Bromley's model is applicable to the linguistic analysis undertaken in this research; it can be extended to account for the organisation's ideologies and the linguistic strategies they use to create and defend their low-tension niche within an increasingly secularised environment. For instance, various elements of the movement's teachings (at least as it is presented to the outside world) and its discourse—including its emphasis on experience; claims of rationality, universality, and instrumentality; its dispute of religious labels; and emphasis on individual authority, autonomy, self-development; and the like—not only align with the subcultures these individuals belong to (the human potential movement and the holistic health movement) but also with New Zealand's dominant cultural dispositions.

Moreover, regardless of the present-day pro-social discourse surrounding meditational practices and the movement's fast-and-loose associations with Buddhism, which essentially allows it to relish the positive image of the tradition (peacefulness, direct link to the Buddha, etc.) and discard its other connotations, Dhamma Medini in New Zealand has arguably enjoyed a certain degree of legitimacy in its host culture from its early years of establishment. According to Dhamma Medini's teacher, this particular centre in New Zealand was officially registered as an 'educational institute' at the local council and hence received no opposition even from their predominately 'Christian neighbours'. Additionally, over the years, the organisation has expanded its services to other secular sectors, for instance, by offering Vipassana courses for large populations of inmates in prisons in 1999 and 2000. More importantly, unlike others religious organisations (such as the Mormon Church, which embodies Bromley's contestant type, or early generations of ISCKON and The Family, which fell under Bromley's subversive groups), Goenka's organisation has not been the target of any noteworthy scandals or lawsuits, which helps preserve its respectable image globally. Furthermore, the movement arguably benefits from a low-tension relation with other religious organisations by the virtue of its proselytisation tactics— word of mouth, as opposed to aggressive strategies. This makes the centre accessible to specific demographics/subcultures and effectively covert to the more culturally/religiously conservative sectors of the population.

Not surprisingly, Goenka's organisation exerts considerable control over disputes and has various interpersonal guidelines and strategies to prevent the spread of controversial ideas among members. For instance, potential claim-makers are placed on deferral lists (the vast majority of disaffiliates were refused participation at one point or another). Behaviour that may lead to the spread of disputes is said to cause 'bad karma', and, according to one participant, the organisation has supplemented a position of a social worker, presumably a psychoanalyst, in an attempt to attend to post-participation psychosomatic episodes. Likewise, the organisation administrates the exit narrative and enforces emic categories that effectively places the failure on the member[17]—hence the significance of self-doubt. As the Dhamma Medini's teacher has it: 'If they stop, it's not the technique that's the problem, it's the person'. Together, these structural features (linguistic and organisational) could be said to constrain the process of exit and its narrative in intricate ways.

Concluding Summary

As the analyses of disaffiliation narratives demonstrate, in the vast majority of instances, disaffiliation did not result in total rejection of the movement's doctrines (the cognitive dimension of exit), nor did it result in complete migration outside of its universe of discourse. Instead, I illustrated that participants reoriented towards explanations and discourses that shared boundaries with the movement's universe of discourse. The disaffiliation trajectories can be figuratively understood as various positions participants take along the traditionalist-postmodernist spectrum: (1) movement towards a traditional

---

[17] Indeed, a critical reflection on the exchanged letters between Damian and the movement's authorities demonstrates this characteristic. For instance, without directly addressing the issues that Damian raised in his letters, their responses consistently centred on the idea that Damian had lost direction, lost touch with the essence of the organisation's mission, and with what it means to be a 'Vipassana meditator'.

Theravada discourse with strict emphasis on morality and the conception of enlightenment as a transcendental reality, and (2) and movement towards the postmodern reconfiguration of enlightenment that places an emphasis on the integration of experience in daily life and relatively relaxed approaches to morality. The next chapter presents a disaffiliation pattern that, in sharp contrast to the abovementioned trajectories, leaps outside the movement's language—deconversion.

6

Deconversion

Breathing New Self into Not-Self

This chapter frames deconversion as the third and final disaffiliation trajectory from Goenka's Vipassana movement. My understanding of deconversion mirrors the conceptualisation of conversion I have carried throughout this book: I consider deconversion as a process of self-transformation that involves a flight from the movement's universe of discourse and its attendant grammar.

Taking Luke's story as an example of a deconversion narrative, the objective of this chapter is to assess the ways in which Luke reconstructs a sense of self, remote from Goenka's universe of discourse. Hence, in addition to exploring the thematic features of his disengagement story, such as cognitive dissonance with the concept of not-self, I examine the structure of his narrative to demonstrate how self-transformation is achieved through narration.

I use the term 'authenticity talk' to refer to a *style* of discourse that functions both as (1) a resource for self-reconstruction post-exit, and (2) a rhetoric that the narrator appropriated to develop a sense of autonomy, empowerment, and self-validation to authorise, legitimise, and rationalise his rejection of a tradition and its system of meaning. I argue that disengagement literature (Coates, 2013; Fazzino, 2014; Hornbeck, 2011) has often misinterpreted authenticity talk to represent actual motives behind exit.

To contextualise these points, I begin this chapter by introducing Luke and by reflecting on the parallels between his narrative and the existing deconversion literature. I subsequently narrow my analytical lens (resume a structural analysis style) and demonstrate the painful process associated with leaving a universe of discourse behind. Next, I introduce the concept of authenticity talk, juxtaposed against other readings of authenticity in the context of exit literature. Consequently, I dedicate some space to the exploration of an example of such literature in detail. Finally, I decontextualise authenticity by reflecting on its historical development. This will be instrumental for gaining the appropriate distance from an intrinsic understanding

Drifting Through Samsara. Masoumeh Rahmani, Oxford University Press. © Oxford University Press 2022.
DOI: 10.1093/oso/9780197579961.003.0007

of the concept as it is understood in everyday culture, paving the grounds for the final examination of Luke's narrative and a better grasp of what he achieved through authenticity talk.

Selected Case Study: Luke

Luke is an ex-Vipassana practitioner in his forties. He struck me as an intellectual, self-reflexive, and a socially engaged activist with a deep fascination with philosophy. 'What is a human being, and what is it to be an I' were utterances that frequently sprang out during our one-hour conversation on 6 August 2015. From my perspective, these expressions were by no means happenstance; rather, they symbolised Luke's concerns, values, and the image he desired to project during the interview.

Luke had the richest résumé in course attendance amongst the participants in this research (of course, except for the two Vipassana teachers). According to his account, Luke had participated in over twenty standard Vipassana courses, served at an equal number, and attended (and served at) a number of longer courses including a thirty-day course, which are only available to select, serious old students who meet a specific set of requirements.[1] These numbers were especially striking, considering that Luke's involvement with this movement did not exceed a period of six years. Needless to say, the gulf between the breadth of our (Luke and my) lived experiences and insider knowledge seem to have crippled our conversation at times—particularly since advanced course materials are not available for examination to outsiders or even to non-advanced old students.

The most salient features of Luke's narrative were that he did not present a self constructed within the movement's universe of discourse, nor did any of the movement's rhetorical strategies outlined in chapter 1 (e.g. the rhetoric of experience, universality, etc.) appear in his language. In fact, Luke made a noticeable attempt to remove himself from the movement's system of meaning and language. In contrast to the narratives of all other participants in this book, Luke's case study represents a single story that leaps outside Vipassana's universe of discourse and lands within a more secular/humanist one. This

---

[1] According to the movement's website, 'thirty-day Courses are open only to serious Old Students committed to this technique who have completed a minimum of six, ten-day courses (one since their first twenty-day course), one twenty-day course, one Satipatthana Sutta course, and have been practicing regularly for at least two years' (Pandhana Dhamma, 2017).

important facet of Luke's language (amongst other points that I will expand on shortly) propelled my conceptualisation of his account as a deconversion narrative. Thus, I extended Gooren's original model to include deconversion as an additional level of religious inactivity (see figure 6.1).

These characteristics in Luke's language effectively brought the process of data collection to a point of saturation—for the purpose of my research was to outline the possible exit trajectories from the Vipassana movement. To this end, this chapter offers the first detailed linguistic examination of deconversion from the Buddhist worldview; how a sense of self emerges from the ashes of not-self. In this regard, the research of Tim Mapel (2007) on 'The Adjustment of Ex-Buddhist Monks to Life After the Monastery' is the closest approximation in addressing exit. However, as the title suggests, Mapel's (2007) work is primarily focused on the process of adjustment post-exit (such as employment, building new relationships, developing in-timacy, etc.), and he does not explore, nor frame, his interviews in terms of deconversion narratives. In fact, as an ex-monk himself, Mapel does not make any reference to whether he or any of the five Western ex-monks in his study had deconverted.

Another noteworthy characteristic of Luke's communicative style was his *critical* approach to the movement he was once affiliated with. This was the common ground upon which Luke and I constructed a relationship during

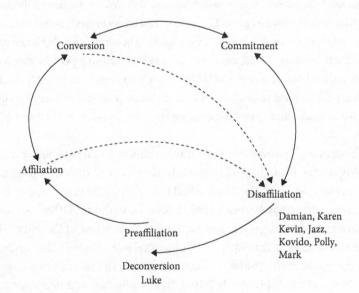

Figure 6.1 Expanding Gooren's model to include deconversion

the interview. Whereas my positionality was implicitly couched in my role as a researcher with an interest in why people leave the movement, Luke demonstrated his position by laying various cues indicating an ex-member identity (Ebaugh, 1988). For example, Luke rapidly criticised the movement's publications on both intellectual and ethical grounds within the first few minutes of the interview (see the passage after this paragraph). This characteristic also distinguished Luke's narrative from all other participants, including Damian who, despite colouring his disaffiliation narrative with various shades of moral criticism, did not reject the technique or its underpinning teachings on intellectual grounds. Moreover, Luke's comments served to explicitly transmit the image of an assertive sceptic and implicitly outlined the moral framework within which he constituted a sense of self and against which he authorised his actions. This background understanding is crucial for contextualising the arguments presented in this section:

L. I did a bit of qualitative research into you know the actual literature published by Goenka or his group, you know to find um to back up my, you know my, my statements about what he does actually teach . . . you know how were these slowly revealed to the, to the people and so on [in] um [ex] and you know some pretty Bizarre, noxious stuff as

5   well . . . so just you know verbal diarrhoea flooded out of these Vipassana research institute . . . but when you actually have a read of it, it's just, as I said Noxious, you know like, um karma theory, people are getting what they deserve, innocent children, well you know that's what they get for [l] you know past crimes in previous lives so on and all that crap you know so um [p] and the worshiping of bones you know in his new pagoda

10   built in the country . . . with donated money funded by the tax payer, to some extent, in a country, to house some bones alleged to belong to some guy who probably didn't exist twenty-five hundred years ago . . . in a country where people are, not only starving but being forcefully dispossessed and murdered by police and so on and all that crap!

Luke's narrative involved all three dimensions of disengagement proposed by Wright and Ebaugh (1993), namely disaffection, disillusionment, and formal disaffiliation; it also featured all four characteristics of deconversion narratives outlined by Barbour (1994). John D. Barbour's (1994) *Versions of Deconversion: Autobiography and the Loss of Faith* is one of the most widely referenced studies on this topic. This influential work has been the conceptual cornerstone for many studies of deconversion in the recent years (Fazzino, 2014; Streib et al., 2011; Streib, 2014). By broadly defining deconversion as a 'loss of faith', Barbour examines a variety of autobiographies ranging from

Augustine, John Bunyan, and John Henry Newman—whose narratives describe a loss of faith, only to be followed by conversion to what their authors perceived to be an 'authentic' Christianity—to a fascinating analysis of Jean-Paul Sartre's *The Word*, in which Sartre used deconversion as a metaphor to interpret personal transformation. This fascinating book also features contemporary accounts of NRM and cult deconversion. Exploring this vast array of narratives, Barbour concluded that deconversion is the 'mirror' image of conversion. He arrived at this insight by examining the overall structure of these narratives and the ways religious language and representations of certain themes, such as a central crisis and emotional upheavals, are broadly shared in both genres. Therefore, one of the strengths of Barbour's book is that he studied deconversion in the light of conversion.

More relevantly, Barbour abstracted four generalisable themes from his close reading of various deconversion autobiographies, concluding that at least three of the following four characteristics can be found in a deconversion narrative. These included (1) 'doubt or denial of the truth of a system of belief', (2) 'moral criticism of not only particular actions or practices but an entire way of life', (3) 'emotional upheaval, especially such painful feelings as grief, guilt, loneliness, and despair', and (4) 'the rejection of the community to which he or she belonged' (Barbour, 1994: 2). The first two characteristics are said to frame the causal factors of the narrative, while the latter pair capture how deconverts frame their lived experiences (Harrold, 2006).

As exemplified in the previous excerpt, Luke's utilisation of moral criticism moved beyond the theme of deception and injustice (as we encountered through the case study of Damian in chapter 4); rather, Luke also drew on a broader humanistic discourse, criticising not only the issues that affected him but also those that he deemed problematic for and harmful to the larger society. In effect, this style of discourse enabled him to deliver his story with more immediacy. Along the same lines, Luke confidently repudiated the technique on grounds of theory and practice (intellectual doubt) using striking narrative asides such as his encounters with other meditators who underwent 'psychotic' episodes after a retreat and stories about a fellow old student who died by suicide. Luke presented these asides in parallel to his experience and suffering:

15 L. I just became suicidal within the first year of practice . . . and bizarrely I thought that going deeper into the practice was my solution to the problem . . . that at least in a Vipassana centre I wouldn't want to spoil the environment by hanging myself there.

Accordingly, Luke constructed a narrative that centralised on crisis and trauma, which he linked to the loss of a stable sense of self resulting from the practice of Vipassana meditation:

L. I guess the psyche is in someway, the practice is in someway, fractures, what seems to be the psyche is, the goal is to fracture the psyche in some particular way and um uproot it, um but there's no, no particular place to put it if you like, [g] once
20   it's been uprooted um I don't know ... I could Never, Ever, [p] place, Place it, or if I did, that that [p] um [p] If [p] if I did, that never lasted for a long time ... the psyche, Where am I in all this if you like
S. yeah yeah
L. notions of you don't exist, you know what I mean and um, oh there's no I, [p] well
25   practically speaking there is an I, if you know what I mean [l] practically speaking I do exist, and um, Really as well, I mean [p] you know we could all say the universe is all gonna end in the future anyway so it all doesn't matter but Practically speaking now, it, it concerns me and my life concerns me
S. mhm
30 L. So, so I won't go along with this notion of, 'oh there's no I'. because, you know who's, who's suggesting it there's no I.
S. yeah
L. it's either goenka or me suggesting that there's no I, So [p] [ex] it's sort of like the god argument, who made god or whatever, so ok who suggested there's no I, well
35   I suggested there's no I, do you follow my?
S. Yeah, yeah, yeah, yeah, yeah
L. so there's always gonna be an observer, and, and then you talk to other meditators and they say, 'well it's the sensations which experiences it' ok well wait a minute if that's the case, [p] [ex] if we're allowing that, what about uncontrolled sensations
40 S. mhm
L. sensations just go, are gonna go and do their own thing does that mean sort of like, being thrown into a pool and struggling for breath if you like you know so [p] um so having, so this whole process having started, inside, outside and Never being able to get a clear answer from them, the first thing that I decided for myself was, with this
45   process having started, you know Manoeuvring the psyche around in a, sort of like um, [p] a traumatic kind of process um, switching from one to the other if you like, um, I figured well the last thing I want is trying to conform to some other person's notion of what's correct
S. mhm

50　L. whether, whoever that might be

　　S. yeah

　　L. that could be anybody, yeah and so I figured you know that's not exactly living a
　　　　human being's life, to just be, trying to conform into somebody else's notion of what
　　　　is right or wrong, or Correct, not even right or wrong just correct and incorrect [l]

In essence, Luke was depicting a state of cognitive dissonance, which he perceived was generated from a disjunction between theory and experience (e.g.
'the notion of you don't exist' vs. 'practically speaking, I do exist'); a disturbance to his sense of self, leading to alienation or a point where one no longer
identified with the body, emotions, sensations, and the mind (e.g. the psych
is fractured and 'uprooted' with 'no particular place to put it'—lines 17–20).
His story emphasised a state of severe instability in which the self is torn between worlds or two understandings of the self: on one end, the self of the
conversional reality; on the other end, the self or the not-self of Buddhist ultimate reality (e.g. 'Manoeuvring the psyche around . . . ' 'switching from one
to the other'—lines 45–46). These two discourses of self coexist in Buddhist
philosophy and, according to Collins (1994), they should not be seen as two
separate ontological states, rather as two approaches or two viewpoints to
the same reality. The first reality belongs to the experience of a layman in his
everyday life; the other (ultimate reality) is revealed in the realm of meditation to the monk. In the ultimate reality, there is no observer of sensations or
thinker of thoughts; in the conversional reality, one assumes individuality
and carries a sense of continuity to which the notion of 'I' is attached (Pagis,
2008: 85). Thus, while the embodied experience and realisation of not-self is
essential to achieving the Buddhist enlightenment, likewise, the layman requires a sense of a stable self to function in conventional reality.

　In conjunction with this Buddhist view, the classic sociological perspective
(of Mead and Cooley) considers a stable sense of self essential for a sane and
healthy life. Although both discourses agree on the premise that the self—
which is the concept given to the individual's identification with his/her body
and thought—is constantly changing, the latter perspective suggests that
the process of self-interpretation and the human tendency to objectify the
self as a whole (on a past-future continuum) is essential for the production
of self-consistency and a sense of stability (Callero, 2003). On the contrary,
by forcing one to concentrate on immediate physical sensations, the goal of
Vipassana meditation is to slowly dismantle the stabilising mechanisms of

selfhood by reducing one's 'tendency to objectify the self as a whole, to connect it to the past or to the future or to turn it into an inter-subjective fact' (Pagis, 2008: 250).

On a thematic level, Luke's critique of the concept of not-self served him an anchor point to construct a rationale for his deconversion narrative. In more general terms, Luke frames his disengagement as a response to the unsettling experience of this detached perspective and its impracticality for living in conventional reality. In this sense, Luke's narrative thematically overlaps with the story of Andrew and Leslie (chapter 3), who also framed their disengagement stories as a resolution to unpleasant meditative experiences. Yet, while Andrew and Leslie resorted to other explanations (such as popular psychology: introversion vs. extroversion) to render the technique unsuitable for their personality type and immediate needs, in contrast, Luke attempted to debunk the theoretical underpinning of the technique all together. This articulation by Luke is likely born out of two decades of retrospective meaning making and consequential to his purposeful engagement with both the insider and outsider literature on this topic.[2]

On a linguistic level, however, Luke rejected the concept of not-self by posing an epistemological question ('who's suggesting there is no I?'). Luke sought to dismiss the concept of not-self—and by extension, Goenka—by proving the ontological existence of the self. To achieve this, Luke objectified the 'self' (e.g. 'what seems to be the psyche'), subjected it to rational inquiry (e.g. 'there is an I, and what does it do?'[3]), and even sought to metaphorically ascribe locality to it (e.g. 'no particular place to put it'—line 19). Note, Luke's choice of terminology here (i.e. 'psyche') is not coincidental; rather it reflects his attempt to release himself from Goenka's language. As I mentioned in chapter 2, Goenka favours the term 'ego' when referring to the concept of the self. On an implicit level, Luke rejected not-self and reinforced the reality of self by performing the role of the Cartesian cogito (e.g. 'who's suggesting there's no I . . . '—lines 31–33). Hence, it could be argued that similar to conversion narratives, Luke's deconversion narrative becomes the site of self-transformation; that the narrator re-enacts or performs the alleged conflict leading to his deconversion (trauma associated with not-self) in order to 'act out his delivery from that conflict' (Stromberg, 1993: 126). My aim in the

---

[2] Such as the work of Paul Fleischman that Luke referenced on two separate occasions during our conversation.

[3] Elsewhere in the interview Luke adds, 'I don't think that . . . it's acceptable to just, to just say "oh there's no I" for Goenka to say "oh there's no I." um there is an I, and what does it do?'

next section is to illustrate how Luke reconstructed a sense of self by progressively evaluating his past and taking an active position against the concept of not-self in his narrative.

Leaving a Universe of Discourse Behind

As mentioned at the outset of this chapter, language drives my understanding of conversion and deconversion. Throughout this book, I have examined the participants' narratives by paying attention to both the content and the subtleties of their language. I have followed Snow and Machalek's (1983, 1984) conception of conversion as a process of migration to a new universe of discourse. The corollary of this view necessitates a conceptualisation of deconversion as a process of self-transformation that involves a flight *from* Vipassana's universe of discourse.[4] This view is consistent with the perspective of many scholars in this field who believe 'conversion and deconversion are two sides of the same coin' (Gooren, 2010: 10); they both involve 'the same process of personal metamorphosis, stressing either the rejected past of the old self or the present convictions of the reborn self' (Barbour, 1994: 3). However, while the two processes can be arguably identical,[5] their narratives are not. This is because, unlike converts, deconverts are not provided with predetermined language, scripts, or guidelines to structure stories and reconstruct a sense of self (Beckford, 1985; Davidman and Greil, 2007).

This assumption that deconverts are not always equipped with a set of prescribed language may not necessarily apply to individuals who exit via consultation with anti-cult movements or 'exit counsellors', for research has shown

---

[4] My understanding of deconversion mirrors the conceptualisation of conversion I have carried throughout this book; it is hinged primarily on the movement across universes of discourse and not simply the movement across social and/or private and religious fields. This is the crucial point that separates my understanding of deconversion from other scholars such as Heinz Streib and his colleagues (2011: 28, Streib, 2014: 271,) who broadly perceive deconversion as 'migration in the religious field' including 'disaffiliation without re-affiliation'. Hence, even though Luke and Damian had both disaffiliated roughly two decades ago, only Luke's narrative was categorised as a deconversion narrative simply because Damian (and other participants) continued to construct, interpret, and represent an image of themselves within the movement's language despite physically departing from the movement and orienting towards a privatised/personal religious field.

[5] Little empirical research has examined the parallels between conversion and deconversion, except to extend the 'new paradigm(s)' of the former onto the latter. For example, Streib (2014) suggests that similar to converts, deconverts should be seen as active agents. Others have suggested that both processes may occur suddenly or gradually. For instance, Ralph Hood and Zhuo Chen (2013) have argued that gradual deconversion (particularly, to atheism) has positive correlations with education and is therefore a gradual cognitive process, whereas sudden deconversion can be associated with emotional factors.

that such narratives are typically shaped within a 'hostage-rescue' (Bromley 1998b: 98; Wright, 2014: 722) or 'brainwashing' discourse, which can be seen as a resource for self-reconstruction post-exit (Coates, 2012). It may also not apply to individuals whose deconversion involved a strong engagement with anti-religious discourse, for instance, the works of Christopher Hitchens, Sam Harris, Daniel Dennet, and Richard Dawkins. In this regard, Fazzino's (2014: 262) research offers a perfect example of former Evangelical Christians, most of whom had considered the works of the abovementioned authors influential to their deconversion process and typically portrayed their exit as a 'liberating experience that evoked feelings of freedom, relief, and happiness'. However, although Fazzino (2014: 260) makes a point of suggesting that her participants' deconversion can be framed as a 'secular conversion', she does not entertain the possibility that her participants' language (e.g. liberating) may have been shaped by the discourse of the books they strongly had referenced in their deconversion narratives. More importantly, most of these studies vouch that their participants—whether influenced by an anti-cult or anti-religious discourse—were ultimately successful in achieving a sense of 'ontological security' (Fazzino, 2014) and reconstructing a sense of self (Coates, 2012) post-exit.

Interestingly, the *content* of Luke's narrative lacked both the optimistic quality of Fazzino's (2014) secular converts and the *explicit* claim that the process of deconversion had brought about a stable sense of self. Note, the following passage developed from a question in which I asked Luke to provide a more descriptive account of his experience:

55　L. oh well if I may say, the, the whole process goes on. it doesn't stop
　　S. yeah
　　L. you know once you start it, it, you know [ex] um in [p] in some ways I know, you
　　　　know it's hard to pick an analogy just to, Just to try and explain it to people, like you
　　　　know a person who doesn't know anything about <u>cars, opening the bonnet and</u>
60　　<u>getting out a hammer on Goenka's advice and making a deep surgical operation</u>
　　　　<u>on the, on the motor</u> you know [hah]
　　S. mhm
　　L. [l] it's not like you can then just say 'oh well that was <u>bad advice,</u> I'm not gonna do
　　　　that anymore' you, you, you try to carry on but there's all this, all this damage
65　　[has] been done if you like
　　S. yeah
　　L. all this interference been had

S. yeah

L. and, and I think if somebody says 'oh you just leave it and move on' well then what
70   were you doing when you were trying to practice? were you not trying to practice it seriously or What? if you try to practice seriously, you're doing something
seriously to Change yourself in some particular way

S. mhm

L. yeah so, um so it, it certainly puts a spanner in the works, for me it was definitely
75   important to get the silly voice of Mr. Goenka out of my head. and not to take any
notice, notice of it Whatsoever!

S. yeah

L. not to make excuses and say 'oh well this does fit into the technique, if you do, if
you just', you can always say 'oh I See! this is what the technique really is'

80 S. aha yeah

L. well no! because [l] if the, if the guy, [p] if the guy can't tell the difference, can't tell
the, [p] [ex] [p] um the, fact that bones don't give off, um vibrations [p] um, [p]
that, that influence the world, I mean if you, if you got somebody talking like that,
you can't, <u>I find it impossible to give that person importance in giving advice</u>, a
85   complete stranger with no responsibility, on his,

S. mhm

L. on sort of the advice that he gives to other people, especially myself!

S. yeah

L. um so, so as I say, but yeah that frame of reference, that feel, <u>that lived experience, that</u>
90   <u>does go on</u>! but <u>where, where, where does, what is</u> the, where does it end up if you've
just been like um stuffing around with your brain, in these Vipassana courses.

S. mhm

L. how do you Stop, stuffing around with your brain? [l] you know what I mean,
where is the right place to land so to speak, what's, what's a correct frame of refer-
95   ence after Vipassana

S. mhm Also

L. um sorry

S. sorry go on

L. you're alright, I was gonna say yeah for me, I, [p] I go through this process of, of,
100   exploring for myself, but <u>the last thing I want to be doing, what I want, is to ask</u>
<u>somebody else to tell me what's right or wrong and</u> so,

S. mhm

L. I'm happy to find that for myself to explore My own to go on my own journey of
life and um but, but I don't want to carry around any baggage from [p] from a
105   stranger [l] if you know what I mean.

Even though the content of this excerpt is infused with a sense of ambiguity, the tone and the structure of the narrative did not. In my view, Luke seemed rather precise in framing what he conceived as a crisis (i.e. inability to find a stable sense of self) and his proposed solution(s) for it: (1) a firm decision to break away from Goenka's language (lines 75–76), (2) retrieving a sense of agency by stripping away Goenka's reliability (lines 81–87), and (3) reconstructing a sense of self by operationalising his value of autonomous seekership through authenticity talk (lines 99–105). In short, whereas the vast majority of disengagers continued to construct and interpret selves within the movement's language,[6] Luke made a conscious attempt to remove himself from the movement's language and reasoning, and, in fact, he considered this break essential to the process of becoming a *former* Vipassana meditator.

In the passage, Luke's effort to achieve agency can be seen in the way he depicted his deconversion as a perpetual battle in which he wrestled with Goenka's authoritative voice. On one side of the ring, Luke portrayed himself as a naive and devout adherent (lines 59–67), permanently marked by the trust he had laid in the hands of his teacher; on the other, the ubiquitous voice of Goenka, the elimination of which Luke considered essential to his revival: 'I could go through the discourses word-by-word, cough-by-cough by Goenka . . . I could indicate those kinds of things um [p] [ex] and I don't, I don't Allow myself to go, to, to replay those voices, that voice or anything like that in my brain'.

In theory, leaving a universe of discourse may seem like an easy task; in practice, this may not be the case. A practical example of this is echoed in Luke's choice of analogy in portraying the challenges associated with reconstructing a stable sense of self post-exit (i.e. 'a surgical operation on the motor'—lines 60–61). As mentioned in previous chapters, one of Goenka's (1997: 5) most memorable expressions involves depicting Vipassana meditation as 'a deep surgical operation on the mind'. In the excerpt, Luke took the same analogy and amended it to serve his own purposes: rendering the technique damaging, and thus justifying his rejection of Goenka's tradition. Although the adaptation of this analogy—from mind to motor—enabled

---

[6] E.g. even Andrew, who had disengaged due to difficult meditative experiences, continued to interpret himself through Vipassana's meaning system. Utterances such as 'I guess when I say I'm strongly physical, I'm probably saying, I'm strongly attached to that physical experience' (chapter 3) clearly encapsulates this point.

Luke to skilfully depict his experience in ways that were both tangible and striking for the listener (myself), nonetheless, it reflected the deep imprints that the movement's language had left behind. This observation does not disqualify Luke's story as a deconversion narrative; it is a mistake to assume deconversion involves a *total* transformation of character, language, and ways of thinking. In fact, Barbour's analysis (1994: 207) also shows that many Christian deconverts continued to use biblical metaphors in their autobiographies. Instead, this observation demonstrates that deconversion or the process of leaving a universe of discourse is not something that can be achieved in the blink of an eye; rather, it is a painful process that requires practice and perseverance as the individual embarks on an ambiguous or unknown ideology (Berger, 2015; Fazzino, 2014; Harrold, 2006).

Deconversion in this light is more akin to a 'learning exercise' (Frankenthaler, 2015: 11), in which the individual learns to 'unlearn' the movement's language, along with its 'idiomatic ways of speaking, thinking, and acting' (Davidman and Greil, 2007: 202). Indeed, Luke's narrative is indicative of an observable movement outside this universe of discourse, which in his case involves recognising the movement's language (i.e. Goenka's voice, terminologies, analogies, and doctrines), developing a critical position against it by engaging in a 'dialogical' practice (Frankenthaler, 2015) through which he attempted to undermine Goenka's voice. Utterances such as 'I won't go along with this notion of, "oh there's no I"' (lines 30–31) clearly encapsulates this point. This is precisely why the process of Luke's disengagement involved a critical engagement with the movement's publication—a typical phase of the deconversion process that has been described as 'paradigmatic work' (Fazzino, 2014: 258).

Further to this end, Luke's narrative featured a constant dialogue through which he gained, developed, and refined *his own* authoritative voice to override Goenka's—a combat which, at times, Luke strived to make convincing by linguistically distancing himself from Goenka, by addressing him formally (i.e. Mr. Goenka—line 75), and eventually referring to him as a 'complete stranger' (line 84). Moreover, the manner in which Luke weaved intellectual criticism into his narrative can also be seen as an attempt to disrobe Goenka of intellectual credibility. For instance, in lines 81–83 Luke made an antagonistic reference to the installation of the Buddha's relics in the (largest dome of the) Global Vipassana Pagoda to critique Goenka's claim that the relics can facilitate the meditator's 'progress'—presumably towards enlightenment—due to the 'vibrations' they scatter in the atmosphere.[7] While such statements can be seen as thematic representations of intellectual doubt, I suggest, relying on a structural reading of the narrative (i.e. the sequential pattern at which his criticisms emerge), that in addition to cementing an identity of a rational ex-member, Luke drew on these rhetorical strategies to either establish his authoritative voice over Goenka's or when he lacked the verbal fluency to communicate (to me) more abstract ideas, including ontological uncertainties and existential anxieties.

Finally, despite all these linguistic attempts, Luke resorted, once again, to present a self primarily anchored in the value of autonomy. To underscore his new self-concept, Luke first depicted and problematised his previous conviction as a novice follower that takes Goenka's advice (lines 59–61). He subsequently created parallels to this theme to lend structural coherence to the narrative (e.g. 'that was bad advice'—line 63; 'impossible to give that person importance in giving advice'—lines 84–85). This plot culminated in a series of statements that indicated Luke's proposed resolution to this conflict:[8] 'the last thing I want to be doing . . . is to ask somebody else to tell me what's right or wrong' (lines 100–101). Here, by emphasising the importance of autonomous seekership in his narrative, Luke simultaneously made his values explicit and conveyed facets of his self-concept as an autonomous agent who is happy to find out the meaning of life on his own. Recall how the same structural pattern occurred in the previous excerpt (e.g. 'the last thing I want is to conform to some other person's notion of what's correct . . . I figured that's not exactly living a human being's life'—lines 47–54).

In other words, Luke's (current) self-concept is constructed and composed through a series of statements that essentially hinged on contemporary understandings of the concept of authenticity: 'being true to oneself', 'going on one's own journey', 'not conforming to others' ideas/advice/guidelines on how to live one's life'. This kind of rhetoric in disengagement narrative is precisely the style of discourse I identified as 'authenticity talk'. I argue that in the context of Luke's deconversion narrative, authenticity talk served him in

[7] In a statement addressed to serious students in 1997, Goenka notes, 'I know from my own experience and the experience of others that if one meditates with the relics of the Buddha, which have such strong vibrations, one progresses more easily'.

[8] By categorising the final paragraph (lines 99–105) of Luke's passage as 'resolution', I am following Labov (1972, cited in Riessman, 2002: 231) who suggests a fully formed narrative includes six properties: 'an abstract (summary of the substance of the narrative), orientation (time, place, situation, participants), complicating action (sequence of events), evaluation (significance and meaning of the action, attitude of the narrator), resolution (what finally happened), and coda (returns the perspective to the present) '.

resuming *his own authoritative voice*, legitimising his exit, and enabling him to construct a self remote from the movement's language.

Authenticity vs. Authenticity Talk

Authenticity is a relatively new construct deeply embedded in Western cultures. As an ideal, this concept is pervasive across the majority of the narratives in this study and particularly stronger among new students and pragmatic leavers: Katrin: 'Being who I truly am'; Michael: 'following my own inner guidance system'; Andrew: 'run it through your own filters, what works for you, you know, find your truth and blah blah'. In a broad sense, authenticity is what is 'original, real, and pure' (Lindholm, 2008: 2). Yet it becomes far more complex once attributed to human beings. As these examples suggest, the concept is amalgamated with questions of identity, ethics, and autonomy. In this sense, an authentic person is one who acts in accordance with his/her desires, ideals, or beliefs that are not only his/hers, but also express who he/she really is (Varga and Guignon, 2016).

Moreover, as implied in the introductory chapter, the concept of authenticity commonly appeared in participants' descriptions of an ideal form of religiosity (i.e. spirituality; see figure I.4). When used in this context, participants perceived Vipassana meditation as a practice that enabled them to access their true authentic selves (e.g. 'I think doing the inner work is critical, it's inner transformation, otherwise all actions are unauthentic'). Against this backdrop, my aim here is to explore authenticity not as a desired ideal, but rather as a rhetorical device—hence, the term 'authenticity talk'—that serves several purposes, including substantiating and legitimising disengagement and deconversion.

Consider, for example, the following excerpt from my interview with Holger, who engaged in authenticity talk as the means to rationalise and legitimise why he had stopped his private practice of meditation. It is important to note that prior to this interview segment (and in response to my question about why he stopped his regular practice), Holger provided a lengthy narrative which related his disengagement to the fact that his meditation space had been highjacked by a stray cat and her five kittens. In narrating this story, Holger adopted a self-deprecating tone (e.g. 'it sounds like a poor excuse, but . . . ') and subsequently added another dimension to this story, which involved the realisation that the pressure he had put on

himself to meditate was actually causing him 'stress'. From this point onwards, Holger argued:

H. <u>I try to understand</u> that if I push, if I put pressure on myself [p] then I'm not acting, [p]
   [v: sentence uttered with ambiguity and almost as a question] out of my own originality? <u>that's what I believe</u>. if you're forced to do something because you think you
   have to, you're doing it for the wrong purpose. Things have to come, you know, things

110   have to come freely [p] to actually [p] be [one] hundred per cent. it's like a Vipassana
   course if somebody says to you, 'you have to do a Vipassana course and sit there for
   ten days' and then you weren't being you, it will not happen. <u>And that's what I believe</u>.

A thematic reading of this passage suggests that Holger draws upon the concept of authenticity in an attempt to *free* himself from the cultural construct
that propels the idea that meditation is beneficial for one's well-being (lines
106–109), for example, by emphasising that the choice to meditate has to be
made by the individual (e.g. come freely) and not guided by external influences. Note, however, how authenticity—or originality to be precise—is first
presented as an ideal ('I try to understand . . . '—line 106) and subsequently
affirmed and reaffirmed through examples and repetition ('that's what I believe' lines 108 and 112). The structure of Holger's narrative indicates that
how he utilised the concepts of authenticity and originality were more or less
an attempt to legitimise his disengagement without having his own agency
undercut by six cats. For, as I have hinted earlier, it seemed that Holger did
not find the narrative of the stray cat convincing and was compelled to provide a more concrete justification for his inaction.

Holger was my first interviewee, and his rationalisation appeared alien to
me from the outset of the data analysis. The reason is related to the simple
fact that 'authenticity' was/is not a prominent discourse in my cultural background. Where I grew up, moral values and social roles are prescribed by
society; what is right and wrong are predetermined and not open for nego-
tiation. For instance, as a child, I was expected to respect my elders in *all*
circumstances, and if I acted contrarily, my behaviour and my justifications
for it would not have been interpreted as original or authentic, but rather as
rude and impolite. In fact, I vividly recall how I dealt with the guilt of not
meditating after my first Vipassana course. I reasoned, 'Goenka suggests that
I must not create more sankharas. And if I'm not meditating to eradicate
them, I may as well not create more by feeling guilty about not meditating'.
The point I raise is that even though Holger and I rationalised our inactions

in different ways—Holger legitimised his inaction by trying to linguistically claim back agency, and I legitimised mine by interpreting Goenka's teachings to suit my own ends—in essence, we both engaged in a dialogical practice and drew from the rhetorical resources we had in our cultural repertoire.

However, because authenticity has become a prominent source of meaning for many individuals in the contemporary West, its rhetorical functions are often taken for granted and the claims and narratives built through this discourse are frequently interpreted as fact. I suggest this is due to the unique characteristics of this discourse, which serves both to (1) legitimise action and (2) provide resource for self-construction. Yet, while the self-constructive properties of authenticity have been addressed in other research contexts such as backpackers' narrative of self-change (Noy, 2004), trans-sexuals' narrative of the 'true self' (Mason-Schrock, 1996), and narratives of self-taught artists (Fine, 2003), exit literature has largely misinterpreted 'authenticity talk'.

Authenticity in Disengagement Literature

Authenticity has been acknowledged in various exit literature as a *desire* that motivates exit (Barbour, 1994; Beckford, 1985; Bielo, 2012; Chalfant, 2011; Coates, 2013; Fazzino, 2014; Harrold, 2006; Hornbeck, 2011). In some instances, a desire for a 'more authentic' lifestyle—for example, living in accordance with the gospel—is noted as a motive for deconversion from one denomination and conversion to another (Bielo, 2012; Harrold, 2006; Streib et. al., 2011: 173). In other cases, particularly among those who make a secular exit, a 'commitment to authenticity' and a desire for an 'authentic identity' is said to have motivated deconversion (Chalfant, 2011; Fazzino, 2014). Overall, and consequential to a casual gaze at the process of deconversion, these studies have interpreted authenticity in exit narratives as some kind of *motivational desire* that leads individuals to overcome doubts and embark on the exit process (e.g. I left a religious group because I wanted to feel authentic).

Likewise, upon examining a dozen of written deconversion narratives, Barbour (1994: 210) concludes that deconversion is 'a metaphor for our times that expresses modernity's search for authenticity, which so often takes the form of a flight from authority, from inherited paradigms of thought and from various pressure to conform'. Unfortunately, beyond these remarks, neither Barbour (1994) nor any of the abovementioned authors have sought to explore the broader cultural transformations brought about by the European Enlightenment that harboured the changes Barbour describes in modern and postmodern modes of self-understandings (Boeckel, 1995).

Whereas most scholars in this field were content to make a causal link between authenticity and disengagement, Dominiek D. Coates (2013) has made a considerable effort to explore the role of authenticity in her article 'Disaffiliation from a New Religious Movement: The Importance of Self and Others in Exit', which examined the narratives of twenty-three former members of eleven NRMs in Australia. Relying on the symbolic interactionist conceptualisation of self[9]—as constructed in the realm of self and others— Coates identified two forms of disaffiliation narratives: the narratives of 'the social selves' and 'the protected selves'. Coates (2013: 2) conceives this distinction on a continuum and in relation to the ex-members' life histories, including their *motivation* for NRM membership.[10] Coates's research shows that even though all the participants in her study had experienced doubt and dissonance during their NRM membership, their social and private selves exhibited distinct ways of managing doubts and negotiating disaffiliation.

Accordingly, the *social selves*, which refers to the accounts of those individuals whose senses of 'selves' are highly dependent on 'stable' others, were more inclined to resolve or to neglect doubts to avoid an 'identity crisis' (Coates, 2013: 6–7). She argues that exit among this group only occurred either when (1) unresolved doubts led to a crisis event or (2) when an alternative 'other' or 'identity solution' became available to the NRM member. In the event that disaffiliation occurred in (1) the context of crises (resulting from heightened doubts) and without the availability of alternative resources, the experience is described as painful and troublesome. In Coates's study, this crisis was commonly related to the member's experience of attaining a higher organisational status within the NRM and subsequently being demoted from that role. In the latter scenario, (2), the social selves deferred disaffiliation until (re-)establishing social networks outside the NRM or after arriving at an 'alternate discursive resource' (or discourses), which provided an alternative

---

[9] Symbolic interactionists posit that a balanced notion of selfhood involves both a sense of uniqueness and a sense of social connectedness. However, not everyone can achieve a reflexive balance between the personal and the social or individuality and connectedness.

[10] According to Coates, those participants labelled as social selves reported high dependence on others, echoing their childhood environments which were controlling or authoritarian. The protected selves had reported histories of 'social anxiety and difficulties in forming social connections', as well as reporting childhood environments that were abusive or neglectful.

interpretive lens through which they could reconstruct themselves and reinterpret their experiences (Coates, 2013: 8–9). To exemplify this, Coates refers to the case of a woman who disaffiliated from a fundamentalist Christian church by engaging in a Christian women's group that provided her with an alternative perspective.

The *protected selves*—which refers to the accounts of those individuals whose sense(s) of self are more internally negotiated and informed by the personal—conceptualised their motivations for NRM affiliation in terms of a desire for self-change and described their NRM membership as an emotionally draining and 'identity disconfirming' experience. Exit among this group was caused by what Coates (2013: 6) calls 'burnout', or the exhaustion associated with unsuccessful attempts at self-change. Hence, she notes (2013:14) that the participants in this category 'described "conformity" to the group demands as a façade behind which their genuine beliefs and feelings remained hidden, albeit to varying degrees'. Unlike the social selves who portrayed disaffiliation as a painful process, the narratives of the protected selves in Coates's research depicted disaffiliation in more positive terms, often regarding exit as a 'relief' or an 'opportunity to be themselves again', accompanied by the 'realisation' that their NRM membership was not the resolution to the self-change they desired.

More importantly, Coates (2013: 15) notes that one of the salient characteristics of this group's narratives was their desire for authenticity alongside the need for a sense of belonging (to the NRM community). For example, Coates (2013: 15) refers to a participant, Adam, who noted, 'I wanted to be part of a community, but I also wanted to be able to express myself fully and honestly, and find my authentic way . . . But there was no room for me to be me'. Another noteworthy example is provided by a woman named Kerry, who, despite suffering the exhaustion of 'having to pretend all the time', continued her membership to remain connected to her family (2013: 15). However, as the story unfolds, Kerry stops 'pretending' and was subsequently expelled from the community. Once again, Coates (2013: 14) frequently cites similar sentiments from Kerry's narrative such as 'I had to pull back. I wanted to be myself again'. Finally, these case studies compel Coates (2013: 6) to conclude:

> The reluctance of the social selves to disaffiliate can be understood as related to the centrality of the NRM to their sense of self, while the 'eagerness'

of the protected selves to disaffiliate may reflect a desire for 'authenticity' as autonomous and independent individuals.

In my view, while Coates offers a compelling approach to the study of disaffiliation narratives, she also confuses (what I have identified as) authenticity talk with an actual motive leading to disaffiliation. That is, if we perceive the disengagers' appropriation of authenticity talk as a narrative device enabling self-reconstruction and legitimacy, then Coates's binary categorisation of social and protected selves easily disintegrates into one. For example, one can conceive Adam's stress on authenticity as an 'alternate discursive resource', enabling this participant to both negotiate disaffiliation and to reconstruct a sense of self post-exit. In the same light, the example based on Kerry can also be seen as an incident in which doubts or dissonances were neglected until they culminated in a crisis (i.e. her expulsion from the NRM). Here, too, Kerry's narrative could be seen as a similar appropriation of authenticity talk, since her story is likewise replete with utterances such as 'I just wanted to be me' (Coates, 2013: 15). Therefore, in both instances, Adam and Kerry were dependent on an alternative discourse rather than purely themselves, as Coates's conclusions suggest. The confusion here is in the fact that the alternative discourse paradoxically promotes uniqueness, individuality, and autonomy. Consequently, what remains from this categorisation are different variations of social selves with distinct approaches to dealing with doubts and the recourses they utilise to exit (i.e. alternative social network, alternative discourse, and those who avoid exit until dissonances result in crisis).

More profoundly, Coates does not take into consideration the important fact that the vast majority of the participants she had categorised as 'social selves' were former members of groups with a strong sense of community such as the Fundamentalist Christian Church; whereas the majority of Coates's participants categorised under the 'protected selves' (including Adam and Kerry) were ex-members of 'personal development' movements and 'psycho-therapy groups'. This pivotal piece of information sheds light on the reasons why individuals who belonged to the first category placed an emphasis on the role of stable others in their membership, whereas individuals in the other group emphasised their individuality.

Indeed, none of the participants interviewed for this book can be seen exclusively on either side of Coates's categorisation; rather, they tend to exhibit both traits. As I have sought to illustrate through a detailed analysis of Luke's narrative (as well as the excerpt presented from Holger), individuals who accentuate authenticity in their exit accounts do so to claim an authoritative voice and to legitimise their action. More importantly, they also draw upon this concept because it provides them with a discursive resource for self-construction. In this sense, authenticity talk worked for Luke in a similar manner that the Vipassana language and terminology, such as 'ego', 'sankhara', and 'conditioning', enabled Elijah to achieve self-transformation and construct a new sense of self in his narrative. Yet, by refusing to objectify the religious disengagers' emphasis on autonomy and authenticity and taking these sentiments at face value, many scholars limit themselves from recognising the rhetorical functions of these concepts. As Boeckel (1995: 386) has rightfully remarked, contemporary social sciences often perceive these widespread models of self-understanding as a 'transhistorical anthropological truth' rather than an ideology with a specific history.

Origins of Authenticity

Charles Taylor (1989, 2003 [1991], 2007) is among the few who has examined the concept of authenticity as a cultural construct in remarkable depth and breadth. For Taylor, the contemporary 'culture of authenticity' represents the idea that 'each one of us has his/her own way of realising our humanity, and that it is important to find and live out one's own, as against surrendering to conformity with a model imposed on us from outside, by society, or the previous generation, or religious or political authority' (Taylor, 2007: 475).

As 'a child of the Romantic period', Taylor (2003 [1991]: 25) associates authenticity with the earlier forms of individualism, namely the 'individualism of disengaged rationality' set forth by Descartes—which demanded that each individual think self-responsibly—and the 'political individualism' of Locke that prioritised the individual's will over and above his/her social obligations. Built on these pillars, Taylor locates the origin of this concept in the eighteenth-century idea that human beings are endowed with a moral compass; an inner voice which they must listen to or keep in touch with to navigate what is right and wrong. Hence, Taylor (2003 [1991]: 26) writes, 'The notion of authenticity develops out of a displacement of the moral accent . . . when being in touch takes on independent and crucial moral significance'.

This of course finds its meaning once compared with earlier theistic moral views in which being in touch meant connection with some source that transcended human beings (e.g. God), whereas now, morality is not to be sought outside of us, rather it is the voice within. Taylor (2003: 27) links this shift to Rousseau, who he also finds responsible for articulating the notion of 'self determining freedom' which is the idea that 'I am free when I decide for myself what concerns me, rather than being shaped by external influences'. Taylor argues that although this understanding of 'self determining freedom' is fundamentally distinct from authenticity, nonetheless the two are intrinsically related and often infused. Finally, Taylor (2003: 28) associates the most recent development or dimension of authenticity to Herder who popularised the principle of originality, which is the idea that 'each of us has an original way of being human'.

Taylor argues that the concept of originality has completely transformed the understandings of authenticity handed down to us from the eighteenth century, simply because, in addition to finding the inner voice and being in touch with it, I now have to live my life in *my own way* and not by imitating (or conforming to) others; if I do, 'I miss the point of my life, I miss what being human is for me' (Taylor, 2003: 29). In other words, the concept of originality suggests that not only should I not live according to the demands of external conformity, rather such a model does not even exist outside of myself; it is something within; something that only I can discover and articulate, and through this process of self-discovery I ultimately define who I am and what my goals and values are.

Note how this way of thinking identically resembles Luke's statements where he strategically bypassed Goenka, devalued his teachings, rendered them irrelevant to sourcing meaning to life (lines 47–54 and 99–101), and thus effectively presented himself as an autonomous agent (e.g. 'go on my own journey of life'—lines 103–104). As I have argued in this case, authenticity talk legitimised Luke's authoritative voice. On another level, however, authenticity talk aided Luke in reconstructing the sense of self, and the dramatic illustrations of a degenerated self in Luke's narrative (i.e. the implication of not-self resulting from the practice of Vipassana) served to justify the need for the kind of validation he sought to accomplish by authenticity talk. Throughout the narrative, Luke strived to depict an image of a fragmented self, a self who had been decapitated and disconnected from the fundamental orientations (e.g. 'what's the correct frame of reference'—lines 89–94) that explained who he was and where he stood in relation to the world (e.g. 'being thrown into a pool and struggling for breath'—line 42), one who now struggles not only to resume a sense of self but also to restore an 'indexical' relationship (Parish, 2009: 145) to himself and the world (e.g. 'where am I in all of this'—line 22).

Consequently, in Luke's case, authenticity talk fulfilled its self-constructing functions on three levels: (1) discursive, which was the narration of the self who does not need Goenka's guidance or advice in finding meaning in life; (2) intersubjective, which was the sense of autonomous self Luke pursued by presenting himself to me during the interview as an ex-member; and (3) the embodied experience, which is the self-transformation that is achieved through the performance of an authentic self through narrative. Thus, the performance of deconversion narrative in this case can be seen as a practice that facilitated the creation of both the experience of authenticity—it quite literally 'represents the effort to restore and maintain the felt reality of self' (Parish, 2009: 147)—and a sense of self situated outside Goenka's universe of discourse.

Furthermore, Luke's narrative structure as a whole resembled the process of becoming an atheist (Smith, 2010). As Jesse M. Smith's (2010: 14) qualitative study has shown, much of an atheist self-concept is 'constructed in terms of what it is not'. That is, an atheist self-concept is first and foremost anchored in the rejection of a religious meaning system and, secondarily, is shaped by appealing to an alternative lens and discourse such as science, reason, and secular thinking (Smith, 2010: 13). Similarly, within the context of his deconversion narrative, Luke represented a self that was first founded upon the repudiation of Vipassana's doctrine (not-self), subsequently strengthened through rational discourse, and finally coloured (or provided with purpose) by authenticity talk. I propose that authenticity talk can be seen as a common ingredient that facilitates the construction of selves that are negotiated/situated outside of religious language. Indeed, while authenticity talk went largely unnoticed in Smith's fascinating analysis, this style of talk was nonetheless evident in a quote he (2010: 17) cited from a participant, Dennis:

> It was very empowering, because—I mean—when you lose the idea of God, it could be like you're lost, like there's no higher purpose . . . but for me it was the idea of setting your own purpose, that it's just you, [that] it comes from within; that's pretty exciting!

Concluding Summary

In the previous chapter, I argued that Vipassana disaffiliation narratives were characterised by (1) the participants' ongoing commitment to the movement's language; (2) their ongoing convictions about the movement's truth claims, including the transformative efficacy of the technique; and (3) a sense of self-doubt, which emerged from their perceived inability to achieve a certain desirable outcome (namely, progress towards enlightenment). Against this backdrop, in this chapter, I have presented Luke's case study as an example of deconversion narrative. By scrutinising the content and the structure of his language, I have demonstrated the ways in which Luke attempted to escape from Goenka's universe of discourse. This example showed that deconversion is a process that requires practice, as the individual learns to unlearn the movement's language and scaffolds a framework against the group's meaning system.

My analysis demonstrated that the performance of deconversion narrative fundamentally induced similar outcomes to conversion narratives (Stromberg, 1993). That is, by evoking his conflict with the notion of not-self during the interview, Luke provided himself with the opportunity to act out his delivery from that conflict, for instance, by performing the role of a Cartesian cogito and by engaging in authenticity talk.

Finally, I supported my claim, that most disengagement literature has mistreated the ex-members' authenticity talk as a motive behind exit, by focusing on the threefold functionality of this discourse in spoken narrative. Since, unlike converts, deconverts are not provided with a predetermined universe of discourse within which to construct a new self, they are likely to seek recourse in their cultural repertoire. Evidently, the wide manifestation of authenticity talk in disengagement literature testifies to the significant role it serves in the process of self-construction post-exit.

Concluding Discussions

In this book, I have examined a pattern of religious disengagement that has been largely neglected by previous scholarship: disengagement in the context of tacit conversion. In the following pages, I provide a general discussion of the study at hand, summarise its main findings, and highlight its contributions to the existing body of knowledge. Concurrently, I address the major limitations and implications of this research for current scholarship and conclude this book with several recommendations for future research.

To explore the nuances of disengagement from Goenka's Vipassana movement, I pursued a qualitative inquiry, undertook fieldwork at Dhamma Medini, and conducted in-depth interviews with twenty-six participants. I have analysed the collected data by embedding Snow and Machalek's (1983, 1984) conception of conversion as a change in one's universe of discourse within Gooren's (2010) conversion career model. Consequently, I simplified Gooren's comprehensive, multifactorial, and multidimensional model into a monolithic, two-dimensional, and workable heuristic framework. This approach enabled me to (1) represent the necessary context for the research, including the cultural, institutional, and linguistic structures that undergird the participants' rejection of conversion; (2) scrutinise the *process* of migration to a new universe of discourse at different levels of religious activity and inactivity; and, subsequently, (3) distinguish patterns of disengagement, including pragmatic leaving, disaffiliation, and deconversion.

Chapter 3 examined disengagement narratives of participants whose conversion career did *not* involve intense levels of commitment to the movement or complete adoption of its universe of discourse. The chapter outlined three linguistic characteristics of pragmatic leavers' narratives: (1) pragmatism, (2) dualistic discourse, and (3) ambivalence. In essence, most of these participants saw themselves torn between inescapable mundaneness and irresistible transcendence. I proposed that these linguistic strategies enabled them to rationalise and negotiate disengagement in ways that avoided rendering their spiritual search/growth as stagnated or stalled. The findings of this chapter supported the concept of 'structural availability' (Dawson, 1999,

Drifting Through Samsara. Masoumeh Rahmani, Oxford University Press. © Oxford University Press 2022.
DOI: 10.1093/oso/9780197579961.003.0008

cited in Chrysside, 2016) and its relevance to the development of commit-ment. Arguing that pragmatic leavers were experience seekers, I showed that their post-disengagement seekership involved orientations towards unde-manding practices that provided more immediate and tangible results. I an-ticipate that future research can test and conceivably expand the linguistic characteristics of pragmatic leavers, particularly within New Age move-ments. Finally, even though many scientists have turned a blind eye to the potential risks and negative effects of meditation, the content of the chapter (i.e. unfavourable meditative experiences) provided substantial evidence to-wards the de-mythification of misconceptions about meditation (Farias and Wikholm, 2015).

Chapters 4, 5, and 6 examined the narratives of individuals who left Goenka's movement after years of intense participation. Accordingly, three trajectories were outlined based on the positionality of the participants' lan-guage in relation to the movement's universe of discourse: (1) drifters in samsara, (2) pursuers of the gateless gate, and (3) deconversion. Chapter 5 detailed the first two trajectories and demonstrated that even though disaf-filiation resulted in reorientation to certain emic concepts such as enlighten-ment, it did not result in a complete migration outside Goenka's universe of discourse or a Buddhist one. On the contrary, chapter 6 examined the process of leaving a universe of discourse and demonstrated how deconversion nar-ratives can also be seen as the site of self-transformation (Stromberg, 1993).

Perhaps one of the controversial elements of these chapters was the propos-ition that deconversion is a rare exit pattern from Goenka's movement. This claim was partly supported by enforcing the linguistic approach to conver-sion on Bromley's (1998b) tripartite typology that links exit patterns and or-ganisational structures. I suggested that, consequential to its ideologies and linguistic strategies (including its epistemic ideology; claims of rationality, universality, and instrumentality; rejection of religious labels and categories; emphasis on individual authority; autonomy; and, more importantly, its propagation of meditation), the movement occupies a low-tension niche within the cultural context of New Zealand, which supports these positions. As a result of this harmony, not only does the movement enforce its emic categories on exit narratives, hence partly engendering self-doubt, but it also continues to influence the world of disaffiliates. My rationale for this claim is based on the fact that, in spite of my efforts, I have been unsuccessful in locating any other person who fits the criteria of deconversion for partici-pant recruitment in this research—through my networks, the participants' networks, the ex-monk Kovido's networks, or even Luke's networks. Clearly, this idea would merit further investigation and requires rigorous application of participant-recruitment methods.

To a large degree, however, these chapters (4, 5, and 6) supported previous scholarship on religious exit (Barbour, 1994; Bromley, 1998b; Coates, 2013; Ebaugh, 1988; Wright, 1991). They demonstrated that even though these participants did *not* consider themselves as converts, nor conceived the movement as a religious institution during their involvement, their disaffiliation involved a reconceptualisation of the organisation and, in some instances, resulted in the retrospective adoption of the Buddhist identity. Over and above the field of religious exit, the implication of this insight more directly forces a re-examination of our understanding of conversion and, by extension, our criteria for participant recruitment. At the outset of this book, I suggested that the field of conversion studies has been limited by taking the informants' self-identification at face value. I argued that for decades, the normative criterion for participant recruitment in conversion studies has been (more or less) boiled down to the question: 'Are you a convert?' (Staples and Mauss, 1987: 138). In this book, I demonstrated that not only does this approach fail to categorically encompass the experience of Vipassana meditators, but it also blurs the subject of study in the face of increasing aversion to labels and, more importantly, in contexts where the category of spirituality prevails over the category of religion.

One of the major contributions of this research is therefore the introduction of the term 'tacit conversion', presented in chapter 2. In the context of Goenka's Vipassana movement, tacit conversion explains the process whereby the adoption of the movement's language paradoxically rendered conversion invisible. I envision that this category can provide an analytical framework for conceptualising the process of personal transformation and commitment in movements with blurred religious/secular boundaries. This notion was developed from the qualitative exploration of this particular movement (in the New Zealand context) by paying attention to its unique institutional and linguistic features. Evidently, there are issues of external generalisability. For instance, conversion to Goenka's Vipassana movement in other cultural settings may not be predominantly tacit. Similarly, tacit conversion may not adequately explain the process of personal transformation and commitment to unequivocally secular movements. Therefore, future researchers wishing to test and expand on this concept must do so by taking account of the distinctive features of the group they study, as the rhetorics explored in this book are not universal although a similar range of discourses can be found in contemporary Mindfulness movements (Rahmani, 2020). Moreover, considering that most individuals in this research self-categorised themselves as religious 'nones'—most of whom ironically expressed and exhibited the highest levels of religious commitment to this movement—this thesis therefore contributes to an understanding of the growing field of unbelief. It provides an empirical basis for understanding the grey space 'in-between' concrete religious identities and non-religious identities such as New Atheism (Zenk, 2013). More importantly, this research should be considered a cautionary tale for social scientists such as Hoverd and his colleagues (2015: 21) who exclusively rely on national census data to foresee the religious landscape of New Zealand drifting on a 'slow boat to apostasy'.

This research responded to the recent call (Gooren, 2010; Stromberg, 2014) to test the rhetorical features of a convert's language as originally proposed by Snow and Machalek (1983, 1984) and later reformulated by Staples and Mauss (1987). Accordingly, the secondary findings of this research refuted Staples and Mauss's long-lasting claim, which considered biographical reconstruction to be the *only* linguistic device unique to the convert's language. As substantiated through examples (in chapter 1), I illustrated that biographical reconstruction and the adoption of a master attribution scheme go hand in hand, both theoretically and empirically. In fact, I argued that is it theoretically unsound to conceptualise one without the other: if one's self-concept undergoes transformation through biographical reconstruction, then one's understanding of the world and one's position in the world should simultaneously be subjected to transformation. However, by distinguishing the *process* of conversion in two shades of conversion and commitment, I also departed from Snow and Machalek's original scheme.

This study continues the call for attentiveness to language and the microdynamics of narratives in studies of religious change. My method of analysis in this book was heavily inspired by Stromberg's (1993) linguistic approach to conversion narratives and by Riessman's (1993, 2002, 2008) guidelines for narrative analysis. I have paid close attention to the content of speech and other modalities of communication, including inflections, tonalities, and delivery of the narrative. I have demonstrated that this multidimensional approach reveals patterns that would otherwise remain obscured by a simple reliance on the communicative content of the language divorced from the contextual features. For instance, chapter 2 demonstrated that committed Vipassana practitioners essentially perform narratives that in many ways resemble 'conversion narratives'. Chapter 4 highlighted the significance of self-doubt in disaffiliation narratives. Chapter 6 argued that previous disengagement literature (Barbour, 1994; Bielo, 2012; Chalfant, 2011; Coates, 2013; Fazzino, 2014; Harrold, 2006; Hornbeck, 2011) has mistreated the ex-member's 'authenticity talk' as a literal motive behind their exit. Instead, I have proposed that it is more fruitful to conceive it as a useful resource for self-construction and as a linguistic device that induces self-validation.

Finally, this research has primarily gazed at the processes of conversion and disengagement through the keyhole of language. As a result, it was insensitive to important factors such as the role of gender and network (Jindra, 2014) in both processes. Therefore, future studies that attempt to elaborate on the existing knowledge of Goenka's Vipassana movement should cast a wider net to gain a more holistic understanding of this tradition.

Vipassana Ten-Day Course Timetable

4:00 a.m.	Morning wake-up bell
4:30–6:30 a.m.	Meditate in the hall or in your room
6:30–8:00 a.m.	Breakfast break
8:00–9:00 a.m.	Group meditation in the hall
9:00–11:00 a.m.	Meditate in the hall or in your room according to the teacher's instructions
11:00–12:00 p.m.	Lunch break
12:00–1:00 p.m.	Rest and interviews with the teacher
1:00–2:30 p.m.	Meditate in the hall or in your room
2:30–3:30 p.m.	Group meditation in the hall
3:30–5:00 p.m.	Meditate in the hall or in your own room according to the teacher's instructions
5:00–6:00 p.m.	Tea break
6:00–7:00 p.m.	Group meditation in the hall
7:00–8:15 p.m.	Teacher's discourse in the hall
8:15–9:00 p.m.	Group meditation in the hall
9:00–9:30 p.m.	Question time in the hall
9:30 p.m.	Retire to your own room—lights out

APPENDIX 2

Participants' Information

Name; Interview date	Sex	Age	Conversion career	#Ten-day courses	Religious identification	Future practice	App. date of first course	App. years since exit
Ian 2014	M	30s	Dropped out Preaffiliation	0	Bright	Not in Goenka's tradition	2006	8
Victor 2014	M	20s	Disengaged Affiliation	1	Unaffiliated	Yes	2013	1
Leslie 2014; 2015	F	40s	Disengaged Conversion	1	Jewish; Panentheist	Another time in life	2014	0; 1
Michael 2014	M	70s	Disengaged Conversion	1	Other	Yes	2014	0
Katrin 2014; 2015	F	30s	Disengaged Conversion	1	Christian–Buddhist	Yes	2014	0; 1
Aroha 2014	F	50s	Disengaged Conversion	1	Everything; Fluid	N/A	2014	0
Brenda 2014	F	30s	Disengaged Conversion	1	Atheist	Yes	2011	3
Andrew 2015	M	40s	Disengaged Conversion	1	Other	No	2006	9
Anne 2014	F	20s	Disengaged Conversion	2	None	Yes	2012	1

(continued)

Name; Interview date	Sex	Age	Conversion career	#Ten-day courses	Religious identification	Future practice	App. date of first course	App. years since exit
Joseph 2014	M	50s	Disengaged Conversion	2 + weekly group sits	Buddhist-Pagan	Yes	1995	18
Matilda 2015	F	30s	Disengaged Conversion-Commitment	2	Other; Buddhist	Yes	2010	
Holger 2014	M	30s	Disengaged Conversion-Commitment	3	None	Yes	2008	2
Mark 2015	M	40s	Disaffiliate Commitment	2+ 1-month retreat	No answer	Maybe	1995	20
Karen 2014	F	30s	Disaffiliated Commitment	3 + 3 service + a number of short courses	Other	Yes	2005	4
Jazz 2014	F	30s	Disaffiliated Commitment	4	Agnostic; Buddhist	Yes	2003	2
Polly 2015	F	30s	Disaffiliated Commitment	5 + 1 service	Baptist	May or may not	2008	4
Kovido 2014	M	60s	Disaffiliated Commitment Ex-monk	Over 15 + 1 year service	Buddhist	Maybe out of curiosity	1979	33
Kevin 2015	M	40s	Disaffiliated Commitment	3	Buddhist	Maybe	1992	16
Damian 2015; 2016	M	40s	Disaffiliated Commitment	Over 10 +20-day course + service	Other/ Maybe even Buddhist	No	1991	19

Luke 2015	M	40s	Disaffiliated Commitment Deconvert	Over 20 + 30-day + service	Atheist	Never	1990 (?)	20
Brian 2014	M	30s	Commitment	3 + service	None	N/A	2013	N.A.
Charlotte 2014	F	30s	Commitment	3+ short course + 20-day service	SBNR	N/A	2014	N.A.
Elijah 2014	M	30s	Commitment	One year service	None	N/A	2013	N.A.
Dylan 2014	M	40s	Commitment	+ series of service	Atheist	N/A	2013	N.A.
Carole 2014	F	60s	Commitment	22 years	None	N/A	1992	N.A.
Ross 2015	M	70s	Commitment	40 years	Not religious; Not Buddhist	N/A	1975	N.A.

Bibliography

Abbey, R. (2014) *Charles Taylor*. London: Routledge.

Anonymous (2012) Goenka Vipassana Cult—Page 3—AFA Forums [Online]. Available from: http://www.atheistfoundation.org.au/forums/showthread.php?t= 16830&page=3 [Accessed 22 February 2015].

Atkinson, R. and Flint, J. (2004) 'Snowball Sampling'. *In: Encyclopedia of Social Science Research Methods Encyclopedia*. London: SAGE. doi: 10.4135/9781412950589

Austin-Broos, D. (2003) 'The Anthropology of Conversion: An Introduction'. *In*: A. Buckser & S. D. Glazier, eds. *The Anthropology of Religious Conversion*. Lanham: Rowman & Littlefield: 1–15.

Barbour, J. D. (1994) *Versions of Deconversion: Autobiography and the Loss of Faith*. Charlottesville: University of Virginia Press.

Barvosa, E. (2008) *Wealth of Selves: Multiple Identities, Mestiza Consciousness, and the Subject of Politics*. College Station: Texas A&M University Press.

Bauman, R. (1975) 'Verbal Art as Performance'. *American Anthropologist*, 77(2): 290–311.

Bechert, H. (1984) 'Buddhist Revival in East and West'. *In*: H. Bechert & R. Gombrich, eds. *The World of Buddhism: Buddhist Monks and Nuns in Society and Culture*. London: Thames and Hudson: 273–285.

Beckford, J. A. (1978) 'Accounting for Conversion'. *The British Journal of Sociology*, 29(2): 249–262.

Bender, C. (2007) 'American Reincarnations: What the Many Lives of Past Lives Tell Us About Contemporary Spiritual Practice'. *Journal of the American Academy of Religion*, 75(3): 589–614.

Bender, C. (2010) *The New Metaphysicals: Spirituality and the American Religious Imagination*. Chicago: University of Chicago Press.

Benjamin, W. (1999) [1982] *The Arcades Project*. Cambridge: Harvard University Press.

Benner, P. (1994) *Interpretive Phenomenology: Embodiment, Caring, and Ethics in Health and Illness*. London: SAGE.

Berger, P. L. (1999) 'The Desecularization of the World: A Global Overview'. *In*: P. L. Berger, ed. *The Desecularization of the World: Resurgent Religion and World Politics*. Washington: Wm. B. Eerdmans: 1–18.

Berger, P. L. and Luckmann, T. (1967) *The Social Construction of Reality*. Garden City, NY: Doubleday-Anchor.

Berger, R. (2015) 'Challenges and Coping Strategies in Leavening an Ultra-Orthodox Community'. *Qualitative Social Work*, 14(5): 670–686.

Bielo, J. S. (2012) 'Belief, Deconversion, and Authenticity Among U.S. Emerging Evangelicals'. *Ethos*, 40(3): 258–276.

Blaikie, N. (2004) 'Interpretivism'. *In*: M. S. Lewis-Beck, A. Bryman, & T. Futing Liao, eds. *Encyclopedia of Social Science Research Methods*. London: SAGE: 509–511.

Boeckel, B. (1995) 'Versions of Deconversion: Autobiography and the Loss of Faith'. *Christianity and Literature*, 44(3–4): 385–387.

Braun, E. (2013) *The Birth of Insight: Meditation, Modern Buddhism, and the Burmese Monk Ledi Sayadaw*. Chicago: University of Chicago Press.

Brekke, T. (2003) 'Conversion in Buddhism?' *In*: R. Robinson & S. Clarke, *eds. Religious Conversion in India: Modes, Motivations, and Meanings*. Delhi: Oxford University Press: 181–191.

Bremborg, A. D. (2011) 'Interviewing'. *In*: Steven Engler & Michael Stausberg, *eds. The Routledge Handbook of Research Methods in the Study of Religion*. Abingdon: Routledge: 310–322.

Brinkerhoff, M. B. and Mackie, M. M. (1993) 'Casting off the Bonds of Organized Religion: A Religious-Careers Approach to the Study of Apostasy'. *Review of Religious Research*, 34(3): 235–258.

Britton, W. B. (2011) *BG 231: The Dark Side of Dharma*. Available from: http://www.buddhistgeeks.com/2011/09/bg-231-the-dark-side-of-dharma/ [Accessed 10 July 2016].

Bromley, D. G. (1998a) 'The Social Construction of Contested Exit Roles: Defectors, Whistleblowers, and Apostates'. *In*: D. G. Bromley, *ed. The Politics of Religious Apostasy: The Role of Apostates in the Transformation of Religious Movements*. Westport, CT: Praeger: 19–48.

Bromley, D. G. (1998b) 'Linking Social Structure and the Exit Process in Religious Organizations: Defectors, Whistle-Blowers, and Apostates'. *Journal for the Scientific Study of Religion*, 37(1): 145–160.

Bromley, D. G. (2004) 'Leaving the Fold: Disaffiliating from New Religious Movements'. *In*: J. R. Lewis, ed. *The Oxford Handbook of New Religious Movements*. Oxford: Oxford University Press: 298–314.

Bromley, D. G. (2006) 'Affiliation and Disaffiliation Careers in New Religious Movements'. *In*: E. V. Gallagher & W. M. Ashcraft, *eds. Introduction to New and Alternative Religions in America: Vol. 1: History and Controversies*. Westport, CT: Greenwood: 42–64.

Bromley, D. G. and Shupe, A. D. (1979) ' "Just a Few Years Seem Like a Lifetime": A Role Theory Approach to Participation in Religious Movements'. *In*: L. Kriesberg, ed. *Research in Social Movements Conflicts, and Change*. Greenwich, CT: JAI Press: 159–185.

Bruce, S. (1999) *Choice and Religion: A Critique of Rational Choice Theory*. Oxford: Oxford University Press.

Bryman, A. (2001) *Social Research Methods*. Oxford: Oxford University Press.

Buckser, A. and Glazier, S. D. (2003) *The Anthropology of Religious Conversion*. Lanham: Rowman & Littlefield.

Bulkeley, K. (2014) 'Dreaming and Religious Conversion'. *In*: L. R. Rambo & C. E. Farhadian, *eds. The Oxford Handbook of Religious Conversion*. Oxford: Oxford University Press: 256–270.

Buxant, C., Saroglou, V., and Tesser, M. (2010) 'Free-Lance Spiritual Seekers: Self-Growth or Compensatory Motives?' *Mental Health, Religion & Culture*, 13(2): 209–222.

Caldwell, P. (1985) *The Puritan Conversion Narrative: The Beginnings of American Expression*. Cambridge: Cambridge University Press.

Callero, P. L. (2003) 'The Sociology of the Self'. *Annual Review of Sociology*, 29: 115–133.

Campbell, C. (2002) [1972] 'The Cult, the Cultic Milieu, and Secularization'. *In*: J. Kaplan & H. Lööw, *eds. The Cultic Milieu: Oppositional Subcultures in an Age of Globalization*. Walnut Creek: AltaMira Press: 12–25.

Campbell, C. (2007) *Easternization of the West: A Thematic Account of Cultural Change in the Modern Era.* London: Routledge.

Carley-Baxter, L. (2008) 'Respondent-Interviewer Rapport'. *In*: P. J. Lavrakas, *ed. Encyclopedia of Survey Research Methods.* London: SAGE: 744.

Carrette, J. and King, R. (2005) *Selling Spirituality: The Silent Takeover of Religion.* Hoboken: Taylor and Francis.

Chalfant, E. (2011) *Thank God I'm an Atheist: Deconversion Narratives on the Internet.* M.A. Thesis. Winston-Salem, NC: Wake Forest University.

Chase, S. E. (2008) 'Narrative Inquiry: Multiple Lenses, Approaches, Voices'. *In*: N. K. Denzin & Y. S. Lincoln, *eds. Collecting and Interpreting Qualitative Materials.* London: SAGE: 57–94.

Chaves, M. (2004) *Congregations in America.* Cambridge: Harvard University Press.

Chryssides, G. D. (2016) 'Conversion'. *In*: J. R. Lewis & I. B. Tollefsen, *eds. The Oxford Handbook of New Religious Movements, Vol. 2.* Oxford: Oxford University Press: 25–35.

Coates, D. (2012) 'The Significance and Purpose of the 'Anti-Cult Movement' in Facilitating Disaffiliation from a New Religious Movement: Resources for Self-Construction or a Justificatory Account'. *International Journal for the Study of New Religions,* 3(2): 213–244.

Coates, D. (2013) 'Disaffiliation from a New Religious Movement: The Importance of Self and Others in Exit'. *Symbolic Interaction,* 36(3): 314–334.

Collins, S. (1994) 'What Are Buddhists Doing When They Deny the Self?'. *In*: F. E. Reynolds & D. Tracy, *eds. Religion and Practical Reason: New Essays in the Comparative Philosophy of Religions.* New York: New York Press: 59–86.

Corradi, C. (1991) 'Text, Context and Individual Meaning: Rethinking Life Stories in a Hermeneutic Framework'. *Discourse & Society,* 2(1): 105–118.

Cowan, D. E. (2014) 'Conversion to New Religious Movements'. *In*: L. R. Rambo & C. E. Farhadian, *eds. The Oxford Handbook of Religious Conversion.* Oxford: Oxford University Press: 687–705.

Davidman, L. and Greil, A. L. (2007) 'Characters in Search of a Script: The Exit Narratives of Formerly Ultra-Orthodox Jews'. *Journal for the Scientific Study of Religion,* 46(2): 201–216.

Davies, C. A. (1999) *Reflexive Ethnography: A Guide to Researching Selves and Others.* London: Routledge.

Deleanu, F. (2010) 'Agnostic Meditations on Buddhist Meditation'. *Zygon: Journal of Religion & Science,* 45(3): 605–626.

Denzin, N. K. and Lincoln, Y. S. (2008) 'Introduction: The Discipline and Practice of Qualitative Research'. *In*: N. K. Denzin & Y. S. Lincoln, *eds. Collecting and Interpreting Qualitative Materials.* London: SAGE: 1–44.

Denzin, N. K. and Lincoln, Y. S., *eds.* (2011) *The SAGE Handbook of Qualitative Research.* 4th ed. London: SAGE.

Ebaugh, H. R. F. (1988) *Becoming an Ex: The Process of Role Exit.* Chicago: University of Chicago Press.

Esin, C., Fathi, M., and Squire, C. (2014) 'Narrative Analysis: The Constructionist Approach'. *In*: U. Flick, *ed. The SAGE Handbook of Qualitative Data Analysis.* London: SAGE: 203–216.

Evans, A., Elford, J., and Wiggins, D. (2008) 'Using the Internet for Qualitative Research'. *In*: C. Willig & W. Stainton-Rogers, *eds. The SAGE Handbook of Qualitative Research in Psychology.* London: SAGE: 315–333.

Farias, M. and Wikholm, C. (2015) *The Buddha Pill: Can Meditation Actually Change You?* London: Watkins.

Faure, B. (1991) *The Rhetoric of Immediacy: A Cultural Critique of Chan/Zen Buddhism.* Princeton: Princeton University Press.

Fazzino, L. L. (2014) 'Leaving the Church Behind: Applying a Deconversion Perspective to Evangelical Exit Narratives'. *Journal of Contemporary Religion*, 29(2): 249–266.

Fine, G. A. (2003) 'Crafting Authenticity: The Validation of Identity in Self-Taught Art'. *Theory and Society*, 32(2): 153–180.

Firth, R. (1999) 'An Anthropological Approach to the Study of Religion'. *In*: R. T. McCutcheon, *ed. The Insider/Outsider Problem in the Study of Religion: A Reader.* London: Cassell: 114–123.

Foxeus, N. (2020) 'Chapter 9 Leaving Theravāda Buddhism in Myanmar'. In: *Handbook of Leaving Religion.* Leiden, The Netherlands: Brill. doi: https://doi.org/10.1163/9789004331471_010

Frankenthaler, L. (2015) 'Dialogical Deconversion: Understanding Undercover Infidelity'. *Journal of Religion and Society*, 17: 1–17.

Gecas, V. (1982) 'The Self-Concept'. *Annual Review of Sociology*, 8(1): 1–33.

Gee, J. P. (1991) 'The Narrativization of Experience in the Oral Style'. *The Journal of Education*, 167(1): 9–35.

Glazier, S. D. (2003) '"Limin' wid Jah": Spiritual Baptists Who Become Rastafarians and Then Become Spiritual Baptists Again'. *In*: A. Buckser & S. D. Glazier, *eds. The Anthropology of Religious Conversion.* Lanham: Rowman & Littlefield: 149–170.

Gleig, A. L. (2010) *Enlightenment After the Enlightenment: American Transformations of Asian Contemplative Traditions.* Doctoral Thesis. Houston, TX: Rice University.

Goenka, S. N. (1997) *Discourse Summaries.* Washington D.C: Vipassana Research Institute.

Goffman, E. (1981) *Forms of Talk.* Philadelphia: University of Pennsylvania Press.

Goldberg, K. (2001) *Inside-Out: A Study of Vipassana Meditation as Taught by S. N. Goenka and Its Social Contribution.* M.A. Thesis. Montreal: McGill University.

Goldberg, K. and Décary, M. (2013) *Along the Path: The Meditator's Companion to the Buddha's Land.* 2nd ed. Onalaska, WA: Pariyatti.

Gombrich, R. F. (1971) *Buddhist Precept and Practice: Traditional Buddhism in the Rural Highlands of Ceylon.* London: Routledge.

Gombrich, R. F. (2006) *Theravada Buddhism A Social History from Ancient Benares to Modern Colombo 2nd Edition.*

Gombrich, R. F. and Obeyesekere, G. (1988) *Buddhism Transformed: Religious Change in Sri Lanka.* Delhi: Motilal Banarsidass.

Gooren, H. (2010) *Religious Conversion and Disaffiliation: Tracing Patterns of Change in Faith Practices.* New York: Palgrave.

Gordon-Finlayson, A. (2012) *Becoming Buddhist: A Grounded Theory of Religious Change and Identity Formation in Western Buddhism.* Doctoral Thesis. Liverpool: Liverpool John Moores University.

Greil, A. L. (1977) 'Previous Dispositions and Conversion to Perspectives of Social and Religious Movements'. *Sociological Analysis*, 38(2): 115–125.

Griffin, C. J. G. (1990) 'The Rhetoric of Form in Conversion Narratives'. *Quarterly Journal of Speech*, 76(2): 152–163.

Griffiths, P. J. (1981) 'Concentration or Insight: The Problematic of Theravāda Buddhist Meditation-Theory'. *Journal of the American Academy of Religion*, 49(4): 605–624.

Hanna, P. (2012) 'Using Internet Technologies (Such as Skype) as a Research Medium: A Research Note'. *Qualitative Research*, 12(2): 239–242.

Harding, S. F. (1987) 'Convicted by the Holy Spirit: The Rhetoric of Fundamental Baptist Conversion'. *American Ethnologist*, 14(1): 167–181.

Harding, S. F. (2000) *The Book of Jerry Falwell: Fundamentalist Language and Politics*. Princeton: Princeton University Press.

Harris, K. (2015) *Leaving Ideological Social Groups Behind: A Grounded Theory of Psychological Disengagement*. Doctoral Thesis. Western Australia: Edith Cowan University. Available from: http://ro.ecu.edu.au/theses/1587 [Accessed 20 January 2015].

Harrold, P. (2006) 'Deconversion in the Emerging Church'. *International Journal for the Study of the Christian Church*, 6(1): 79–90.

Hart, W. (1987) *The Art of Living: Vipassana Meditation as Taught by S. N. Goenka*. Onalaska, WA: Pariyatti.

Harvey, G. (1999) 'Coming Home and Coming Out Pagan (But Not Converting)'. In: C. Lamb & D. Bryant, eds. *Religious Conversion: Contemporary Practices and Controversies*. London: Cassell: 233–246.

Harvey, P. (1990) *An Introduction to Buddhism: Teachings, History and Practices*. Cambridge: Cambridge University Press.

Healy, J. P. (2008) *Attraction, Affiliation and Disenchantment in a New Religious Movement—A Study of Individuals' Experience in a Siddha Yoga Practice*. Doctoral Thesis. Sydney: University of New South Wales.

Healy, J.P. (2011) 'Involvement in a New Religious Movement: From Discovery to Disenchantment'. *Journal of Spirituality in Mental Health*, 13(1): 2–21.

Heelas, P. and Woodhead, L. (2005) *The Spiritual Revolution: Why Religion Is Giving Way to Spirituality*. Oxford: Blackwell.

Heirich, M. (1977) 'Change of Heart: A Test of Some Widely Held Theories About Religious Conversion'. *American Journal of Sociology*, 83(3): 653–680.

Hey, J. (2006) 'Religious Identity: In Praise of the Anonymity of Critical Believing'. *Implicit Religion*, 9(1): 54–73.

Hidas, A. M. (1981) 'Psychotherapy and Surrender: A Psychospiritual Perspective'. *Journal of Transpersonal Psychology*, 13(1): 27–32.

Hindmarsh, D. B. (2005) *The Evangelical Conversion Narrative*. Oxford: Oxford University Press.

Holmes, J. (1997) 'Story-Telling in New Zealand Women's and Men's Talk'. In: R. Wodak, ed. *Gender and Discourse*. London: SAGE: 263–299.

Hood, R. W. and Zhuo, C. (2013) 'Conversion, Deconversion'. In: S. Bullivant & M. Ruse, eds. *The Oxford Handbook of Atheism*. Oxford: Oxford University Press: 537–552.

Hornbeck, J. P., II (2011) 'Deconversion from Roman Catholicism: Mapping a Fertile Field'. *American Catholic Studies*, 122(2): 1–29.

Hoverd, W. J., Bulbulia, J., Partow, N., and Sibley, C. G. (2015) 'Forecasting Religious Change: A Bayesian Model Predicting Proportional Christian Change in New Zealand'. *Religion, Brain & Behavior*, 5(1): 15–23.

Hoy, D. C. (1993) 'Heidegger and the Hermeneutic Turn'. In: C. B. Guignon, ed. *The Cambridge Companion to Heidegger*. Cambridge: Cambridge University Press: 170–194.

Hunsberger, B. and Brown, L. B. (1984) 'Religious Socialization, Apostasy, and the Impact of Family Background'. *Journal for the Scientific Study of Religion*, 23(3): 239–251.

Hunsberger, B., Pratt, M., and Pancer, S. M. (1994) 'Religious Fundamentalism and Integrative Complexity of Thought: A Relationship for Existential Content Only?' *Journal for the Scientific Study of Religion*, 33(4): 335–346.

Hurworth, R. (2005) 'Interpretivism'. *In*: S. Mathison, *ed. Encyclopedia of Evaluation*. London: SAGE: 209–210.

Jacobs, J. (1987) 'Deconversion from Religious Movements: An Analysis of Charismatic Bonding and Spiritual Commitment'. *Journal for the Scientific Study of Religion*, 26(3): 294–308.

Jacobs, J. (1989) *Divine Disenchantment: Deconverting from New Religions*. Bloomington: Indiana University Press.

James, W. (1902) *Varieties of Religious Experience*. London: Longman, Green.

Jindra, I. W. (2014) *A New Model of Religious Conversion: Beyond Network Theory and Social Constructivism*. Leiden: Brill.

Jorgensen, J. (1996) 'The Functions of Sarcastic Irony in Speech'. *Journal of Pragmatics*, 26(5): 613–634.

Kärkkäinen, E. (2007) 'The Role of I Guess in Conversational Stancetaking'. *In*: R. Englebretson, *ed. Stancetaking in Discourse: Subjectivity, Evaluation, Interaction*. Amsterdam: John Benjamins: 183–220.

Kincheloe, J. L. (2001) 'Describing the Bricolage: Conceptualizing a New Rigor in Qualitative Research'. *Qualitative Inquiry*, 7(6): 679–692.

Kincheloe, J. L., McLaren, P., and Steinberg, S.R. (2011) 'Critical Pedagogy and Qualitative Research'. *In*: N. K. Denzin & Y. S. Lincoln, *eds. The SAGE Handbook of Qualitative Research*. London: SAGE: 163–177.

Knapp, M., Hall, J., and Horgan, T. (2014) *Nonverbal Communication in Human Interaction*. 8th ed. London: Wadsworth, Cengage Learning.

Kvale, S. (1995) 'The Social Construction of Validity'. *Qualitative Inquiry*, 1(1): 19–40.

Kvale, S. (2007) 'Epistemological Issues of Interviewing'. *In*: S. Kvale, *ed. Qualitative Research Kit: Doing Interviews*. London: SAGE: 11–22.

Laverty, S. M. (2008) 'Hermeneutic Phenomenology and Phenomenology: A Comparison of Historical and Methodological Considerations'. *International Journal of Qualitative Methods*, 2(3): 21–35.

Lévi-Strauss, C. (1966). *The Savage Mind*. Chicago, IL: University of Chicago Press.

Lewis, J. R. (2013) 'Free Zone Scientology and Other Movement Milieus: A Preliminary Characterization'. *Temenos*, 49(2): 255–276.

Lewis, J. R. (2016) 'Seekers and Subcultures'. *In*: J. R. Lewis & I. B. Tollefsen, *eds. The Oxford Handbook of New Religious Movements*. Oxford: Oxford University Press: 60–71.

Lindahl, J. R., Kaplan, C. T., Winget, E. M., and Britton, W. B. (2014) 'A Phenomenology of Meditation-Induced Light Experiences: Traditional Buddhist and Neurobiological Perspectives'. *Frontiers in Psychology*, 4: 1–16.

Lindahl, J. R., Fisher, N. E., Cooper, D. J., Rosen, R. K., and Britton, W. B. (2017) *The varieties of contemplative experience: A mixed-methods study of meditation-related challenges in Western Buddhists*. https://doi.org/10.1371/journal.pone.0176239

Lindholm, C. (2008) *Culture and Authenticity*. Oxford: Blackwell.

Lofland, J. and Skonovd, N. (1981) 'Conversion Motifs'. *Journal for the Scientific Study of Religion*, 20(4): 373–385.

Lofland, J. and Stark, R. (1965) 'Becoming a World-Saver: A Theory of Conversion to a Deviant Perspective'. *American Sociological Review*, 30(6): 862–875.

Lomas, T., Cartwright, T., Edginton, T., and Ridge, D. (2014) 'A Qualitative Analysis of Experiential Challenges Associated with Meditation Practice'. *Mindfulness*, 6(4): 848–860.

Loss, J. (2010) 'Buddha-Dhamma in Israel: Explicit Non-Religious and Implicit Non-Secular Localization of Religion'. *Nova Religio: The Journal of Alternative and Emergent Religions*, 13(4): 84–105.

Malmkjær, K. and Williams, J. (1998) *Context in Language Learning and Language Understanding*. Cambridge: Cambridge University Press.

Manen, M. V. (1990) *Researching Lived Experience: Human Science for an Action Sensitive Pedagogy*. Albany, NY and London: State University of New York Press.

Manning, C. J. (1996) 'Embracing Jesus and the Goddess: Towards a Reconceptualization of Conversion to Syncretistic Religion'. *In*: J. R. Lewis, *ed. Magical Religion and Modern Witchcraft*. New York: State University of New York Press: 299–326.

Mapel, T. (2007) 'The Adjustment Process of Ex-Buddhist Monks to Life After the Monastery'. *Journal of Religion and Health*, 46(1): 19–34.

Mason-Schrock, D. (1996) 'Transsexuals' Narrative Construction of the "True Self"'. *Social Psychology Quarterly*, 59(3): 176–192.

Maxwell, J. A. and Chmiel, M. (2014) 'Generalization in and from Qualitative Analysis'. *In: The SAGE Handbook of Qualitative Data Analysis*. London: SAGE: 540–553.

McLeod, J. (2001) 'Hermeneutics and Phenomenology: The Core of Qualitative Method'. *In: Qualitative Research in Counselling and Psychotherapy*. London: SAGE.

McMahan, D. L. (2008) *The Making of Buddhist Modernism*. Oxford: Oxford University Press.

Mead, G. H. (1967) *Mind, Self & Society from the Standpoint of a Social Behaviorist*. Charles W. Morriss, *ed.* Chicago: Chicago University Press.

Medini Dhamma (2014) *Vipassana Meditation Centre* [Online]. Available from: http://medini.dhamma.org/centre-2/ [Accessed 22 February 2014].

Medini Dhamma (2017) *Vipassana: The Technique* [Online]. Available from: http://medini.dhamma.org/vipassana/vipassana-technique/ [Accessed 22 February 2017].

Melnikova, N. (2014) *The Modern School of Vipassana—A Buddhist Tradition?* Doctoral Thesis. Brno: Masaryk University.

Montgomery, R. L. (2014) 'Conversion and the Historic Spread of Religions'. *In*: L. R. Rambo & C. E. Farhadian, *eds. The Oxford Handbook of Religious Conversion*. Oxford: Oxford University Press: 164–189.

Morgan, D. L. (2008) 'Snowball Sampling'. *In*: L. Given, *ed. The SAGE Encyclopedia of Qualitative Research Methods*. London: SAGE: 817–818.

Nieuwkerk, K. van, (2014) "Conversion' to Islam and the Construction of a Pious Self'. *In*: L. R. Rambo & C. E. Farhadian, *eds. The Oxford Handbook of Religious Conversion*. Oxford: Oxford University Press: 667–687.

Norris, R. S. (2003) 'Converting to What? Embodied Culture and the Adoption of New Beliefs'. *In*: A. Buckser & S. D. Glazier, *eds. The Anthropology of Religious Conversion*. Lanham: Rowman & Littlefield: 171–182.

Noss, J. B. (1975) [1963] *Man's Religions*. 3rd ed. New York: McMillan.

Noy, C. (2004) 'This Trip Really Changed Me: The Backpackers' Narrative of Self-Change'. *Annals of Tourism Research*, 31(1): 78–102.

O'Connor, H., Madge, C., Shaw, R., and Wellens, J. (2008) 'Internet-Based Interviewing'. *In*: N. Fielding, R. M. Lee & G. Blank, *eds. The SAGE Handbook of Online Research Methods*. London: SAGE: 271–289.

Okely, J. (2012) *Anthropological Practice: Fieldwork and the Ethnographic Method*. London: Berg.

O'Reilly, K. (2009) *Key Concepts in Ethnography*. London: SAGE.

Pagis, M. (2008) *Cultivating Selves: Vipassana Meditation and the Microsociology of Experience*. Doctoral Thesis. Illinois: University of Chicago.

Pagis, M. (2009) 'Embodied Self-reflexivity'. *Social Psychology Quarterly*, 72(3): 265–283.

Pagis, M. (2010a) 'Producing Intersubjectivity in Silence: An Ethnographic Study of Meditation Practice'. *Ethnography*, 11(2): 309–328.

Pagis, M. (2010b) 'From Abstract Concepts to Experiential Knowledge: Embodying Enlightenment in a Meditation Center'. *Qualitative Sociology*, 33(4): 469–489.

Paloutzian, R. F., Richardson, J. T., and Rambo, L. R. (1999) 'Religious Conversion and Personality Change'. *Journal of Personality*, 67(6): 1047–1079.

Pandhana Dhamma (2017) *Vipassana Meditation: Course Requirements for Old Student Courses* [Online]. Available from: https://www.padhana.dhamma.org/en/courses/course-requirements-for-old-student-courses/ [Accessed 22 February 2017].

Parish, S. M. (2009) 'Review Essay Are We Condemned to Authenticity?' *Ethos*, 37(1): 139–148.

Patterson, W. (2013) 'Narratives of Events: Labovian Narrative Analysis'. *In*: M. Andrews, C. Squire, & M. Tamboukou, *eds. Doing Narrative Research*. London: SAGE: 27–46.

Payne, G. and Payne, J. (2004) *Key Concepts in Social Research*. London: SAGE.

Pigrum, D. (2008) 'Rhetoric'. *In*: L. Given, *ed. The SAGE Encyclopedia of Qualitative Research Methods*. London: SAGE: 793.

Pollio, H. R., Henley, T. B., and Thompson, C. J. (1997) *The Phenomenology of Everyday Life: Empirical Investigations of Human Experience*. Cambridge: Cambridge University Press.

Popp-Baier, U. (2001) Narrating Embodied Aims. Self-Transformation in Conversion Narratives-A Psychological Analysis [Online]. *Forum: Qualitative Social Research*, 2(3). Available from: http://search.proquest.com/docview/867759076/abstract [Accessed 6 January 2016].

Popp-Baier, U. (2002) 'Conversion as Social Construction: A Narrative Approach to Conversion Research'. *In*: C. A. M. Hermans, G. Immink, & J. Van Der Lans, *eds. Social Constructionism and Theology*. Leiden: Brill: 41–62.

Popp-Baier, U. (2008) 'Life Stories and Philosophies of Life: A Perspective for Research in Psychology of Religion'. *In*: J. A. Belzen & A. Geels, *eds. Autobiography and the Psychological Study of Religious Lives*. Amsterdam: Rodopi: 39–74.

Priest, R. J. (2003) 'I Discovered My Sin!' *In*: A. Buckser & S. D. Glazier, *eds. The Anthropology of Religious Conversion*. Lanham: Rowman & Littlefield: 95–108.

Radford, D. (2015) *Religious Identity and Social Change: Explaining Christian Conversion in a Muslim World*. London: Routledge.

Rahmani, M. (2020) 'Secular Rhetoric as a Legitimating Strategy for Mindfulness Meditation'. *In*: S. Newcombe & K. O'Brien-Kop, *eds. Routledge Handbook of Yoga and Meditation Studies*. Routledge. https://www.taylorfrancis.com/chapters/edit/10.4324/9781351050753-21/secular-discourse-legitimating-strategy-mindfulness-meditation-masoumeh-rahmani

Rahmani, M. and Pagis, M. (2015) *Vipassana Meditation | WRSP* [Online]. Available from: http://www.wrldrels.org/profiles/VipassanaMeditation.htm [Accessed 22 February 2017].

Rambo, L. R. (1993) *Understanding Religious Conversion*. New Haven: Yale University Press.

Rambo, L. R. (2003) 'Anthropology and the Study of Conversion'. *In*: A. Buckser & S. D. Glazier, *eds. The Anthropology of Religious Conversion*. Lanham: Rowman & Littlefield: 211–222.

Rambo, L. R. and Farhadian, C. E. (2014) 'Introduction'. *In*: L. R. Rambo & C. E. Farhadian, *eds. The Oxford Handbook of Religious Conversion*. Oxford: Oxford University Press: 1–24.

Rapley, T. J. (2001) 'The Art(fulness) of Open-Ended Interviewing: Some Considerations on Analysing Interviews'. *Qualitative Research*, 1(3): 303–323.

Rawlinson, A. (1997) *The Book of Enlightened Masters: Western Teachers in Eastern Traditions*. Chicago: Open Court.

Richardson, J. T. (1985) 'The Active vs. Passive Convert: Paradigm Conflict in Conversion/ Recruitment Research'. *Journal for the Scientific Study of Religion*, 24(2): 163–179.

Richardson, L. (2000) 'Evaluating Ethnography'. *Qualitative Inquiry*, 6(2): 253–255.

Ricoeur, P. (1981) *Hermeneutics and the Human Sciences: Essays on Language, Action and Interpretation*. Cambridge: Cambridge University Press.

Riesebrodt, M. (2010) *The Promise of Salvation: A Theory of Religion*. Chicago: University of Chicago Press.

Riessman, C. K. (1990) 'Strategic Uses of Narrative in the Presentation of Self and Illness: A Research Note'. *Social Science & Medicine*, 30(11): 1195–1200.

Riessman, C. K. (1993) *Narrative Analysis*. London: SAGE.

Riessman, C. K. (2002) 'Narrative Analysis'. *In*: A. Michael Huberman & Matthew B. Miles, *eds. The Qualitative Researcher's Companion*. London: SAGE: 216–270.

Riessman, C. K. (2008) *Narrative Methods for the Human Sciences*. London: SAGE.

Robinson, B., Fyre, E. M., and Bradley, L. J. (1997) 'Cult Affiliation and Disaffiliation: Implications for Counseling'. *Counseling and Values*, 41(2): 166–73.

Roof, W. C. (1993) *A Generation of Seekers: The Spiritual Journeys of the Baby Boom Generation*. San Francisco: Harper San Francisco.

Schuller, B. and Batliner, A. (2014) *Computational Paralinguistics: Emotion, Affect and Personality in Speech and Language Processing*. Sussex: John Wiley & Sons.

Schwandt, T. A. (2000) 'Three Epistemological Stances for Qualitative Inquiry'. *In*: Norman K. Denzin & Yvonna S. Lincoln, *eds. Handbook of Qualitative Research*. London: SAGE: 189–213.

Selim, N. (2011) *Doing Body, Doing Mind, Doing Self: Vipassana Meditation in Everyday Life*. M.A. Thesis. Netherlands: University of Amsterdam.

Sharf, R. H. (1995) 'Buddhist Modernism and the Rhetoric of Meditative Experience'. *Numen*, 42(3): 228–283.

Sharf, R. H. (2015) 'Is Mindfulness Buddhist? (And Why It Matters)'. *Transcultural Psychiatry*, 52(4): 470–484.

Shoenberger, N. A. and Grayburn, C. (2016) 'Born into Deviance: Disaffiliation Processes for First- and Second-Generation New Religious Movement Members'. *Journal of Religion and Society*, 18: 1–18.

Shuman, A. (2011) 'Exploring Narrative Interaction in Multiple Contexts'. *In*: J. A. Holstein & J. F. Gubrium, *eds. Varieties of Narrative Analysis*. London: SAGE: 125–150.

Skonovd, N. (1981) *Apostasy, the Process of Defection from Religious Totalism*. Doctoral Thesis. Davis: University of California.

Smith, J. M. (2010) 'Becoming an Atheist in America: Constructing Identity and Meaning from the Rejection of Theism'. *Sociology of Religion*, 72(2): 1–23.

Smith, N. H. (2004) 'Taylor and the Hermeneutic Tradition'. *In*: R. Abbey, *ed. Charles Taylor*. Cambridge: Cambridge University Press: 29–51.

Snow, D. (1976) *The Nichiren Shosou Movement in America: A Sociological Examination of Its Value Orientation, Recruitment Efforts, and Spread*. Doctoral Thesis. Los Angeles: University of California.

Snow, D., Zurcher, L., and Ekland-Olson, S. (1980) 'Social Networks and Social Movements: A Microstructural Approach to Differential Recruitment'. *American Sociological Review*, 45(5): 787–801. doi:10.2307/2094895

Snow, D. A. and Machalek, R. (1983) 'The Convert as a Social Type'. *Sociological Theory*, 1: 259–289.

Snow, D. A. and Machalek, R. (1984) 'The Sociology of Conversion'. *Annual Review of Sociology*, 10: 167–190.

Somers, M. R. (1994) 'The Narrative Constitution of Identity: A Relational and Network Approach'. *Theory and Society*, 23(5): 605–649.

Souto-Manning, M. (2014) 'Critical Narrative Analysis: The Interplay of Critical Discourse and Narrative Analyses'. *International Journal of Qualitative Studies in Education*, 27(2): 159–180.

Spickard, J. V. (1998) 'Rethinking Religious Social Action: What Is 'Rational' About Rational-Choice Theory?' *Sociology of Religion*, 59(2): 99–115.

Spickard, J. V. (2011) 'Phenomenology'. *In*: M. Stausberg & S. Engler, *eds*. *The Routledge Handbook of Research Methods in the Study of Religion*. London: Routledge: 333–345.

Spiro, M. E. (1982) [1970] *Buddhism and Society: A Great Tradition and Its Burmese Vicissitudes*. Berkeley: University of California Press.

Staples, C. L. and Mauss, A. L. (1987) 'Conversion or Commitment? A Reassessment of the Snow and Machalek Approach to the Study of Conversion'. *Journal for the Scientific Study of Religion*, 26(2): 133–147.

Stark, R. (1996) *The Rise of Christianity: A Sociologist Reconsiders History*. Princeton: Princeton University Press.

Stark, R. and Bainbridge, W.S. (1985) *The Future of Religion: Secularization, Revival and Cult Formation*. Berkeley: University of California Press.

Stark, R. and Finke, R. (2000) *Acts of Faith: Explaining the Human Side of Religion*. Berkeley: University of California Press.

Statistics New Zealand, *Concerning Language* [Online]. Available from: http://www.stats.govt.nz/browse_for_stats/people_and_communities/Language/concerning-language-2004.aspx [Accessed 22 February 2016].

Stets, J. E. and Turner, J. H. (2006) *Handbook of the Sociology of Emotions*. New York: Springer.

Stone, G. P. (2005) 'Appearance and the Self: A Slightly Revised Version'. *In*: D. Brissett & C. Edgley, *eds*. *Life as Theater: A Dramaturgical Sourcebook*. New Brunswick: Transaction: 141–62.

Stone, M. (2013) *The Dark Side of Meditation*. Available from: https://vimeo.com/70483499 [Accessed 22 February 2017].

Strauss, C. L. (1966) *The Savage Mind*. Chicago: University of Chicago.

Streib, H. (2014) 'Deconversion'. *In*: L. R. Rambo & C. E. Farhadian, *eds*. *The Oxford Handbook of Religious Conversion*. Oxford: Oxford University Press: 271–296.

Streib, H. and Hood, R. W. J., *eds*. (2016) *Semantics and Psychology of Spirituality: A Cross-Cultural Analysis*. New York: Springer.

Streib, H., Silver, C. F., Csöff, R. M., Keller, B., and Hood, R. W. (2011) *Deconversion: Qualitative and Quantitative Results from Cross-Cultural Research in Germany and the United States of America*. Göttingen: Vandenhoeck & Ruprecht.

Stromberg, P. G. (1993) *Language and Self-Transformation: A Study of the Christian Conversion Narrative*. Cambridge: Cambridge University Press.

Stromberg, P. G. (2014) 'The Role of Language in Religious Conversion'. *In*: L. R. Rambo & C. E. Farhadian, *eds. The Oxford Handbook of Religious Conversion*. Oxford: Oxford University Press: 117–139.

Sutcliffe, S. J. (2004) 'The Dynamics of Alternative Spirituality: Seekers, Networks, and "New Age"'. *In*: James R. Lewis, *ed. The Oxford Handbook of New Religious Movements*. Oxford: Oxford University Press: 466–490.

Sutherns, R., Bourgeault, I. L., and James, Y. (2014) *Exploring the Concept of Embodied Research: Does It Take One to Know One?* [Online]. SAGE Research Methods Cases. Available from: http://srmo.sagepub.com/view/methods-case-studies-2013/n164.xml [Accessed 30 October 2014].

Taylor, B. (1976) 'Conversion and Cognition: An Area for Empirical Study in the Microsociology of Religious Knowledge'. *Social Compass*, 23(1): 5–22.

Taylor, C. (1989) *Sources of the Self: The Making of the Modern Identity*. Cambridge: Cambridge University Press.

Taylor, C. (2003) [1991] *The Ethics of Authenticity*. 11th ed. Cambridge: Harvard University Press.

Taylor, C. (2007) *A Secular Age*. Cambridge: Belknap Press of Harvard University Press.

Travisano, R.V. (1970) 'Alternation and Conversion as Qualitatively Different Transformations'. *In*: G. P. Stone & H. A. Faberman, *eds. Social Psychology hrough Symbolic Interaction*. Waltham, MA: Ginn-Blaisdell: 594–606.

Van Maanen, J. (2011) *Tales of the Field: On Writing Ethnography*. 2nd ed. Chicago: University of Chicago Press.

Varga, S. and Guignon, C. (2016) 'Authenticity'. *In*: E. N. Zalta, *ed. The Stanford Encyclopedia of Philosophy*. Available from: http://plato.stanford.edu/archives/sum2016/entries/authenticity/ [Accessed 4 July 2016].

Veer, P. van der (2012) 'Market and Money: A Critique of Rational Choice Theory'. *Social Compass*, 59(2): 183–192.

VRI Dhamma (2012) *Vipassana Research Institute, Words of Dhamma* [Online]. Available from: http://www.vridhamma.org/en2012-12 [Accessed 22 February 2014].

VRI Dhamma (2014) *Talks and Answers to Questions from Vipassana Students 1983–2000.* [Online]. Available from: http://www.vridhamma.org/uploadedfiles/BenefitofMany.pdf [Accessed 1 June 2014].

Wallace, B. A. (2002) 'The Spectrum of Buddhist Practice in the West'. *In*: C. S. Prebish & M. Baumann, *eds. Westward Dharma: Buddhism Beyond Asia*. London: University of California Press: 34–50.

Wallace, G. (2009) 'Dying to Be Born: A Meditation on Transformative Surrender Within Spiritual and Depth Psychological Experiences'. *In*: D. Mathers, M. E. Miller, & O. Ando, *eds. Self and No-Self: Continuing the Dialogue Between Buddhism and Psychotherapy*. London: Routledge: 143–152.

Weber, S. L. (2003) 'An Analyst's Surrender'. *In*: J. D. Safran, *ed. Psychoanalysis and Buddhism: An Unfolding Dialogue*. Boston: Wisdon: 169–188.

Weiss, R. S. (1994) *Learning from Strangers: The Art and Method of Qualitative Interview Studies*. New York: Maxwell Macmillan International.

Wilcke, M. M. (2002) 'Hermeneutic Phenomenology as a Research Method in Social Work'. *Currents: New Scholarship in the Human Services*, 1(1): 1–10.

Wolcott, H. F. (2008) *Ethnography: A Way of Seeing*. Walnut Creek: AltaMira Press.

Woodhead, L. and Heelas, P. (2000) *Religion in Modern Times: An Interpretive Anthology*. Oxford: Blackwell.

Woolfolk, R. L. (1992) 'Hermeneutics, Social Constructionism and Other Items of Intellectual Fashion: Intimations for Clinical Science'. *Behavior Therapy*, 23(2): 213–223.

Wright, B. R. E., Giovanelli, D., Dolan, E. G., and Edwards, M. E. (2011) 'Explaining Deconversion From Christianity: A Study of Online Narratives'. *Journal of Religion and Society*, 13: 1–17.

Wright, S. A. (1983) *A Sociological Study of Defection from Controversial New Religious Movements*. Doctoral thesis. Storrs: University of Connecticut.

Wright, S. A. (1984) 'Post-Involvement Attitudes of Voluntary Defectors from Controversial New Religious Movements'. *Journal for the Scientific Study of Religion*, 23(2): 172–182.

Wright, S. A. (1987) *Leaving Cults: The Dynamics of Defection*. Washington, DC: Society for the Scientific Study of Religion.

Wright, S. A (1991) 'Reconceptualizing Cult Coercion and Withdrawal: A Comparative Analysis of Divorce and Apostasy'. *Social Forces*, 70(1): 125–147.

Wright, S. A. (2007) 'The Dynamics of Movement Membership: Joining and Leaving New Religious Movements'. *In*: D. G. Bromley, *ed*. *Teaching New Religious Movements*. Oxford: Oxford University Press: 187–210.

Wright, S. A. (2014) 'Disengagement and Apostasy in New Religious Movements'. *In*: L. R. Rambo & C. E. Farhadian, *eds*. *The Oxford Handbook of Religious Conversion*. Oxford: Oxford University Press: 706–735.

Wright, S. A. and Ebaugh, H. R. F. (1993) 'Leaving New Religions'. *In*: D. G. Bromley & J. Hadden, *eds*. *Cults and Sects in America*. Greenwich, CT: Associations for the Sociology of Religion and JAI Press: 117–38.

Yamada, K. (2005) [1979] *The Gateless Gate: The Classic Book of Zen Koans*. Los Angeles: Simon and Schuster.

Yamane, D. (2000) 'Narrative and Religious Experience'. *Sociology of Religion*, 61(2): 171–189.

Yü, D. S. (2014) 'Buddhist Conversion in the Contemporary World'. *In*: L. R. Rambo & C. E. Farhadian, *eds*. *The Oxford Handbook of Religious Conversion*. Oxford: Oxford University Press: 465–487.

Zenk, T. (2013) 'New Atheism'. *In*: S. Bullivant & M. Ruse, *eds*. *The Oxford Handbook of Atheism*. Oxford: Oxford University Press: 245–262.

Zinnbauer, Brian J., Pargament, Kenneth I., Cole, Brenda, Rye, Mark S., Butter, Eric M. Belavich, Timothy G., Hipp, Kathleen M., Scott, Allie B., and Kadar, Jill L. (1997) 'Religion and Spirituality: Unfuzzying the Fuzzy'. *Journal for the Scientific Study of Religion* 36(4): 549–564.

Index

For the benefit of digital users, indexed terms that span two pages (e.g., 52–53) may, on occasion, appear on only one of those pages.

Figures are indicated by *f* following the page number